DOCUMENTS OF SOCIAL HISTORY

Editor: Anthony Adams

MASTER AND ARTISAN IN VICTORIAN ENGLAND

MASTER AND ARTISAN IN VICTORIAN ENGLAND

The Diary of William Andrews and the Autobiography of Joseph Gutteridge

EDITED AND WITH AN INTRODUCTION BY
VALERIE E. CHANCELLOR

EVELYN, ADAMS & MACKAY

9 Fitzroy Square, London W.1.
SBN 238.78918.7
Printed in Great Britain by R. & R. Clark Ltd., Edinburgh

CONTENTS

Preface

I should like to thank Mr A. A. Dibben, the Coventry city archivist, who first drew my attention to the diary of William Andrews and who kindly granted permission for its publication. The assistant archivist, Mr D. J. H. Smith and the staff of the Coventry and Warwickshire Collection were also extremely helpful in suggesting material on which further research into the lives of Andrews and Gutteridge might be based. My thanks are also due to M. Maurice Lambot and to my former colleague at the Coventry College of Education, Mr Peter Searby, with whom I discussed various points.

By far the most valuable general work on Coventry in the nineteenth century is *The Industrial Revolution in Coventry* by John Prest (1960). For the Coventry silk industry, the works of Sir Frank Warner and Horace Miles (an unpublished thesis), were foremost among those consulted. Other information was gleaned from the Reports of the Commissioners and the Coventry newspapers of the period, notably the *Coventry Morning Daily Telegraph*, the *Coventry Herald* and the *Coventry Standard*. Various other pamphlets, articles and collections of newspaper cuttings, including those written and compiled by William Andrews himself, provided much detail of the local background. They are too numerous to mention individually, but they are to be found in the Coventry City Record Office and the Coventry and Warwickshire Collection.

V.E.C.

Introduction

Joseph Gutteridge 1816–1899, and William Andrews 1835–1914

Joseph Gutteridge's autobiography recounts the joys and struggles of life as seen through the eyes of one who was an artisan and generally content to remain so; in contrast, William Andrews' diary records the progress of an aspiring master, ultimately the proud possessor of his own successful business. Both men passed nearly all their long lives in Coventry, well away from the centre of national events. They saw or experienced few incidents of a sensational character, or if they did, they have not chosen to record them. The interest of their recollections lies in the illuminating picture of everyday English provincial life and its changing industrial organisation in the Victorian era which they present.

It is a curious fact that at a time when the prosperity and importance of Coventry was somewhat in decline, the fathers of both Gutteridge and Andrews chose voluntarily to settle there after serving in the regular army. Joseph Gutteridge, the elder, came of a Coventry family and decided to remain in his native city when he received his discharge as a soldier there after the Battle of Waterloo in 1815. The following year saw the birth of the son who was named after him. Andrews' father came originally from Scotland, but grew to love Coventry while stationed at the local barracks, and settled there permanently when he had served his time. His son's recorded interest in parades of soldiers and the Rifle Volunteers may be a reflection of his military background.

It would appear that in spite of this initial similarity, Gutteridge's home background was slightly less prosperous and settled than that of Andrews. Yet his education was by no means neglected by the standards of the time. His autobiography recalls his early happy experience at a dame school run by a Quakeress. Later, although hampered by illness, he received more formal schooling at Baker, Billing and Crowe Charity School before being apprenticed as a weaver at the age of thirteen at the factory where his father worked. There he was able to keep up his interest in mechanics and natural history. His chief handicaps at this period were a cruel and unreliable stepmother who forced him to leave home by her tantrums, and the loss of a father who might have instilled greater financial caution into his son had he lived.

In contrast, Andrews was always able in his youth to rely on the encouragement of both his parents. His father was in business in the city and he was able to send his son to Mr Mander's day school for private pupils nearby. A surviving note-book of 1848 shows that young William received a good grounding in mathematics, enabling him to approach such subjects as land surveying and astronomy with some degree of understanding. He was apprenticed at the age of thirteen to Messrs Bray in the designing department, and his diary records the series of prizes, including visits to the Great Exhibition of 1851 and to Paris, which he won during his subsequent studies at the Coventry Schools of Art and Design. Andrews had the advantage of a secure and respectable home, but its prosperity in comparison to the Gutteridge household must not be over-rated. What money he had to set himself up in business, he saved for himself.

Indeed, it is difficult to avoid the impression that the subsequent disparity in worldly success and wealth between Andrews and Gutteridge did not stem from their background and education, but from their totally differing characters. Gutteridge was a charming, kindly, but often imprudent man. His autobiography records the quixotic romanticism which caused him to rush into marriage before he had finished his apprenticeship and before he had been able to purchase his own loom. Later his honesty and devotion to principle caused him to refuse a dole available to freemen of the city when it entailed an avowal of religious beliefs which he did not possess, though his wife and children were starving at the time. Love of his fellow men and an interest in intellectual and spiritual rather than worldly matters are predominant features of his book. His obituaries record the crowds of friends at his graveside and their fond memories of the modest, gentle old man who used to show the natural history specimens in his home-museum in Yardley Street to all who were interested.

William Andrews was a man nicely calculated to take full financial advantage of the Gutteridges of this world. His diary gives full details of his urge to excel as a student, his thrifty efforts to save, and his early identification, when appointed manager by Messrs Cash, with the interests of his employers so that he even excelled them in resisting the demands of workers that they should sign the price list which was intended to guarantee the weavers a fair wage. Andrews never married and during the critical slump of 1860–61 he was able to seek work abroad with savings in his pocket. His quest for work was hard, but he records it with rarely a trace of self-pity. After his return to Coventry, his urge to be his own master became dominant. Although he was well paid, as befitted one of the very few successful managers in Coventry during a partial depression in trade, he was determined to succeed in business on his own account, and succeed he did. Andrews had few real friends, though he was reputed to be pleasant and even entertaining in conversation to those who knew him well, and the diary records some of his lighter moments spent in the enjoyment of wine or in purchasing an expensive frock coat in Paris. He even reveals a vein of youthful romanticism at times. His comparison of himself with King Alfred and his enjoyment of Byron's verse suggest that he saw himself as the lonely individual struggling against a harsh fate. In later years the qualities indicated in the diary evidently hardened. Contemporaries paint a picture of a man who was widely respected, but also feared and disliked. They comment on his hard and unsympathetic manner, his growing taciturnity and his tendency to snub those who tried to make polite conversation with him. The best recorded of his qualities in the obituary in the *Coventry Herald* was that, 'He was intellectually honest; he was not the victim of sham sentiment; putting aside the occasional expression of strong prejudice, he seemed emotionless.' It is a measure of his lack of humour that his one or two mild public jests were actually remembered and recorded in his obituaries.

The careers of Andrews and Gutteridge are to a great extent a reflection of the ferocious ambition of the one, and gentle, scrupulous unworldliness of the other. In talents they were not dissimilar. Gutteridge was a gifted mechanic as well as a skilled weaver. In 1867 he was one of four workmen delegates from Coventry chosen to visit the Paris Exhibition, and to report back to the Society of Arts. Later he was entrusted by his employer, Mr Stevens, with the task of demonstrating the weaving of silk pictures (Stevengraphs) at the Bradford Exhibition of 1870. Andrews was not only a talented designer, but also excelled as card stamper, reader-in and figure weaver. Both men faced a difficult industrial situation in the Coventry of their time.

The city was surrounded by common land, protected from encroachment by building, which hampered its expansion. At the beginning of the century it had been a stopping place for stage-coaches, but the growth of the railways rather bypassed it and it was much over-shadowed by its growing neighbour, Birmingham, which was expanding rapidly, unshackled as it was by the restrictions of a notable past. The two main Coventry industries were silk and watch-making. The former catered mainly for a lower middle-class trade in plain and a few fancy goods, the production of luxury goods being confined to London and to centres on the continent in Switzerland and France. The Coventry silk industry was still organised on largely traditional lines in the mid-nineteenth century. Entrepreneurs provided the silk for Coventry merchants who in turn distributed it from their warehouses to the weavers. The latter wove it in their own homes and were paid according to a list of prices. This was intended to ensure that a fair wage was paid for the labour involved and that labour was not sold too cheaply during the not infrequent slumps caused by general economic depression or particular hazards such as changing fashion or seasonal variations in demand. Following the riot which occurred against Mr Beck's attempted installation of the first power-loom in Coventry, technical improvements in silk manufacture were much delayed in the city. Even go-ahead employers were reluctant to introduce the fully developed factory system.

The brothers Cash tried in their new venture at Kingfields, in which Andrews was involved, to soften its rigours. The weavers were allowed individual cottages with larger, well-lighted rooms in the upper storeys for weaving, while one engine supplied power to the whole concern. This innovation allowed the weavers to retain the independence of working in their own time, but proved hopelessly uneconomical since power had to be supplied regardless of whether all the looms were working or not. The old-fashioned organisation of the industry could not withstand the onslaught of foreign competition which was unleashed by the coming of free trade between England and France on the signing of the Cobden Treaty of 1860. In a desperate attempt to preserve their trade the masters attempted to resist the price list and the result was a crippling strike and lockout. After 1861 the industry did modernise and men of enterprise and modern outlook of the Andrews' type were able to survive and even to prosper. As a whole, however, the silk industry remained in decline and the numbers employed in it continued to fall.

Gutteridge gives a vivid account of the suffering during the periods of industrial unrest and depression which he endured. In the general slump of the 1840's he was unemployed, partly because he refused to accept work he considered beneath him in the tainted atmosphere of a factory. On several occasions his family were on the verge of death from cold and hunger. Even later after a period of recovery and comparative prosperity for the silk industry, he and his second wife suffered severe privation in the crisis of 1860. Gutteridge never had the ambition to rise much beyond the status of an ordinary artisan, although he longed for the chance to use his unusual technical knowledge and skill to the full. He continued to work until the slump of 1890 left him without employment. He then faced such financial strain that he was nearly forced to sell his collection of natural history specimens, although the great aim of his life was to keep this together. However, the publication of his book and the raising of money for a small annuity by his friends and admirers prevented this disaster.

Unlike Gutteridge, Andrews contrived to turn even adversity to his advantage. His reaction to the crisis of 1860 was to seek work from the silk manufacturers of France and Switzerland and incidentally to learn something of their organisation and expertise. On his return he had little difficulty in finding a job and in rapidly increasing the business of his employers. With very little capital, but with some good contacts, he later set up business on his own and the diary ends with his first success. In 1868 he took a partner, Mr T. Burbidge, so that he could enjoy a little more leisure. But after the latter's retirement in 1874 he continued the business on his own account. One sign of his success is that on several occasions he was a member of delegations on behalf of the silk manufacturers in their representations to the governments of the day. However, in 1890, Andrews closed his business down, declaring it not worth keeping on. It appears that he had made more than enough money to keep him in retirement. He continued to live in style for the last twenty-four years of his life and died at his residence, 'Steeplecroft', from whence he was accorded an oppulent funeral.

Much of Andrews' later life was devoted to his interest in politics, both local and national, and it is perhaps significant that he and Gutteridge held notably divergent views on this subject. One of the chief features of the latter's autobiography is his unflinching political moderation and devotion to the Liberal cause. Although he suffered severely in the 1840's, Gutteridge makes little allusion to Chartism or to revolutionary sentiments then current in some sections of the working class. In the 1860's he remained true to the ideals of free enterprise and free trade in spite of the miseries which Gladstone's policies brought to Coventry. Small wonder that his book found a resting place in the library at Hawarden and that Mr Gladstone arranged for the author to receive £70 from the Royal Bounty fund. *Lights and Shadows in the life of an Artisan* was generally well-received, it seems, partly because of the author's quietist outlook. His obituaries reported his reputation as 'a gentleman among the working classes' and 'a splendid example to the young'. Gutteridge was even held up as a model to the restive workers of France. Writing in the *Journal des Debats*, one Augustin Filon declared him to be the 'embodiment of individualism' and far more praiseworthy than those who busied themselves with strikes and other mischiefs. Socialists, he was sure, would not read Gutteridge's book. This review, reported in the *Coventry Telegraph*, brought a swift response from a reader who asserted that Socialists admired Gutteridge and had read his work with enjoyment. He pointed out that in one passage he criticises the exploitation of labourers by the capitalist class as against religion and against nature, and concluded that in happier times Gutteridge would have been able to use his talents more fully and would have been a citizen honoured by the world instead of just by Coventry. In fact Gutteridge was probably not so passive an employee as his readers supposed. There is evidence that he may have taken an active, if minor, role in the strike of 1860.

Andrews' diary is unlike Gutteridge's book in that the author's political attitude is implicit rather than openly expressed. We know, however, that he was later believed to be a 'Tory of Tories' and that he publicly questioned the motives and opinions of those Unionists who left the Liberal party after Gladstone's first Home Rule Bill, apparently because he considered them too radical. He was always a good party man and helped to organise the Conservative Party in Coventry. However, it is notable that Andrews did not stand on a party programme when elected to the city council. This may have been because Coventry was, even before 1832, a place where all freemen could vote in parliamentary elections, and since all men could become freemen after completing an apprenticeship on payment of a due, the tradition of a wide electorate and an electorate of radical mind was well established. However that may be, Andrews was successful as councillor for Gosford for nineteen years. When the government of the city was reorganised in 1890, he still headed the poll for the area, although he was the only Conservative among the six successful candidates. At the time he issued a manifesto which was regarded as 'savouring of the egoist'. It recorded his successes in saving public money by a reorganisation of the city's debts, and his work for water supply, irrigation, the installation of gas and road widening. It was some measure of his personal unpopularity that he was not made an alderman until 1896, although he was later offered and refused the office of mayor. He continued to make efficiency rather than any party slogan the keynote of his career in local politics. To the fury of those who disregarded him, he was completely vindicated in his criticism of a new and expensive water supply as open to contamination, and this, together with his rudeness, may account for the many ungenerous remarks recorded of him. In his later years he was much derided for his fanatical support for gas as opposed to electricity and for his attempts to stop city aid for technical education on the grounds that such things were best left to individual masters and apprentices. His attachment to ruthless efficiency and common-sense can be contrasted to Gutteridge's equally marked devotion to brotherly love in the world.

These features can also be discerned in the religious outlook of the two men. Gutteridge thought deeply about questions of religion and morality. The sufferings and injustice which he saw about him caused him to lose his faith in God, though he never abandoned the moral principles of Christianity. He was at this period influenced by the local philosopher, Charles Bray, the friend of the novelist George Eliot, and the apostle of what Gutteridge came to term the 'when you are dead you are done with' theory. Bray's stoic creed did not have any lasting appeal for him, and after the death of his first wife Gutteridge became interested in spiritualism. Finally he came to accept the idea of a Supreme Being and Creator. When he died, the funeral sermon was preached by the Rev. G. Heaviside at the Great Meeting House who lamented the 'mere accident' which had made Gutteridge temporarily an atheist. It appears, then, that he was reconciled to Christianity before his death.

Of Andrews' religious beliefs we know but little, for all speculation on the topic is absent from his diary. However, it would appear that he set store by formal religious observance. One of his first acts on completing his apprenticeship was to purchase a seat at the Congregationalist Chapel at Vicar Lane, and he was soon involved in setting its finances straight. Later it would appear that Andrews drifted away from non-conformist worship and attached himself to the Church of England, his funeral service being conducted by a canon of St Michael's (now Coventry Cathedral). Perhaps he found the established church a suitable mileu for one of his affluence and social position. As it happened, it also accorded with his interest in local antiquities. When the church was restored during the years 1885–1890, Andrews was a member of the committee which raised funds for the work. Moreover, he engaged in the controversy as to the effect of ringing the bells on the fabric of the tower. As a result of his own efforts in surveying it, he wrote several papers on the restoration of the bells and steeple. When the work of restoring the steeple actually begain in 1886 he was called upon to lay the first stone above the foundations, saying in his speech that he hoped this glorious monument would still stand after the deaths of those present and that they were not unworthy of their great predecessors who had built the tower and steeple. This is one of the few touches of idealism to be found in the known writings or speeches of Andrews, and even this illustrates his concern for the practical and concrete rather than with abstract speculation.

In spite of their divergent outlook and opinions, Andrews and Gutteridge had many interests in common. Gutteridge, it is true, was the more widely read, but in other respects their leisure activities are equally matched. Both men were great walkers. Though Andrews covered the greater distances on the Continent and was the more adventurous, Gutteridge's autobiography records his enjoyment of strolling through the English countryside. Both were interested in astronomy, though Andrews appears to have been the more methodical in his observations, at least before he got his own business. Indeed, his hobby may have been a great solace to him since it is often mentioned during periods of unemployment or depression in business, though admittedly he had more leisure to record what he saw at such times. Again both men were interested in geology and natural history in general. Here it was Gutteridge who made the more comprehensive observations and who formed a splendid collection of fossils as well as botanical and other specimens. Nevertheless, Andrews was sufficiently well-informed to use his hobby in determining his policy on drainage and water supply in the city, and he also wrote many papers on natural history and archæology. He was also the president of the Warwickshire Naturalists and Archaeologists Field Club for several years. Both men enjoyed activities which were practical rather than academic. Gutteridge was always dexterous with his hands, and in his later years amused himself by making violins and tailoring his own clothes. Andrews painted local scenes and was also a keen photographer, being so successful that the Science and Art Department particularly asked him to exhibit some of his work in the Paris Exhibition of 1890.

The general importance of the lives of Andrews and Gutteridge in relation to the history of their own times is that they illustrate so clearly how the ideals of free enterprise and free competition worked in Victorian society. In character they certainly differed, but in family backgrounds, talents and education, they were remarkably similar. For over forty years they worked within the same industry in the same city. Yet the one remained an artisan to face what the preacher at his funeral sermon termed 'the horror of his environment', and to live to an impoverished old age. The other made money from his own business at a time of general depression in the silk industry and lived and died in comfort. One was respected and loved; the other respected and feared, even hated. It is ironic that Gutteridge was commended in several of his obituaries for his individual struggles as the epitome of free enterprise: 'He has taught what can be accomplished even by the humblest person when he is content to bring to bear on any given subject unflagging, persevering and painstaking labour', as the *Coventry Times* put it. No such comments were made about Andrews' far more marked rise from his early environment. Perhaps this absence of a patronising tone in the obituaries illustrates that in death as in life Andrews was the far more formidable figure.

Notes on the Texts

The diary of William Andrews runs from 1850 until shortly before the author's death in 1914. However, daily entries cease after he succeeded in setting up his own business in 1863 and the pressure of work accordingly increased. Thereafter, he recorded merely a few brief facts about his itineraries on holiday and these have been omitted in this edition as being of little interest or importance. The manuscript exists in two note-books in which there is little variation in writing until Andrews' last illness took its toll. This leads to speculation that the earlier portion of the diary may have been copied out by the author, possibly during his retirement when he compiled various scrapbooks of newspaper cuttings and other mementoes. One or two slips in writing apparently confirm this. The fact that the diary contains little of personal comment or information may be the result of this possible rewriting, though this could equally well be the result of Andrews' reserved and uncommunicative character. The text is given here exactly as it was written except for standardisation of spelling, dates, and a few changes in punctuation to make the sense more readily intelligible. These changes are of a minor nature since Andrews' manuscript bears testimony to his meticulous efficiency. Mostly the diary speaks for itself, but a few notes have been added for the guidance of the reader.

Joseph Gutteridge's autobiography also began as a diary, but first appeared in print as a series of articles in the *Coventry Herald.* It enjoyed some success and was subsequently published as a book (under the title *Lights and Shadows in the Life of an Artisan*) in 1893, helping in a small way to relieve the author's penurious old age, though it did not run to a second edition. The work bears some traces of its journalistic origin, containing several diffuse sections on Gutteridge's hobbies which break up the narrative. These have accordingly been shortened in two places in the present edition. It is hoped thereby to give the work greater cohesion without omitting anything of major interest concerning the author's life. On the whole Gutteridge describes events so fully that detailed notes seem unnecessary. However, two respects in which he may mislead the reader are pointed out at the end of his book.

THE DIARY OF
WILLIAM ANDREWS

The Diary of William Andrews

1850

SUNDAY AUG. 18: Visited Berkswell and Baddesley Clinton with J. Iliffe.
SUNDAY SEP. 1: Saw 3 women and 6 men baptised in the canal at Longford today.[1]
SEP. 2: Nuneaton railway opens today, saw the first train. Later in the day about 30 passengers had to ride on top of carriages, there not being room enough inside.[2]
SEP. 3: They began to fill Swanswell pool today.
SEP. 13: Had a book 'The Nile Boat' presented to me at the annual meeting of School of Art by Thos. Cope Esq. as 2nd prize for ribbon design.[3]
SEP. 15: Visit the new Harbury cutting with C. Peters and Sidney Peters.
OCT. 14: Swanswell is nearly completed.
OCT. 10: Ratcliff's factory hands parading the streets today.
OCT. 16: Saw a large red beech tree removed from bottom of Hertford St. to cemetery today; the crowd cheered.
SUNDAY NOV. 3: Walked with J. Rowley via Coundon, Corley, Astley, and Seaswood Pool to Nuneaton.
NOV. 4: Walk with S. Rowley via Hartshill, Oldbury to Atherstone and back to Nuneaton – train to Coventry.
NOV. 14: Have served 2 years of my apprenticeship today.
SUNDAY NOV. 24: Went to Trinity Church and saw some very old books, Fox's Book of Martyrs, a New Testament etc., saw a stone fall from the steeple and smashed to pieces.
TUESDAY DEC. 10: Saw a Catholic preaching tonight opposite our house in Fleet St.[4] A young man got up and argued with him and told him that he could not prove from the bible that there was a purgatory. He was just searching for a chapter and verse from St. Paul when a turf flew into the air and fell perpendicularly upon his head; upon which he went up Smithford St. followed by 400 or 500 people, down Little Park St., Cow Lane, Grey

Friar's Lane and was then taken by the police to the lock-up.
DEC. 20: Slight Aurora Borealis.

1851

JAN. 22: Aurora Borealis.
MONDAY FEB. 3: See Barnard's Panorama of the Mississippi at St. Mary's Hall.
SATURDAY MAR. 15: Give over work and warehouse closed at 5 o'clock tonight (an unusual circumstance).
MAR. 16: Walk to Stoneleigh Park with J. Archer.
MAR. 25: Go to the School of Art early this morning, the first time of morning study.
MAY 28: Begin to make dark colours today.
JUNE 3: The Committee of School of Design today award me a prize to go and visit the Hyde Park Exhibition.[5]
JUNE 4: W. H. Bray enquires about the prize and promises me a holiday to go.[6]
JUNE 18: Go to the School of Design at 4 o'clock. There is a meeting of the committee – W. H. Bray, L. Dresser, S. Newsome, S. Whitten and another. I am presented with a prize of 30/- to visit the Exhibition. The following prizes were awarded, Hough 40/-, W. A. 30/-, R. Lowe 30/-, Carter 30/-, Amos 20/-, Shaw 20/-, J. Newsome 20/-, Total 190/-.
TUESDAY JUNE 24: Godiva procession.[7] City crammed with people.
JULY 12: Went to a Mr. Mackintosh to have my phrenological bumps examined.
JULY 15: Went to Leamington by a Vicar Lane excursion, 43 railway carriages, walk to Chesterton.[8]
JULY 27: Went over to Wiberleys to arrange about going to London.
28: Great eclipse of sun today. Cloudy, could not see it, was dusky at middle of eclipse about 3 o'clock.
SAT. AUG. 1: Coventry to Nuneaton and then by excursion to London. Leave Nuneaton 1 o'clock, arrive Euston 5h. 45m., drive to Battersea.
SUN. AUG. 2: River to London Bridge, walk round by Tower and City, back by river at 2 o'clock, Mr. and Mrs. Porteous to tea with us.
MONDAY AUG. 3: Exhibition, afterwards round by Buckingham Palace, Serpentine, Kensington Gardens. Mr. and Mrs. Caldicott come up today.
TUESDAY: Steamer to Gravesend and return.

WEDNESDAY AUG. 5: Go by myself to warehouse in Wood St. then to Guildhall, Thames Tunnel, ascend St. Paul's Dome, Westminster Abbey, National Gallery, British Museum, Zoological Gardens.

THURSDAY: Exhibition with father, home to Battersea from Hungerford Pier.

FRIDAY AUG. 7: To Hungerford Pier, bus to Euston, Coventry 10 minutes past 4, to warehouse in evening.

AUG. 13: Lammas Day. The lammas riders pull down a wall at back of Draper's Fields.[9]

AUG. 28/51: J. Iliffe finishes his apprenticeship today.

SEP. 11: I am 5 ft. 7 in. high.

SEP. 19: Steeple of R. C. Church now building.

NOV. 4: Annual meeting of School of Design, receive prize Boswell's Life of Johnson.

NOV. 17: Have a decayed tooth drawn by Lukyn.

SUNDAY NOV. 30: Walk to Corley Moor and back this afternoon.

DEC. 14: Sketch Baginton Oak.

DEC. 15: Another tooth drawn by Lukyn.

DEC. 16: Some outhouses on fire in Stivichall Park tonight, went with father to see.

DEC. 22: C. Peters leaves us today to go into business himself.

DEC. 25: Walk with father to Wyken this afternoon – see the church.

DEC. 29: Holiday. Go to Birmingham and Dudley.

1852

JAN. 5: Mr. Bray's mother taken very ill. My height is 5 ft. $7\frac{1}{2}$ in.

14: Old Mrs. Bray dies at 10 o'clock this evening.

19: Mrs. Bray buried in Stoke Church Yard.

FEB. 19: Aurora Borealis tonight – a splendid display.

MAR. 10: R. C. steeple finished today.

SUNDAY APRIL 11: Saw 9 people baptized in canal at Longford today.

APR. 12: Pillar of light in sky after sunset.

19: Same appearance in sky.

MAY 3: Saw Jupiter's satellites for first time with small telescope.

26: Mr. Gifford, master of School of Design, informs me that I am to have a medal for drawing.

JUNE 10/52: Row the last few days about the money for the booths in the green with the freemen.

JUNE 15: Went with J. Owen to Kenilworth to search subterranean passage. Took his bulls-eye lantern. Went up the passage 59 yards, the roof had there fallen in. It was 3 ft. 4 in. high and arched over with stone, but in some places patched with brick. Floor of hard stone, was not quite straight but turned about a little and went slightly up hill – was a little under 3 ft. wide. The passage is under the wall on west side of castle.

SUNDAY 20: Visit Kenilworth, Gaveston's mount, Guy's Cliffe and Milverton.[10]

SUNDAY JULY 11: Coventry luggage station burned to the ground.

SUNDAY AUG. 8: Scot's Greys attend Vicar Lane Chapel.

AUG. 26: Fussel, the new master, comes to school of Design.

SEP. 9: The Old Mill Dam at new buildings being now demolished.

13: Annual meeting of School of Design. A medal is presented to me at St. Mary's Hall by Mrs. Cope. Others beside myself were Hough, S. Owen, R. Lowe, W. Carter, H. Amos (dead). Coventry had 6 medals, Birmingham 8, Spitalfields 9, Nottingham 7, Macclesfield 3. The medals were adjudged by W. Eastlake and Maclise on May 20th.

SAT. OCT. 2: Very busy at warehouse – presented with 2/6.

OCT. 14: Draughting class at School of Design begins the season.

SUNDAY 24: Walk with J. Archer to Coombe Pool.

28: Buy a foot ribbon rule.

OCT. 30/52: J. Iliffe leaves warehouse today. He has been out of his time little more than a year. He has been with them $8\frac{1}{4}$ years, and has had £50 for his year's service. He goes to Courts and Taylor of West Orchard.

NOV. 1: Commence my new duties as head man at warehouse. W. H. Bray elected member of City Council.

NOV. 11: Heavy rain all night and all today. About 5 o'clock in afternoon a stream of water began to pour down Hill St., increasing till eleven p.m. when it was 2 ft. deep in front of our house (No. 15). The street looked like a river, cellar 4 ft. deep. Water disappeared suddenly at 1 a.m.

17: Go to London with father today by excursion, lodge at William St. Hampstead Road, walk round West End to see preparations for Duke of Wellington's funeral.[11]

NOV. 18: Leave lodgings at 7 o'clock, stood at corner of Cockspur St. The funeral took 2 hours to go past. Street frightfully crammed, 5,000 troops present. We went to Greenwich in the afternoon and home to Coventry at night.

21: Floods again – water in front of our house 1 foot deep.

DEC. 19: Walk through Stoneleigh Park with J. Archer.

27: Walk to Newnham Regis today. Total extent of country walks this year 269 miles.

1853

JAN. 11: W. Hough commences his duties as draughting master in place of W. Burbery, gone to Macclesfield.

JAN. 22: Finish a design for Sharp and Odell for the Dublin Exhibition. 4 designs done by F. Clark, W. Owen, W. Hough and W. A.

MAR. 27: Go with J. Archer to Austy and Shilton. Heavy drifting snow storms.

APR. 30: Finish drawings and designs for the exhibitions at Marlborough House.

MAY 4: My weight is 9 stone 4 lb.

9: Have a tooth drawn, lower jaw, right side, the rearmost double tooth – the 5th tooth I have had drawn.

19: I pay the weavers this week for the first time.

SUNDAY JUNE 5: Hot ride to Leamington, then walk to Stratford and back, then visit to Jephson Gardens. Returning from Leamington some cows got on line. We nearly had an accident.

JUNE 7: Thos. Owen dies today, age $22\frac{3}{4}$, of inflammation of the bowels. The last time I saw him was on Jan. 23. He complained of a cold and has been ill nearly ever since.

12: Saw T. Owen buried in Hill Field Church at half past one.

13: Mr. Fussel, master of School of Art, informs me that I am to have another medal.

JULY 2: Heard a farewell sermon to the Scot's Greys at Vicar Lane. They are going to the camp at Chobham.

14: Began to rain heavily at 2 a.m., kept on till noon and slightly the rest of the day – streets flooded 2 or 3 feet deep in various places.

JULY 20: The hole that is being made for the new gasholder was filled with water by the flood last Thursday. A steam engine is now pumping it out.

JULY 31, SUNDAY: Revd. Henry Ollard preaches his farewell sermon at Vicar Lane tonight.

AUG. 1: Farewell service at Vicar Lane. Heard Mr. Ollard's farewell address. Testimonial, a gold watch and purse of £53-13-1d.

9: My 1853 medal has arrived at Coventry.

28: Saw the comet tonight, the nucleus very bright, tail about 3 degrees long, a very beautiful object.

30: Get holiday from warehouse. Go with father to Brinklow and sketch church, then to Wiberley's to Foleshill Wake.

SEP. 27: Make a water colour drawing of Keresley Church.

OCT. 11: Bargain with Mr. Joseph Bray for me to do the draughting.

16: Visit Jackman at Whitley Abbey and am shown through the rooms.

NOV. 17: In future I am going to find my own pocket money which I earn by draughting.

23: Receive 25/- from Mr. Sanders for water colour of Keresley church.

DEC. 4: Advent Sunday. Go with father to Sowe church. Hear Perkins preach.

23: Weight 128 pounds. My income this year £4.14.5. Total of country walks 366½ miles.

1854

JAN. 4: Snow a foot deep all over England.

JAN. 5: Enter myself as a member of the Coventry Mechanics Institution, 2/6 per quarter.

JAN. 8, SUNDAY: Become a seat-holder at Vicar Lane Chapel.

FEB. 20: Opened an account for myself at the Coventry Savings Bank. Deposited £5.

FEB. 21: Annual meeting of School of Art at St. Mary's Hall. I am presented with my medal, the second I have gained. The Revd. Drake in the chair. A successful meeting. My medal was for 6 ribbon designs. It was gained last May.

28: Go to a soiree at St. Mary's Hall held by School of Art.

MAR. 5: Noticed a star of 5th magnitude in Taurus N.W. of Aldebaran disappear behind the moon at 9h. 5m. This occultation was not mentioned in the almanacks. Sky very clear and excellent view of disappearance. The star became twice half extinguished and then instantly disappeared. At 9.45 the star had not emerged and sky became hazy, at 10 sky clouded.

MAR. 24, FRIDAY. Walked to Brandon and back before breakfast.

28: War proclaimed.

30: Saw the new comet tonight, its nucleus – star of 1st magnitude.

MAR. 31: Comet's tail about 2 degrees long.

APR. 1: Comet just below a Arietis, tail vertical.

3: Comet's tail inclined to left.

4: Last sight of comet with naked eye.

7: Saw comet with 1 inch aperture. It is becoming faint and distant.

APR. 10-13: Light Dragoons leave Coventry this morning for Turkey via Canterbury, Calais and Marseilles. Headquarters arrive from Birmingham.

11: Comet still visible with telescope, tail short and faint. Headquarters leave, the band has broken up and put in ranks.

18: 5th Dragoons pass through Coventry en route for Turkey.

19: Finish my drawings at School of Art for summer exhibition.

26: A general fast on account of the war.

MAY 25: A tremendous hail storm this afternoon, ground was white with it, gathered it in handfuls after the storm.

29: The School of Art has obtained no medals this season.

31: Mr. Rafter, the Master of the Coventry School of Art, offers me a situation as assistant master, but I decline it, not having the time on account of my apprenticeship.

JUNE 19: Godiva procession. When the first half had started, it rained heavily. Second half did not start till one hour later.

29: Went over with father to Fillongley Grange to Mr. Hollick's.

JULY 23; SUNDAY: Went a walk this evening and at 6 o'clock a cow attacked me in a field at Coundon and a tall hedge being behind me and no way of escape, I was obliged to fight her and caught hold of her left horn with my right hand and after a violent struggle drove her off, but she had dislocated my right shoulder. Dr. Bicknell set it 3 hours later.

MONDAY, 24: Stay at home.

TUESDAY, 25: Go to warehouse again this afternoon.

AUG. 2: Exhibition of prize drawings of Schools of Art of Great Britain at St. Mary's Hall, the drawings are very good – the Coventry drawings, 12 sheets, are exhibited by side of the others. These are mostly very poor, but the best four sheets are my own.

13: Leave off my sling today – my arm is getting better.

20, SUNDAY: Go with J. Archer and J. Sansome to Stoneleigh.

28: Shoulder joint still stiff.

SEP. 28: Mr. Ollard visiting Coventry. He preaches tonight at Vicar Lane. Deut. 8, Chap. 5, Ver. . .

OCT. 2: Bells ring in Coventry today to celebrate the Alma victory and procession of a band and flags round the city.

21: My shoulder is well now.

NOV. 1: Foggy morning, fog afterwards rose and formed very low clouds, could see them tumbling over the summit of St. Michael's steeple.

NOV. 17: Finish my drawings at School of Art. 1. Perspective.* 2. Ornament outlined from round.* 3. Ornament shaded from round.* 4. Foliage from the flat. 5. Flowers shaded from nature.* Flowers painted from flat. *P.S. Gained a medal each for these four.

DEC. 15: A meeting of the members of Mechanics Institution tonight to consider a proposal of the Religious and Useful Knowledge Society to amalgamate with us.[12] A very stormy meeting came to no definite conclusion.

DEC. 26: Visit Birmingham, Dudley and the Caverns.

28: Mr. R. Caldicott stops me in the street and informs me that they have awarded medals to 4 of my drawings out of the 6. Total income this year for draughting etc. £8.14.2. Amount in the Savings Bank Dec. 31/54 £9.3.5.

1855

JAN. 15: The medals gained at the November Exhibition in London are Andrews 4, Laxon 2, Lower 1, Bagshaw 1, Owen 1, Grimes 1, Wilcox 1, total 11.

18: About 80 wounded men from the Crimea arrive in Coventry from Liverpool where they had just landed.

19: The wounded go by rail to Cheltenham and another lot arrive.

31: Mr. Rafter informs me that the government have granted me a prize studentship for one year at School of Art.[13]

FEB. 9: Mr. Rafter informs me that the government have purchased two of my drawings, one of them the Florentine scroll shaded in chalk for 20/-, the other a pilaster from the gate of the Madeleine in outline for 10/-.

FEB. 17/55: Canal frozen 6 inches thick.

MAR. 18, SUNDAY: Go on an errand to Beston's at Berkswell. He tells me a curious piece of information.

20: Height 5 ft. 9 in. Weight 131 lbs.

21: General fast on account of the war.

29: Receive the 30/- today for my two drawings.

APR. 10: Make a water colour drawing of Stivichall Church which my father presents to Mrs. Gregory.

19: Finish my drawings for the May Exhibition. 1. Anatomy. 2. Historical Styles. 3. Woody nightshade.

MAY 1: Meeting of members of Mechanics Institute, a majority of votes in favour of amalgamation.

3: Snow storm for an hour or two tonight, very cold.

4: Snow on ground in patches.

12: Very cold. Obliged to have fires at warehouse.

JUNE 6: Mr. Bray says I can have 2 or 3 days holiday next week – thinks it will do my health good. I have had scarcely any holiday during my apprenticeship. Decide to go to Nottingham.

JUNE 10; SUNDAY: Left home at 3h. 45m. a.m. Fine morning. Walk to Rugby, arrive at station at 7h. Take train at 7h.30 for Nottingham, arrive at 10 o'clock. Arrive at my uncle's at 11.45, afternoon over the Mapperley Hills.

11: Visit ruins of Castle, the meadows and R. Trent. At evening visit the School of Design (Fussel, master, formerly of Coventry).

12: Trentbridge, Wilford Ferry, Clifton Park, back to Trentbridge. Caught a chub with a stick.

JUNE 13: Leave Nottingham 8.40, leave train at Sileby, visit granite quarries, refresh at Old Red Lion, Sileby, reach Coventry at 4 o'clock.

30: Mr. Rafter comes to the warehouse today to inform me that the government have awarded me a prize of £8 to go to Paris Exhibition.

JULY 4 AND 5: Buy maps and Guide Book of Paris.

7: Buy a continental railway guide.

10: Get my passport.

12: Leave Coventry at 4.45 afternoon for London. Sleep at 55 Goswell St.

13: After having been three times to Paymaster General's Office and twice to Marlborough House, I received £3 at 12 o'clock. Under weigh from below bridge at 1 o'clock, reach Boulogne at 11 at night, sleep at British Hotel.

SAT. 14: Walk round Boulogne, leave at 7 a.m., Paris 3 p.m., go to Hotel du Rhone, 13 in party.

JUNE, 15: Visit Versailles and St. Cloud whole of day.

MON. 16: Visit offices at 14 Rue du Corgue. See Mr. H. Cole, visit Exhibition.

17: Visit Exposition des Beaux Arts.

18: Exposition Industrielle.

19: Churches, Palais Luxembourg, Invalides.

20: Churches, Jardin des Plantes, Fortifications.

21: Leave Paris 7 o'clock, Rouen 11h. 18m., leave Rouen 3.50, Dieppe 5h. 15m., bathe in the sea, sleep on steamer.

SUN. 22: Under weigh 12.45 a.m., Newhaven 6.20, morning, London 11h., Kensington Gardens. Leave Paddington 2h., Leamington 6.10, Coventry 8 o'clock.

JULY 23; MONDAY: Warehouse again.

AUG. 10: Walter Iliffe, a new apprentice on trial, is sent home tonight. He is too lazy and insubordinate.

AUG. 15: Weight 9 stone 4 lbs.

SEP. 5: Mr. Joseph Cash calls on my father to ask what I mean to do when I am out of my apprenticeship. He says he wants a designer.

8, SAT: I ask for a holiday on Monday. Mr. Bray refuses, says he cannot spare me.

9, SUN: Visit Warwick, Fenny Compton, Burton Hills, Avon Dasset, Leamington. See Mary Allan alive for the last time.

15: Go and see Messrs. Cash today. They think of an arrangement for three years, the first six months to be in Paris.

20: Visit Cash's. They offer me £100 per year and the first six months to study in Paris or London.

24: Messrs. Bray want me to stay with them.

27: Tell Messrs. B. that I am inclined to think Cash's will be best for me. Go to Cash's to show a design.

OCT. 1: Cash sends for me. I visit him at evening. The journey to Paris is to be deferred until after 3 months. I am doing a red, white and blue design for them. School of Art meeting tonight. I am presented with my medal and 'Barnard's Water Colours'. Sir J. Paxton in the chair.[14] When I went up to the platform to receive it, there was great applause.

OCT. 3: Take my design to Cash's.

9: Take my red, white and blue design to Cash's. They seem well satisfied with it.

12: Read today in a paper that Mary Allan of Leamington was seriously injured last Thursday down a well.

15: Go to Cash's today and make final arrangement. The engagement is for 3 years at £100 per year. It is to be binding on me, but not on them. A written agreement was not considered necessary.

19: W. H. & C. Bray advertise today for a warehouseman in my place.

20: Mr. Allan comes over and informs us that his daughter, poor Mary, died last night at 8.45.

22: Go to Leamington tonight and see Mary Allan dead. She looks much older.

25: I and Rowley go to Leamington today and bury Mary Allan. We carried the head of the coffin, two of her young men carried the foot.

NOV. 6: Go with my father and buy a watch at Rotherhams for myself, No. 90841, £5 net.

7: Buy a palette knife and case of instruments.

8: Messrs. Bray have engaged a young man named Croxall in my place.

14: Finish my apprenticeship today.

15: Fetch my indenture from Mr. Davis.

16: Have holiday this morning, see the fox-hunting at Cubbington.

NOV. 17/55: Finish with Messrs. Bray. They behaved kindly to me at parting. They told me that if I did not succeed at Cash's to come to them and they would do what they could for me. They made me a present of 5/-. I promised to send them my address when I am in Paris.

NOV. 19: Commence at Cash's this morning – working hours 9 till 1 and 2 till 6 – a decided improvement from the hours at Bray's.

25: With a violent swing of my arm with a walking stick I dislocated my shoulder in a lane between Willenhall and Baginton. It was easily set later in the day.

29: Mr. Cash informs me that I shall probably go to Paris about end of January.

30: New large reading room opened at Coventry Institute.

DEC. 8: My shoulder is nearly well.

10: Go to work again this morning. My income this year, including £9-10-0 from government, was £21-7-9. This does not include any salary from Messrs. Cash. On completing my apprenticeship my savings amounted to £16.12.2.

1856

JAN. 10: Go with father tonight to ordnance summit, Corley, to see if the great fire on the Malverns was visible, but we could not see it.

17: Go to Neville's to be photographed. The price for the two is 7/- and 3/6.

22: Letter from Vasselon to Mr. Cash saying that he is ready to receive me. It is arranged that I shall go on Saturday week.

26: A letter of introduction this morning from Ellis Everington to their agent at Lyons.

31: Receive half a year's salary £50, go to the bank and leave my signature to be sent to London for a passport.

FEB. 1: Go with father by 8 o'clock train to London, go to Jones Lloyd and get a recommendation to the Foreign Office for a passport, take it to Foreign Office, get two £10 circular notes from London on Westminster Bank.

FEB. 2: Get my passport, also an introduction from Mr. H. Cole of Haden of Lyons, leave London Bridge Station at 6 p.m., Newhaven at 10 p.m.

FEB. 3, SUNDAY: Land at Dieppe 6 a.m., custom house closed, had to wait some hours for my bag. Ramble on the cliffs, a grand procession in the town of Henry IV – something like the Godiva show. Leave Dieppe 5 p.m., train does not go any further than Rouen. Stay at Hotel d'Angleterre.

FEB. 4: Leave Rouen 6 a.m., Paris 10.30, stay at Hotel de la Poste. Go and see Vasselon this afternoon. Expect to commence work on Wednesday morning.

FEB. 5/56: Go and see Vasselon again. It is the carnival today, a procession of bulls. I see the Emperor and Empress at the balcony of the Tuileries.[15] We cheered them.

FEB. 6: Start work with Vasselon, at work all day, hours 8 morning till 4.30 afternoon without any interval except 5 minutes, luncheon on the spot about noon.

7: I obtain 25 fr. 15 c. for English sovereigns.

8: Take a room for a month at 20 fr. 12, Hotel St. Roch, Rue Des Jeuners. Pay my account at Hotel de la Poste 16 fr. 50 c., 50 c. waiter.

9: Remove to my new lodging.

10: Sunday omnibus to Passy Walk, St. Cloud, Boulogne, Sevres, Passy to Paris, then to Louvre.

12: Take a ticket for 15 days table d'hote chez Noury 17 fr. 50 c.

15: Go to English class at 6 Rue Jacob.

17; SUNDAY: Go with Adrien, the Frenchman, to Pere la Chaise and then visit the fort of Vincennes.

19: Working hours increased from 4.30 to 5.30 p.m.

21: Theatre St. Martin, only one play – lasted from 7 till 12.

24; SUNDAY: Go a round of churches.

27: Visit some looms at work in Rue Faubourg du Temple.

MAR. 2; SUNDAY: Champ de Mars, Neuilly, Courbevoie, Mont Valerien, Suresnes, Bois de Boulogne, Champs Elysees.

3: Buy a tireligne (draughtsman's pen) 2 fr.

4: Buy a thermometer 3 fr. Go to a lecture at conservatoire des arts et metiers.

MAR. 8: Go to a lecture at Conservatoire: soude et potass (soda and potassium).

9; SUNDAY: Visit Louvre and Pantheon.

11: Grand Italian Opera tonight. Pit ticket 5 fr. Grisi in Norma.[16] J. Cash in Paris today.

16; SUNDAY: Prince Imperial born this morning, grand illuminations, visit Hotel Cluny.[17]

17: 21 years of age today, treat my fellow artists with drinks all round.

20: Attend the funeral of my landlord at the cemetery Montmartre, escort of Garde Nationale.

21; GOOD FRIDAY: fast day, am unable to obtain either breakfast or lunch.

23; SUNDAY: St. Denis, Enghien, Montmorency.

24: Fete de Paques. Hotel des Invalides, Neuilly, boat on the Seine with Roussel.

30; SUNDAY: Jardin du Luxembourg, Meudon Sevres, Ville d'Avray steeple chase. Saw accident on the road in returning – vehicle smashed, wounded horse and man with broken thigh dying. Peace signed today – grand illumination at night.[18]

APR. 1: General illumination of all the private houses in Paris, but not public buildings. To see the illuminations I take omnibus from Louvre to Barrière de l'Etoile, walk from Etoile to Bastille, then omnibus to Madeleine, then walk to hotel.

6; SUNDAY: Rive droite to Versailles Palais, Parc, Trianon, Rive gauche a Sevres, walk to Passy, omnibus home.

APR. 11/56: Perceive a soreness in my throat tonight.

12: Throat worse.

13: Take a dose of rhubarb and repeat it in the evening. Visit St. Germain.

14: Throat worse – go for advice to Smith, Medicin Anglaise, 8 Rue Castiglione. He says it is one of the glands of the throat swelled. Charge moderate, 5 fr. English chemist (Roberts) charges 7½ fr. for medicine, etc. (thieves), double the value of the articles.

15: Receive letters from Messrs. Cash informing me that they will probably require me at the end of month.

16: Throat getting better.

17: Throat well – light evening now, walk in Montmartre.

19: Theatre de L'Ambigu – The Deluge – very wonderful.

20; SUNDAY: Visit Fontainbleau. Very beautiful, large carp in the ponds.

21: Go to the Grand Opera, 'Les Hugenots'.

SUN. 27: Visit Pere La Chaise in the morning, afterwards to Neuilly to dine with Mr. Vasselon and then in boat on the Seine.

29: Receive instructions from Coventry to return at the end of the month.

30: Decide to start day after tomorrow, leave off work at noon today.

MAY 1: Have my new frock coat today, 120 fr.

2: Leave Paris 5 evening, Dieppe 9.40, leave Dieppe 11.15.

3: Arrive Newhaven 6.30 morning, Coventry 3.42 afternoon, journey of 22 hours. Visit Cash's in evening. In France the vegetation is a month in advance.

MAY 5; MONDAY: Go to work at Cash's again.

11; SUNDAY: Go to Vicar Lane again.

27: Sworn in as freeman this morning.

29: Festival Day to celebrate the peace. 800 children go in procession through the streets with flags, etc.

JUNE 3: Commence again at the School of Art.

8; SUNDAY: Go with J. Archer to Binley and Coundon.

JULY 2: Go with Atkins, Matthew and Hardiman to Kenilworth to the Flower Show, have half holiday.

21: Go to London today to the Crystal Palace.[19]

22: Go over Leaf's house, then to Woolwich and over the Dockyard and Greenwich Hospital – Drury Lane Theatre in the evening.

23: Go over Ellis's house and to Crystal Palace and up the tower. Return to Coventry.

AUG. 2: Leave Coventry this morning with father and Mr. Anstey for

Scotland. After an intensely hot journey arrive at Glasgow at 2.30 next morning.

3; SUNDAY: Hear Norman McLeod preach at Barony church, see my uncles Sam, John and Hay.

4: Leave Glasgow 7 a.m., Balloch Bowling, Loch Lomond, Rowardennan. Commence the ascent at 11 o'clock. We arrive at summit of Ben Lomond at 2 p.m., arrive at the Inn at 5 – a fearful hard day's work, thermometer all the way up to 90° and 85° in the shade at summit. Up the lake to Inversnaid tonight.

AUG. 5/56: Walk to Loch Katrine, then by steamer to the end of the lochs and walk through Trossachs, back same way to Inversnaid, then across to Tarbet, walk to Arrochar and back then up the loch to Inverarnan.

6: Leave Inverarnan by chaise through Glen Falloch, Tyndrum, Glenorchy, Dalmally Pass of Awe, Tainault to Oban.

7: By steamer to Staffa and Iona. Back to Oban in the evening.

8: Thunderstorm early this morning. Leave Oban by steamer, disembark at Crinan and through the canal to Ardrishaig, then by steamer to Glasgow, arrive 6.30 p.m. and to Stirling, arrive 1 a.m.

9: Go round Stirling and through the Castle. Afterwards to Edinburgh and Dalkeith.

10; SUNDAY: To church this morning. To the Roman camp in afternoon. See my Uncle and my father's Aunt Hill.

11: Visit Roslyn Castle and Chapel, then to Edinburgh Castle, Holyrood, etc.

12: Visit my Aunt Margaret, W. Porteous, Mrs. Hill, etc. Leave Dalkeith for Edinburgh, meet Anstey at the Castle. Leave Edinburgh at 8 p.m. for England.

13: Arrive Liverpool 5.20 a.m., walk through town and docks, arrive Coventry at 4.45 afternoon.

14: At work again this morning.

SEP. 12: Finish my drawings.

15: The drawings all arranged in St. Mary's Hall today. Inspector comes.

16: Inspector goes through the drawings, mine are very good, but deficient in quantity. I exhibit in two stages only. The award is: Mallinson 7 medals, Adams 2, S. Owen 2, Miss Cash 1, H. Owen 1, Reeves 1, Grimes 1. We are examined tonight in model drawing and perspective.

SEP. 19: Cash's factory hands are all paid off tonight. They finished by giving three cheers for the master.

20: Factory closes today.

27: Still closed. Put out a handbill today announcing that we intend to return to weekly wages.

28; SUNDAY: Heavy rain today. It ceased at 4h. 5m. afternoon. At 4.15 it began to blow tremendously. A whirlwind was passing over. It had been very calm for the preceding ten minutes. It made a noise like half a dozen express trains making past and lasted about one minute. As far as the eye could reach upwards the air was filled with thousands of leaves blowing furiously in all directions. It came over St. John's church, passed over our house (taking about a dozen slates off the adjoining houses), then across the barracks where it took about 30 yards clean out of the barrack wall, then over the Paddy Croft, Warwick Row, Grey Friars Green and Ogden's nursery and the Park gardens, cutting trees in two and tearing them up by the roots. Its breadth did not exceed 100 or 150 yards. The other parts of the city knew nothing of the occurrence. During the wind the flame of the kitchen fire was drawn up the chimney with blue flame and a roaring noise.

MONDAY, 30: About 100 hands and pickers up returned.

OCT. 10: Annual meeting of School of Art. I am presented with a book on Middle Age Art. They forgot the medals.

12: Receive my medal.

26; SUNDAY: Berkswell by train, walk to Kenilworth and back to Coventry.

31: Receive a box of colours and a box of instruments for the two examinations which I passed when the inspector was here.

NOV. 2; SUNDAY: Walk out with Archer and Tester.

22; SATURDAY: Mr. John Cash gives me my half year salary without asking – also voluntarily gives me half an hour to take a stroll up the Warwick Road.

30; SUNDAY: Go and look at the land today where Cash's are going to build the houses near Foleshill.

DEC. 14; SUN.: Go with Tester and Archer to Baginton.

23: A meeting of the seat holders at Vicar Lane Chapel tonight to consider about purchasing a new organ and paying off the £100 debt on the building.

24: Visit Mr. and Mrs. Allan at Leamington and also see Mary's grave.

My income this year £102. 9. 7.

Expenses in England	£37.18. 7.
Expenses in France	£25. 2. 0.
	£63. 0. 7.

At home paid 10/- per week for Board and Lodging. I have travelled during the last eighteen months 3,500 miles away from Coventry and 500 in Warwickshire. Total 4,000.

1857

JAN. 2: Saw an occultation of Jupiter well this afternoon. Saw it well and all four satellites were visible. The planet was rather paler than the moon. Jupiter was visible at 3.30 this afternoon.

13: Meeting of Committee at Vicar Lane tonight to consider alteration of organ, etc. I am appointed secretary.

19: Saw emersions of Jupiter's 1st and 3rd satellites. Our time appears to be about seven minutes fast on Greenwich.

26: 22 arches of the Spon End viaduct fell in during last night.

FEB. 5: Mander, book-keeper at Cash's unwell. I am doing his work.

15: Most Sunday afternoons go a walk up the Warwick Rd. with Archer and Tester.

24: Commence to prepare dark coloured designs for next winter.

MAR. 18: Meeting of the Committee tonight at Vicar Lane. A catastrophe takes place and the meeting is dissolved.

27: Parliamentary election today. Ellice, Paxton, Mellor, Phillimore, Treherne. Ellice and Paxton returned by overwhelming majorities. Procession round the city afterwards.[20]

APR. 5; SUNDAY: Go and see the houses which are being built at King Fields.

7: See a small telescopic comet near a Persei – very faint (D'Arrests comet) quite invisible to the naked eye.

10; GOOD FRIDAY: Visit Kenilworth Castle and Honily.

MONDAY, 13: Mr. Cash informs me at ten this morning that I am to go immediately to London. I leave at 1 o'clock, London at 5. See my father at Euston Square. We go up Primrose Hill.

14: Meet Mr. Cash at 8.30 this morning at the Milton Club, 14

Ludgate Hill. We go round the West End and look in the windows – dine at the Milton, accompany him to station at 5 p.m. Polytechnic in evening.

15: Visit British Museum, afterwards Woolwich Rotunda, etc.

16: Crystal Palace – evening Princess Theatre to see Charles Kean in Richard II.

17: Kew Gardens, Richmond Hill.

18: Leave London 10.50. Arrive Coventry 2.5. Mr. Cash pays all my expenses, 36/-.

19; SUNDAY: See a small comet in Perseus exactly like the other.

MAY 6: At Cash's we have a half holiday and all walk through Baginton, Stoneleigh to Bubbenhall. Tea at Malt Shovel, skittles, walk home through the meadows to Ryton Bridge.

11: Receive case of instruments and box of colours from the Department. The colours were very common and worth perhaps 6/- instead of 20/-. Instruments good, but rusty. These were due to me on completing my year of prize-studentship.

MAY 18: Hear that Mr. Sibree offers to resign his ministry if the committee will give him £120 a year and the endowment of Dunn's house. Hear they intend to offer him £100 per year net (afterwards they offered it to him and he refused it).

JUNE 16: Uncle William Andrews arrives in Coventry.

22: Go haymaking in Mr. Joseph Cash's field.

23: Same.

24: Same – rick slipped over. We commenced at 7 p.m. to rebuild it. Finished at 10½ p.m.

29: Visited Chatsworth by an excursion today. Walk from Rowsley.

JULY 7: Commence designs today for the competition.

11: Uncle William gives Cash's notice and leaves today.

AUG. 4: Half day's holiday. Visit Bubbenhall, Ryton meadows.

9: Stormy. 7 sheep killed on the green by lightning.

13: Very stormy night, continuous flashes of blue lightning, sometimes 7 or 8 in succession and 30 or 40 in a minute, a second storm at 11 p.m. Was at School of Art finishing my last drawing – probably my last night at the School of Art.

17: Hear from my uncle from Scotland, doing very bad and would be glad to return to Coventry.

AUG. 26: Finish my ribbon designs. Mr. Cash gives me permission to show the ribbon.

29: Rafter, the master of School of Art, alters his mind about the ribbon, is doubtful about it, refers me to Mr. Caldicott the secretary, etc.

31: Call on Mr. Caldicott. He says that I may send the piece of ribbon, they will be glad to see it, etc. I mount the designs ready.

SEP. 1: Send the designs, 6 for ribbons, 3 for trimmings and 3 for watches. Mr. Rafter calls me into his room tonight. I find Owen there, the two make strong protest about my sending the piece of ribbon. I agree to withdraw it solely at their request, to prevent any ill-feeling, etc.

SEP. 2: Speak to Mr. Cash. He blames me for submitting to dictation last night. Call on Mr. Caldicott. He is annoyed at the conduct of Rafter and Owen, and refuses to have the ribbon taken out, and says it shall be decided by the Committee. The Committee meet at twelve and decide to have it taken out. Prizes awarded – myself first prize for ribbon design 8 votes, Owen had but 5 and Cowsill 1 – there were no other competitors. Owen the prize for trimmings, Gillings for watches, Stubbes for warehouseman's ribbon design.

SEP. 3: Go and see the designs at St. Mary's Hall.

4: Hear there is a screw loose about Gillings' watch design.

7: Inspector comes today to examine the drawings. I pass examinations in free hand drawing and model drawing tonight with a view to a studentship under the new regulations.

8: Pass examinations tonight in geometry, perspective and drawing from memory. It is decided that Gillings shall not have the prize for watches as he did not do the design.

10: Replace the piece of ribbon in my frame at the hall and place my name to my designs.

11: I am successful in gaining the prize studentship. Medals awarded by the inspector: Andrews 3, S. Owen 1, Nevill 1, E. Whiteman 1, Whitten 1, Cryer 1, Dalton 2, Frost 2, Rollason 1.

23: Leave Coventry at 8 a.m. for Manchester to go and see Art Treasures Exhibition, stay with Lunes at night.

24: Exhibition again. Afterwards Peel Park and Museum, evening a few friends at Lunes.

25: Leave at 7 a.m. Liverpool, then by Tynwald steamer to Douglas, arrive 6 p.m., fine voyage.

26: Bad weather, Kirkonchan, Douglas Head, sea rough.

SEP. 25/57; SUNDAY: Kirk Braddon half way house to Peel – ruins of St. Trinians, sea visible on other side of island.

28: Douglas Head all morning sketching, after Kirk Braddon and Nunnery, evening moonlight walk on beach.

29: Leave Isle of Man at 9 a.m., Liverpool 4 p.m.

30: Leave Liverpool 9.10 a.m., Coventry 1.30.

OCT. 2: Meeting of Committee at Vicar Lane tonight – resolve to commence the organ.

6: Annual meeting of School of Art at St. Mary's Hall. I am presented with my medal, the prize of £10 for the best ribbon designs for professional designers, and a book, the life of Stephenson. There was great applause. The prize for watch design awarded to R. Lowe.

7: A general fast day on account of India.[21]

15: The Messrs. Cash send for me to counting house, and state that they intend to open a new warehouse at King Fields and propose to have me to manage it, offer me a house free and £100 per year and to be paid extra for what designs I do for them.[22] They promise me that if I do not succeed I am to return to my old place as designer and give me till the beginning of next week to consider it.

17; SATURDAY: Go to King Fields this afternoon to look at the house – don't like it very much.

19: Talk with John Cash again today. We arrange that I am to have the house rent free and gas and coals and £120 the first year. Sister Anne is to go and keep house with me.

21: Commence to make preparations.

23: The gas is being laid in.

26: Go and buy a dozen chairs, 2 tables, a carpet, etc.

27; TUESDAY: Remove from home today to the house, No. 8 King Fields and commence house-keeping.

31: Open the business at King Fields this morning.

NOV. 6: I am offering 3/10 per piece for weaving 24 Orientals – gross lengths, etc.[23]

7: The weavers residing here are dissatisfied with the price I offer – 4 of them go as a deputation to Joseph Cash. I hear that he tells them he has nothing to do with it and that they must apply to me (the business is carried on in my name). 8 of them afterwards go to Coventry. I go and see Messrs. Cash. They tell me to be firm and to hold out and to decline to sign any list.[24]

8: Mr. Sibree's memory fails him in his sermon this morning.

9: C. Dresser chosen mayor today. Mr. Joseph Cash sends for me at

9 o'clock tonight. The tenants complain much about the price I am offering. He tells me to give way a little and try and pacify them.

NOV. 10: Weavers are applying to me for work. I have two warpers going now.

11: Bennoch and Twentyman of London have failed. Hear that Barbwell is in with them for £21,000 and nearly all the small trimming manufacturers are in to some extent.

21: Have a gas stove put in my warehouse.

27: Stopped warping because of putting the shafting through the shop.[25]

28: Finish the flower garden in front of my house.

DEC. 2: Recommence warping.

10: Meeting tonight at Vicar Lane principally composed of women. It is decided that Mr. Sibree (is to go), all the deacons and four old friends are to be a committee to choose a new minister.

19: Since I have been in business I have warped 1,000 pieces of ribbon of which 300 pieces are already delivered to Hertford St.

22: Have 20 looms going.

31: Weather fine and mild. We have had no winter yet.

Income this year: Salary	100		
Prize	10		
Odd	1	8	6
	111	8	6
Expenditure:			
Furniture	17	10	6
Journey through Isle of Man	3	7	10
Board at home, house-keeping, etc.	39	3	7
	60	1	11

In bank Dec. 31st, £106 13 11.

1858

JAN. 24; SUNDAY: Go with J. Archer round by Baginton.

FEB. 13: Messrs. Cash job a lot of my goods this week. Mallinson is turned away. He does not suit.

15: Messrs. Cash talk of removing my warehouse to other premises as early as they can.

18: At work till 1 a.m. this morning designing.

MAR. 9: Meeting of Finance Committee at Vicar Lane Chapel. I am invited and attend. Income of chapel about £220, there is debt of £16 on incidental expenses fund. Shillito is to have £150 a year and Sibree £80.

13; SATURDAY: Make a plan today of Vicar Lane Chapel. Aurora Borealis tonight.

15: Great eclipse of sun today. Make every preparation to observe it. See the sun very well previous to commencement, clouds come over, do not obtain a glimpse till after the totality is over. It was about as dusky as at 6 o'clock in the evening.

17: It was cloudy everywhere on Monday except at Fotheringay in Northamptonshire.

21: It is announced that Mr. Shillito will accept the call given to him by the Vicar Lane congregation.

APR. 3: Send in 330 pieces this week.

APR. 4/58; SUNDAY: Mr. Shillito preaches his opening sermon.

10: It is decided today that I am to remove from King Fields to a house at Draper's Fields.

MAY 1: The estimated value today is silk in warehouse £454, silk with weavers £556, do. factory £220, do. dyer £21. Total £1251.

5: Day holiday – visit Chester and see the Cup race. 28 ran.

21: I am to remove next week, take down warping frames.

JUNE 2: Quarrels in the city about the fair.

3: Remove to Draper's Fields.

6: Fair is held in Hales St.

14: The Queen arrives this afternoon. We have seats in the station yard.[26]

16: A meeting of my weavers is held this evening at the Prince William Henry public house.

18: Have a deputation from the general weavers committee this morning. I decline to sign the list.

19: The deputation comes again. I still refuse.

21: The deputation goes to see Mr. Joseph Cash this morning.

26: Go to Stoneleigh Abbey this afternoon, go through the house, see the Queen's apartments, the grounds, etc.

29: Another meeting of my weavers tonight at the Prince William Henry.

JULY 2: A final deputation wait on me this morning to know if I will sign the list. I decline. They threaten that they will have a meeting at St. Mary's

Hall. They had a paper signed by most of my hands – 'That we are of opinion that the conduct of Mr. Andrews as reported by the deputation that have waited on him is most despicable, and we are determined to use every means,' etc., etc.

JULY 6: M John Cash insists I hold out saying that if I cannot, he will shut up the business.

19: Visit Stoneleigh this afternoon with Coventry Institute. Go over the Abbey.

21: Receive two letters from the Department of Science and Art. One informs me that I have gained the National Medal this year. The other that it is to be of bronze instead of silver.

AUG. 10: Go and hear Spurgeon preach at Wyken Square this evening.

20: The contest of the weavers committee with Smith terminates today. Smith gives in.

21: The committee come to see me – I defy them. They go to Mr. Joseph Cash; he defers them till Mr. John comes home next week. See Mr. Joseph tonight. He tells me to give in.

22: Smith calls at my house tonight and talks with me about the committee.

23: A triumphal procession of factory weavers through the city. They have succeeded in forcing most of the factory owners to sign a list for piece work.

AUG. 24: Mr. John Cash returns.

25: Mr. John decides that I am to sign the list. It is much to my annoyance as it was by their advice I refused at first.

26: Committee come today. I request them to defer it till tomorrow.

27: I sign the list this morning, but add to my name the address Draper's Fields so that my signature will be no longer binding when I no longer live in Draper's Fields.

29: Wrote last week to the Department of Science and Art enquiring if I can have the medal in silver by paying for the metal.

30; MONDAY: A combination of 9 ribbon factory owners has been affected. They put out a handbill on Friday making a determined stand for weekly wages and threaten to close all their factories.

SEP. 1: See a comet in the North tonight. It was visible to the naked eye as a star, but with a telescope a large tail could be seen.

4; SATURDAY: Lock out of the factories. 900 hands thrown out.

5: Comet's tail visible to the naked eye.

9: Tail getting brighter, nucleus 2nd mag.

13: Tail 4′ long.

14: Factory hands still out.

15: Stopping warping dark colours.

SEP. 30/58: Comet now very bright, tail about 20′ long.

OCT. 1: Factory strike just in the same state. Both parties hold out.

2: Mr. John Cash asks me about my future prospects. I tell him I have no decided ones, he says he cannot give me any more salary – this is because at commencing the business it was understood that I was to have an annual present if the business turned out satisfactory.

4: Have been running about 25 looms this season, they are now standing at change of colours but the weavers are not willing to wait. 10 have already got work (the factories are idle).

5: The comet passes over Arcturus tonight ½′ from the nucleus. 1 hour in passing over, tail is 30′ or 35′ long. Commence to warp light colours.

9: Hart closes his Bedworth factory today.

11: Annual meeting of the School of Art. I receive the ordinary bronze medal for the last time. I have done no drawings this year.

15: Comet has gone away now.

17; SUNDAY: Vicar Lane reopened.

25: Have 24 looms going now.

27: The lockout is at an end. The masters have given in.

NOV. 11: Mr. Cash tells me that it is their intention to give me a percentage on the profits.

15: Commence to give out single hand work.

19: It is decided today that I am to use tram instead of singles, so I am to have my own way at last.[27]

NOV. 21; SUNDAY: Tester is living in Coventry for a few weeks. We go up the Warwick Road 'as of yore'.

24: Thermometer at 8 a.m. stood at 18°.

DEC. 11: Am very busy now.

13: Exhibition of National Drawings at St. Mary's Hall. My silver medal has come – I had declined to accept a bronze one – the department in order to keep faith with myself and others had a few silver medals struck instead of bronze medallions.

Income this year	£123	1	0d
Expenditure	83	2	11
Cash in bank	146	12	0

1859

JAN. 7; FRIDAY: The new organ at Vicar Lane opened tonight.

10: Recognition service for Mr. Shillito tonight.

26: Snowed a few minutes this morning, the first we have had this winter.

FEB. 10; THURSDAY: Have sent in already 315 pieces this week.

12: Weather very mild lately.

23: We have no frost for several weeks.

MAR. 4: Season extremely mild. Could see a fire some miles off tonight, sky all red.

6; SUNDAY: Go to Wolston Heath, scene of five farm buildings burned. Cow burned to death.

23: Weather still mild.

24: Sent in 380 pieces this week. Weather warm.

MAR. 30/59: Ground white with snow first time this winter.

31: Intense frost last night. Sent in 408 pieces this week.

AP. 3: Frost last night (the last this season).

5: Intensely hot weather.

9: Go with father to London tonight.

10; SUNDAY: Go and hear Gordon Cumming this morning. Hyde Park afternoon, Westminster Abbey in the evening.

11: Go round the city and West End. Return to Coventry by evening express.

21: Have sent in 518 pieces this week.

22; GOOD FRIDAY: Visit Kenilworth and Honily.

23: Weigh in 300 pieces today.

29: War begins between Austria and France.[28]

MAY 2: Stock-taking today. My books are taken away and a new set given me.

3: A frost last night.

8: Occultation of Saturn tonight, saw emersion, planet was much fainter than the moon.

19: Half holiday. Go to Canley, Gibbet Hill and Stoneleigh.

JUNE 10: Send in my income tax paper for first time. Have filled it up for £120.[29]

13: Mr. John Cash tells me that my percentage on the goods will amount to about £40 or £50 per year.

17: Write to Paris to J. Roussel, send my passport to London for visa.

23: Receive answer from Paris, decide to go, ask for holiday.

24: Coventry fair.

JUNE 25: Leave Coventry at 3.35 p.m., via London, Calais, Dover, Lille, Amiens.

26; SUNDAY: Arrive Paris 9 a.m. Go to Hotel St. Roch. Find Wepfer directly. Spend the day with him.

27: Go to Roussel and order 6 designs, dine Chez Noury. Weather intensely hot.

28: See exposition of pictures. Champs Elysees, afterwards Bois du Boulogne, see Empress. Dine Salle Montesquieu.

29: Select the designs, leave Paris 7.40 p.m.

30: At Coventry at noon.

JULY 2: Send written report of journey to Messrs. Cash.

15: Go with father to agricultural show at Warwick.

SEP. 12: Go with a School of Art party to Stratford-on-Avon.

14: Appeal against House Tax this morning, get exempted. Jeffcoat and Soden on bench.

27: Go to Bubbenhall with Mathew, Holland, Owen, J. Iliffe.

OCT. 5: I joined the Volunteers yesterday.[30]

12: Splendid Aurora tonight, the rays were a deep crimson and converged to a point near zenith.

18: We drill for the first time in the barrack yard this afternoon.

19: A steam factory is being built at King Fields.

21: Hard frost last night, ice $\frac{3}{8}$ of an inch thick.

22, 23, 24: Hard frost.

25: Tremendous cyclone tonight and tomorrow. Annual meeting of School of Art. I should have received a silver medal, but Mr. Caldicott, the secretary, forgets it.

26: Royal Charter wrecked, 400 lives lost. I fetch my medal this morning.

28: My name is in the papers with the other students who received prizes.

NOV. 14: I step 1950 steps in a mile.

19: Go to Warwick and consult Matthews about my shoulder. He advises me not to do any shooting with the rifle.

21: Send in my resignation to the secretary of the Rifle Volunteers with much regret.

DEC. 17: Temperature this morning 9° at 1 o'clock, 15° at 9 p.m.

18: 7 p.m. 9°.

21: Thaw sets in.

24: Hawley and Hill send me a turkey.

27: Go to Wiberley's to supper.

Income this year (to Jan. 8/60)	£163	3	0
Expenditure: Pocket money	£5	2	11
Clothes	10	14	9
Private bills, subscriptions, part of journey to Paris, Income tax, etc.	6	5	3
Furniture	7	3	2
Housekeeping	46	8	0
Not accounted		9	7
Total	76	3	8

Saved this year £87 12 9

I am now worth £267.

1860

JAN. 2: John Archer was taken ill last spring with inflammation of the lungs. He was very seriously ill, but in the summer to all appearance he perfectly recovered. Late last autumn he burst a blood vessel, and was again seriously ill, but he rallied considerably. But just before Xmas he was taken much worse. Dr. Dresser was sent for but gives him no hopes of recovery. I visit him very often.

21: I see J. Archer alive for the last time. He is quite prepared and resigned to die. I left him asleep.

25: J. Archer dies this morning at 1 o'clock. He burst a blood vessel and in five minutes all was over. His last words were 'Call my mother.' I saw his body this afternoon.

30: We bury John Archer in the cemetery today, I and 5 other bearers. Mr. Shillito officiates. J. A. was 11 days younger than myself.

FEB. 5; SUNDAY: The bearers who carried J. Archer attend Vicar Lane together this morning.

7: Saw the partial eclipse of moon this morning. The dark part of the moon was very bright, the dark patches were plainly visible on it.

11: Mr. Gladstone made his statement in the House last night. The duty is to come off foreign ribbons immediately.[31] Our Coventry ribbon manufacturers seem confident of holding their ground against the foreigner. The idea seems to be that our coal and machinery will beat them.

12; SUNDAY: Go with Mr. Archer and Robert Archer and show them where the names are carved on the tree at Stivichall Common.

16: Coventry ribbon factories are on half time. Most of the outdoor looms are standing.

27: I am making an effort to give out goods at 3/- instead of 3/11, but am not very successful.

29: Mr. Joseph Cash informs me that it is not their intention to carry on permanently with the business at Draper's Fields.

MAR. 22: Trade is still no better. I have only 10 looms going instead of 50.

AP. 2: Saw Venus at 1h. 30m. today. Have only 6 looms going, now 5. Messrs. Cash tell me this morning that trade being so bad, they intend to give up the outdoor trade, consequently will be enabled to dispense with my services, and give me a month's notice. They state that they will shut the house up or that perhaps I can remain in it after. This does not coincide with the promise they made me when I consented to undertake their King Fields business, namely that if I was not successful, I should return to my place with them as designer.

AP. 13: Trade no better.

14: Saw Venus at 1 o'clock East of the sun.

20: Trade no better and of 100 looms in Cash's factory at West Orchard, 60 are standing.

MAY 3: Saw Venus at 10½ h. a.m. E. of the sun, 12 hours before sunset. Remove today the greater part of my furniture to my father's in Fleet St.

7: Sister Anne goes to Dell's. Settle today with Messrs. Cash. They pay me till May 5th. May 19th would have completed my half year.

8: Hear Cash's have now only 17 looms standing to the factory.

11: Advertise in the local papers today for a situation.

18: Ditto.

19: J. Iliffe takes the house in Draper's Fields today.

21: I present Mr. Sibree with two sketches today for his lecture. Go to Warwick and see the Volunteer Review.

22: Clear out from Draper's Fields today.

23: Receive £2 from J. Iliffe and give up the keys of the house.

24: Occultation of Jupiter at 4h. 34m. afternoon. Could perceive the planet with 2 inch aperture.

25: Mother ill in bed with bad knee.

MAY 27/60: Mother rather worse. Aunt Ann comes to see her.

28: Mother rather better.

30: Mother's knee breaks today.

JUNE 5: Ribbon trade said to be getting worse, manufacturers are not so confident of being able to compete with the foreigner. Great doubt prevails.

7: Mother sick and seems worse. Dr. Powell is sent for and he and Dr. Bicknell hold a consultation. Powell says she is dangerously ill.

8: Give advertisement to T. Robinson to insert in Basler Nachrichten as he is going on the deputation to Basle.

10: Mother getting better.

14: Call on C. Peters today. He strongly recommends me to go to Basle.

15: Aunt goes home today.

16: Mr. John Cash gives me a good written character today.

19: Mother comes down stairs.

21: Man killed by lightning this afternoon on Grey Friars Garden.

23: Review of 19,000 Volunteers in Hyde Park. Coventry Volunteers go.

24: Go with father by Kenilworth and Stoneleigh Park.

28: Trade still no better.

30: Coventry Volunteers practise at the target at Allesley tonight for the first time.

JULY 2: Call on Mr. T. Robinson. He says he advertised twice in the Basler Nachrichten.

JULY 2: I have now been out of employment since May 5th. I have advertised twice in Coventry papers for a situation and have not obtained a single reply. Trade is getting worse and I have given up all hope of obtaining employment in Coventry at present. I have also advertised twice in a Basle paper without result. My mind is now made up. I decide to go on the continent and seek employment and see the world. I will be like King Alfred. I will penetrate the enemy's camp and see what I can discover. If I am not successful, I can but return to England. Cash's have had for some considerable time in their employ a Swiss designer named Seiler from Basle, also Owen who was beaten by me in the professional designer's competition in 1857 at the School of Art.

JULY 3: Call on old masters W. H. and C. Bray. Mr. W. H. Bray is very civil and promises to write me a character. I go behind the butts tonight and see the target practice.

7: Call on Seiler at Cash's today. He refuses to give me any letters of introduction to Basel, but Mr. John Cash has informed me that if I can find out all that the foreigners are doing, there will be no difficulty in my obtaining employment with them when I return.

JULY 12/60: I have managed to obtain a couple of letters of introduction to people on the continent. I bid my friends good-bye today.

13: Leave Coventry this morning, arrive at London, visit the Tower and Thames tunnel.

14: Leave London 9 a.m. by steam boat for Ostende. Arrive 8 p.m. Rough off Margate, rain off Ostende. Stay at Ship Hotel, find a Coventry man staying there, Mr. Friedlander.

15: Ostende to Bruxelles, stay at Hotel de Brabant.

16: Rail to Gemappe, Waterloo walk to Bruxelles 19 miles.

17: Leave Brussels 1.15, Liege, at Verviers enter Prussia, Cologne 10 p.m. Hotel Freidrich at Viersen. They charge me 5 francs for a dinner which I had not 10 minutes allowed to eat.

18: Go to Crefeld, eclipse of sun.

19: Search for employment at two places – unsuccessful. Return to Cologne, Hotel de Hollande.

20: Leave Cologne 6 a.m. Konigswinter, Drachenfels, have 2 hours at Coblentz, arrive at St. Goar.

21: At St. Goar, ramble about, remarkable echo. Afternoon ramble, the village Rheinfels, etc.

22; SUNDAY: St. Goar, Prinz von Preussen, St. Goarhausen, villagers dancing, Swiss valley.

JULY 23/60: Leave St. Goar, the Rhine, Mainz – Austrian troops – Mannheim, Heidleberg.

24: Heidleberg, Baden, Basel. Stay at Gasthof z. Wildemann.

25: Basel. Look over the city.

26: Basel. Wasting my time about letters of introduction, go for a walk across the French frontier at Burgfelden or St. Louis.

27: Am shown over the establishment of Emanuel Burgy this morning. Go for a walk over Baden frontier.

28: Commence searching for employment. I offer my services to start with to the principal firm Sarasin & Co. I find the principal smoking a cigar in his counting house. As soon as I tell him who I am, he also offers me a cigar and we smoke. I explain to him without reserve who I am and that there is a row in Coventry between masters and men and that it is hopeless for me to seek employment in England. At first they refused to employ me, then hesitated, and finally told me to call again on Monday. He seemed to be rather afraid of employing me, and remarked that 'Les Anglais sont tres habilles.' I take a room at a boarding house for a month at 20 fr. or 70 fr. including board. The address is Siegfried, Geometer, 31, St. Johann Vorstadt, Basel.

JULY 29/60; SUNDAY: Attend service at Cathedral, walk by Huningen.

30; MONDAY: Call on Sarasin for an answer, but he cannot give me a place. Call on Bischoff Freres near the museum.

31: Call on de Barry, Sulger and Stuckelburger, Bischoff fils, without success.

AUG. 1: Call on Freivogel, Kochlin without success.

2: Call on Kochlin again, Trudinger. See Mr. Hawley today from Coventry.

3: Call on Bischoff freres again and Les fils d'Isaac Dreyfus without success.

4; SATURDAY: Call on Fischer & fils, am to go Tuesday morning for answer. Weather very rainy.

5; SUNDAY: French chapel, afternoon fete of Huningen.

6: To Muttenz by rail, walk back.

7: Call on Fischer again. I resolve to delay further search for a week and go and see the Alps.

8: Leave Basel. Rail to Liestal, walk Liestal to Sissach, rail Sissach to Lanfelfingen. Sun Inn at Lanfelfingen, walk over the Jura by the Unter Hauenstein pass to Olten. First view of Alps from summit of pass. Olten Gasthaus zum Kreutz. See Alps beautifully, Lake of Luzern, Bay of Uri, Fluellen, dine at Altdorf and walk to Wasen, Cow Inn.

AUG. 10/60: Walk through cloud and rain to Andermatt. Rain all day. Hotel St. Gotthard very dear.

11: Walk from Andermatt over St. Gotthard pass to Airolo. Hear Italian spoken.

12; SUNDAY: From Airolo through rain to hospice.

13: Hospice comfortable, civil and reasonable. Walk from hospice to Altdorf 33¼ miles. Hotel de L'Ours at Altdorf good and cheap.

14: Altdorf to Luzern, see lion, rail to Basel.

16: Recommence my search today for employment. Call on Sarasin & Co., Oswald & Co., Horandt & fils, Richter Linder without success.

17: Rain all day. Stay at my lodgings.

18: Search at six houses without success.

19; SUNDAY: Encounter the weavers deputation from Coventry in the street.[32]

20: Call at Bachofen & John, Forcart Weis & Burckhardt Wiedt, J. J. Linder. Visit the deputation at the Black Bear Hotel tonight.

21: I have now been in Switzerland nearly 4 weeks and am beginning to despair of obtaining work, but am woken up early this morning by young Oswald for Oswald & Co. and walked off to his atelier and set to work at designing. I visit the deputation again tonight.

22: Designing at Oswald's again. They also give me a draft to do. Deputation leaves Basel tonight, most of their information they obtain from me.

23: Still at Oswald's. Oswald cannot make up his mind.

25: Engage this morning with Oswald for three months at 100 francs per month. Go to the police office with a note from Oswald about a permit to reside in Basel.

26; SUNDAY: Fete of St. Jacob.

27: Oswalds is about 2 miles from my lodgings. I remove today to fresh lodgings on the other side of the river at Klein Basel so as to be nearer my work – Muller 190 Basel.

28: My new lodgings turn out very bad, and are full of fleas. Made acquaintance of Ernst Wirz today.

29: My new lodgings have made me very ill. I ask permission of Oswald to return to Siegfried and obtain it. Go to the police office this afternoon at 3 o'clock to have an interview. Pay 1 franc.

31: Make a bargain with Siegfried again, 25 fr. per month for cafe with supper, 25 fr. per month for dinner – no wine. Remove back to Siegfried's this evening.

SEP. 4: Am rapidly recovering my hand at designing after being away from it for nearly 3 years.

SEP. 6/60: Fete of the Basel University today. Torchlight procession.

7: Am now settled down steadily to work at Oswald's.

9; SUNDAY: English church at 3 Kings Hotel.

10: Receive intelligence that the great strike at Coventry is finished. The manufacturers have obtained a victory and the famous weavers' list is destroyed. Whilst the weavers at Coventry had stopped every loom in the trade, here in Basel the looms have been working till 9 p.m. to supply the English market.[33]

15: It is agreed that I am to stay $\frac{1}{2}$ an hour longer at Oswald's every night to teach his son Matthias English. I am to have something extra for it.

19: A buyer from Leaf's of London comes today and persuades Oswald that striped styles are no go, that checks are wanted.

21: Receive my 'permis de sejour' but they have kept the passport.

23; SUNDAY: Go to Dilinger. See the Alps in the distance and the sunset.

30: Go to Huningen with Wirz.

OCT. 1: Oswald fils tells me that his father thinks it would be a good thing for me if I were to give lessons in the English language in the evenings, and says he would let me give over at 6 o'clock.

4: I speak to Siegfried today. He is quite willing to allow me to give lessons.

10: Two of the Jura summits are white with snow.

12: Snowed a little. The grapes in the neighbourhood are not yet cut.

13: This week it has rained for 48 hours continuously and again for 24 hours.

17: Receive a letter from J. & J. Cash today asking me to buy racks and pinions for them.

18: Write to Cash's civilly asking them to use some other means to get their racks and pinions, as such a transaction might compromise my position here. Receive a letter from C. Peters asking what is doing in Basel.

19: Advertise in the Basler Nachrichten today that I give lessons in English at 1 franc a lesson.

22: Grapes are being cut now, new wine is already to be had.

25: Vines are brown now.

26: English buyers here today. Weather very fine now.

27: The woods on the Jura are a fine rich brown colour and the leaves are falling. Buyer for Bradbury Greatorex Mclarf here today; Leaf's buyer was here a month ago.

OCT. 28; SUNDAY: Go to Augst and see Roman ruins, broken columns, etc.

29: The annual Basel fair commences today.

NOV. 1: Receive my second month's salary, 100 francs. Oswald gives me 15 extra for teaching his son English.

2: No frost yet, geraniums are still in the open air, weather seems to be steadily becoming colder and Rhine lower.

3: A frost tonight, the first this season. Grapes are all cut now.

4; SUNDAY: Visit St. Crishona.

6: Sharp frost every night, wind N.E. Warm my chamber for the first time.

7: Grounds covered with snow which does not thaw.

11: Still sharp frost every night. Receive a letter for Hawley.

12: Woodcock from Bannerman's is here.

13: Receive letter from Crawford of Coventry.

14: Receive a letter informing me that John Cash and Seiler have visited Basel and stayed two or three days.

15: Frost gone. Weather very mild and rainy-warm wind.

18; SUNDAY: Go with Wirz and visit the Jewish cemetery at Hagenheim.

20: A buyer from Glasgow here.

29: Graham from Green and Graham here.

30: Meet Shaw the buyer in the street.

DEC. 1/60: Weather mild. Receive my salary – 10 fr. extra.

3: Receive letter from Rollason about Owen. Johnson the buyer here.

5: Turner for Cook, Son & Co. here. Murdoch's nephews and Slater here about 3 weeks ago.

8: Oswald sends me today to 3 Kings Hotel to see Turner of London. Johnson and Bancel from Leaf's here. Barometer very low.

9: Brown from Morrison's here.

10: Hyde from Sir John Watt's here. Brown and Chapman from Morrison, Dillon & Co.

11: See the above buyers today, but do not succeed in selling them any goods.

16; SUNDAY: Go to Therwyl and Renach.

18: Ratcliff & Lester arrive here.

20: Ratcliff & Lester leave.

21: We could see well to work till ½ past 4 this afternoon, although it was cloudy.

22: 4 inches of snow.

23; SUNDAY: Go to Lorrach and Tullingen.

25: 6 inches of snow fell in the night – thermometer 9 degrees below zero at noon. Rained and froze where it fell which proves there was a warmer current above.

26: Thaw.

1861

JAN. 1; TUESDAY: Go to Mutlenz in the rain.

6; SUNDAY: To Mulhausen with Dicky the Scotchman.

7: Thermometer 11 Reaunur° below zero on the bridge this morning. Dine with William Townsend at Trois Rois. Visit Wahl's works.

8: At Oswald's we gradually become slacker and for the last three weeks we have done nothing at all.

9: 7 – 10 degrees of cold every morning on the bridge.

10: Oswald says I must try and obtain employment in another house.

11: Call on Burgy this morning. He promises to see what he can do.

14: 10° of frost. Call on Richter-Linder. He will make no definite promise.

16: 10° of frost this morning, 9½ at noon.

17: 12° this morning, 9½° at noon. Ice floating in the Rhine. It freezes as it runs.

19: Brosher of Wirz (Hermann) goes to see Burgy today for me. He promises to employ me if he possibly can. Richter makes me an offer.

22: Go to Burgy. He had not made up his mind. Go at once to Richter and accept his offer – 100 francs per month. I am to go next Monday.

25; FRIDAY: Go to St. Crishona and see Jeffries. Magnificent view of Alps.

28; MONDAY: Start work with Richter-Linder.

29: Go to Oswald's tonight and receive my certificate of good character. Hear that Oswald has given up his business (not having been successful) and has sold all his looms to Magalon.

FEB. 7: In the three Coventry parishes are 18,000 persons depending on Ribbon Trade of which 9,000 are workers, of them only 2,500 are in employment.

12: Turner (from Cook's) was here a few days ago. He only came to look for job lots.

14: Brown and Chapman here (Morrison).

17; SUNDAY: Go to Metteuz – find the ruins at last.

18: Carnival. Ascend the Gempenfluh.

FEB. 20/61: Last of Carnival. Go to masked ball.

21: A great storm in England today. In Basel warm and muggy, not much wind. We have just got the south edge of the cyclone.

27: Weigh 27½ kilos.

MAR. 4: Cousin Isabella dies today of a decline brought on by her bad foot.

10; SUNDAY: Go to Reinach with Dicky and Lister and visit Mr. Isles the Scotchman.

15: Weather very cold.

17: Warm sunny afternoon.

19: Go to the Burgvogtei this evening to try and form an English club.

24: Fine warm weather.

29; GOOD FRIDAY: Train to Mutteuz – Mutteuz 2 p.m., Arlesheim 3.45.

AP. 1; EASTER MONDAY: Holiday this afternoon. Go to Grenzach.

7; SUNDAY: Ramble in the marshes below Neudorf. See dancing at Huningen in the square.

8: Double windows taken off. Buds are just bursting and trees are just beginning to show the faintest tinge of green.

14; SUNDAY: In afternoon rail to Mutteuz. Walk by Schonmatte, Genpenstollen, mount the summit of the Gempenfluh (765 metres) for the first time, then by Gempen (music there), Dormeck, Dormeck Bruck, Reinach, Therwyl, Oberwyl, Birmingen, Basel.

APRIL 21/61: Hear the cuckoo for first time this season. Go to Ruhrberg and Wyhlen this afternoon.

23: St. George's day. Traditionally this is always reckoned a cold day to Basel and it is cold today.

28: Trees are just coming into full leaf and are a brilliant green.

MAY 1 TO 7: Weather cold.

9: Ascension. Holiday today. Go to Grenzach.

10: Very hot.

12: Go to Grenzach.

19; SUNDAY: Religious service today at the camp.

22: A son of H. Spencer of Coventry comes to visit the fabrique of R. Linder. He came with Woodcock, the buyer.

23: Call on Johnson, W. Bancell (of Leaf and Sons) at the 3 Kings Hotel today to ask them about the possibility of a situation in France as they have a branch at St. Etienne. They think it will be best for me to remain in Basel at present.

26; SUNDAY: Go in Baselland and see the looms at Seltisberg, Lupsingen, Ziefen, Reigoldswyl Ziefen, Bubendorf, Liestal.

28: Thermometer 80° Fahrenheit in the shade.

JUNE 1: I have obtained a holiday to visit Italy. I start early this morning.

I have no baggage but a knapsack. Rail Basel to Bern, Bern to Thun. Rain at Thun. Late in evening visit the camp. Altwegg not there. Hotel de la Couronne at Thun.

JUNE 2/61; SUNDAY: Rain all morning. Concert in church. See Altwegg. Afternoon clears up. Steamboat to Spitz. Heavy rain again. Walk Spitz to Frutigan (12 miles), arrive 7½ p.m., Hotel de l'Aigle. Have not yet seen the Alps because of the weather. Swiss officer in hotel.

JUNE 3; MONDAY: Leave Frutigan 6 a.m., over the Gemmi pass, cross a fallen avalanche, arrive at Leuk (30 miles) 4 p.m., pass over bridge on the road, from which a stone occupied 4 seconds in falling to the bottom of a ravine. Travellers at hotel. Amusements. Fine warm day.

4: Leave Leuk 7½ a.m. Walk to Breig 18 miles – very hot. Arrive 1½ p.m. Leave Brieg 3 p.m., walk to Sinjelon Hospice 18 miles in 4h. 25m. arriving at 7½ p.m. Rained the last hour. Stay at Hospice with the monks.

JUNE 5: 2½ inches of snow has fallen during the night, snowed all morning. Dinner at Hospice. Start at 1½ p.m. in the snow, walk to Domo d'Ossola 24 miles arriving at 8¾ p.m. When I started from Hospice, it snowed – lower down road rained, then fine for some distance, but rain for the last hour.

6; THURSDAY: Leave Domo 6 a.m. by omnibus, arrive Pallanza 11 a.m. where I dine. Boat to Isola Bella, steamer to Arona. Rained in morning, fine rest of day.

7: Rail to Magenta, staying on way 1½ hours at Novara. Field of Magenta, rail to Milano, Albergo della Ancora. Fine day. Evening go to Theatre della Stadera performance 'Il Trovatore'.

JUNE 8; SATURDAY: Deliver letters of introduction M. Gilbert. Attend service in the cathedral on account of the death of Cavour.[34] Evening in the country with M. Schuler to see silk worms. Am shown wonderful echo. Fine day. At night Theatre della Cannobiana.

9: Leave Milan at noon, arrive at Genoa 9 p.m. Fine.

10; MONDAY: Fine. Genoa, English ships. Italian fleet etc. Genoa to Torino. Hotel de la Ville at Turin.

11: Fine. Musee des Armes, Galerie des Tableaux etc., Torino to Chivasso.

12; WEDNESDAY: Fine. Chivasso market day. Chivasso to Ivrea, Ivrea to Verres by dilligence, walk in 3 hours to Chatillon 9 miles. Good wine here.

13: Fine. Walk to Chatillon to Aosta 15 miles in 5 hours including a stopping of ½ hour. See Roman antiquities. Stay at Jardin des Plantes.

14; FRIDAY: Leave Aosta 7 a.m., arrive at St. Bernard Hospice 2 p.m. 6 feet in snow. Leave Hospice 5 p.m., row about passport at St. Pierre, arrive at Hotel des Alpes at Osières 9¾ p.m. Day's walk 36 miles.

15; SATURDAY: Walk Osières to Pissevache 13 miles in about 4½ hours. Rail Pissevache to Villeneuve, see castle of Chillon, rail Chillon to Lausanne. Stay at Ouchy.

16; SUNDAY: Lausanne. Rail through Yverdon, Neuchatel, Bienne, Basel. My 15 days excursion has cost me 180 francs all told. I have only had occasion to speak English once during the tour. I have traversed 177 miles of the road on foot.

JUNE 17; MONDAY: My skin is the colour of mahoganny with the Italian sun. I find Owen from Coventry (my old fellow student) in Basel on a visit. I also see Seiler here today. He has left Cash's and has now returned to his native town of Basel. There have been many changes in Coventry since I left it a year ago. Cash's have now only one designer (Woodward). Weather very hot. Thermometer in my room (with a north aspect) 80° Fahrenheit all night.

22: Very hot. Thermometer in my room generally 80° to 86°.

JUNE 29: Two buyers from Rylands Manchester here today. They give a large order for No. 4 Taffetas. Mr. Richter pays me for the 15 days I have been absent by his own will. Morrison's buyer here. Campbells (Glasgow) buyer here.

30: Rain all day. Go to English church at 3 Kings.

JULY 3: See a magnificent comet tonight near the great Bear. The tail was 90′ long and reached past the zenith at 11 p.m. It has arrived suddenly and appears to be moving from left to right. Stars of the 1st magnitude looked pale beside it. Position this evening.

JULY 7/61: Go by Horn Chrishona, Ruhrberg, Herthen, Warmbach to Rheinfelden. Return by train.

3: The comet gets small by degrees and beautifully less. The earth is said to have passed through the tail on Sunday, June 30th. The following week we had cold and dull weather. I remember noticing on July 3rd the most unusual circumstance that the tail on the preceding side was much shorter. Did the earth carry away a piece of the tail?

JULY 15: Visit today Landskrone and Mariastein.

21: Visit Haltingen, Eimeldingen, and Stein.

26: I weigh only 60 kilos.

30: Bancell & Johnson (Leafs) here. They complain much of the bad trade in England.

AUG. 2: Thermometer 84° in the shade today.

4: I go with Richters dyers on their annual excursion to St. Urban today. The comet is now barely visible to the naked eye.

AUG. 11/61; SUNDAY: Visit Schauenburg.

13: Thermometer nearly 26° Reaumur, or 89°F. Every day from 85 to 90 in shade.

16: 26½° Reaumur today.

18: Rail to Rhinefelden. Walk to Magden, Meisprach (dinner), Buirs, Farnsburg, Rickenbach, Wintersingen, Sissachfluh, Hingen, Lausen, Leistal, Schontal, and rail to Basel.

25: Basel to Wyhlen by rail, on foot to Ruhburg, Inzlingen, Riehen Weil, Leopoldshobe, Huningen, St. Louis, Basel.

28: Visit the summer casino this evening with some friends.

SEP. 1: Mount the Passwang today, 1207 metres.

8: Visit Birseck Schloss.

14; SATURDAY: Leave Basel 7h. 30m., walk up Wiesenthal to Schopfhein, dine at Engel, then to Zell, Schonau and Todnau. Steep at Todnau (Bar), 30 miles walk.

15: Todnau over mountains to Freilburg 18 miles. See Cathedral, return to Basel by train.

22: E. Wirz leaves Basel for Manchester.

29: Walk through Eltingen. Cannot find the path up the Blauen so am obliged to flank it on the left. Arrive at Blauen village in the rear, no inn, descend to Zwingen to dine. Return to Blauen village, find the path up on the south side easily, arrive at summit, view of Alsace, Vosges, Kaizerstuhl, Black Forest, etc. Return by Hofstetten, Fluhen, Benhen and Neuwylen.

30: R. Linder has asked Horandt about a situation for me, but it is no go. However, I decide to leave at end of October and chance it.

OCT. 4: Weight is 60½ kilos.

8: Apply at the Blue House today. J. F. Sarasin & Co. Fischer (the head of the firm) is very civil, but unable to find me a situation. He questioned me whether we had not many taffetas in the looms at Richter Linder's and seemed much afraid of his competition and price.

9: Apply at Koechlin's today, but no use.

10: Have to go before the Income Tax Commissioners today for inadvertantly not having paid my tax in response to the notification in the local press, which I knew nothing about. I find them very civil. I have to pay 3 francs tax and ½ franc fine.

11: Apply at De Barry today (no use).

12: Apply today at Freer & Co. at Aarau (civil and short), J & I Frey (civil enough, makes fancys), Herzog (civil, a large establishment), H. A. Senn, Zofingen (civil), Sutter (jealous). I cannot obtain employment. I return to Olten by rail, then to Langenbruch.

13; SUNDAY: Rains steadily this morning. I cannot reach Basel without passing the Jura which is enveloped in cloud. I walk in the rain to Mumliswyl, and commence to climb the Passwang mountain (1207 metres), as I ascend the rain becomes finer. I reach the clouds near the Wasserfaulle. I remain ½ hour in a wood for shelter, then scale the summit. I am now above the clouds and rain and look down on them with bright warm sunshine and blue sky above me. All Switzerland South of the Jura is covered with clouds underneath me like a sea of snow. North of the Jura it is very fine weather, the ridge separating the two sorts of weather like a wall. Above the clouds the Alps tower perfectly clear extending 120′ along the horizon. I remain 2 hours on the summit, then descend to Reigoldswyl and Liestal, rail to Basel. We have had a long series of fine weather. It is now the middle of the vintage and new sweet wine is to be had.

OCT. 20: Vintage over. Sweet wine no longer to be had.

26: Tell Richter today I will leave next week.

28: The annual fair in Basel commences today.

30: Receive letter of introduction today from Kiefer to Hardroft at St. Etienne.

31: Obtain my passport.

NOV. 1: Receive two letters of introduction from Lardet. Geraniums in the open air look as well as in summer.

3: Geraniums taken in. Snow in the Black Forest.

4: Leave Basel early this morning. Snowed for the first time, the Jura white. Arrive at Geneva. Hotel du Lac.

5: Leave Geneva and bid farewell to Switzerland. Lyons, St. Etienne.

6: Engage a lodging at No. 11 Rue St. Louis au Deuxieme for a month.

7: Remove to my lodging, search and find my Swiss friend, Kohler. Weather much warmer here than in Basel.

NOV. 8: Call with letter on Felix Brionde (froide) and Gustave Bancel (civil), and Hartoff (very civil). Engage for pension, dinner and supper, at 2 francs per day.

13: I have now been here 8 days, have ransacked the town but can get no employment.

16: Visit Firminy today, see the River Loire. Receive letters of introduction from Lyons.

18: Leave my heavy luggage at my lodging and go to Lyons.

18-23: Have spared no effort but can obtain no situation in Lyons, trade being so wretchedly bad.[35]

23: Return to St. Etienne, write to the Blue House at Basel, the head of that firm told me that I might do so if I was not successful in France.

26: Go with Bally and Nussbaumer to Rochetaille. Fine scenery.

27: Receive answer in negative from Sarasin of Basel.

28-29: F. Franklin and R. Philips here from Coventry.

DEC. 1: Review of troops.

2: Rail from St. Etienne to Nevers.

3: Nevers to Paris.

4: See Roussel and Wepfer also Vasselon, my old master.

10: Have found no employment; decide to leave tomorrow.

11: Leave Paris this afternoon, leave Dieppe 8.40 p.m., weather fine, heavy south-west gales rises, our steamer 'The Paris' rolls heavily, at 12.30 midnight the main shaft snaps, the deck sometimes makes an angle of 35° with the horizon, we burn blue lights and send up rockets, another boat comes alongside, to bear us company. At 3h. 15m. the broken engine is disengaged and we start working one paddle wheel only, land at Newhaven 8 a.m.

DEC. 12; THURSDAY: Reach London 11.30 and am once more in England.

13: Visit Crystal Palace, see Blondin.[36] My weight is 9 stone 9 lbs.

14: I have already called on 10 houses in the city in search of employment.

15; SUNDAY: See my sister, Helen. I find myself a complete stranger in my native land. My ideas and habits have so changed that I have become a foreigner. The wretched foggy climate here, the different food and the rough habits and manners of the inhabitants quite sicken me. I begin to wish I were back on the continent.

16-17: No success in finding a situation.

18: Go to Spitalfields, call on Kent and Stone, also Soper and son, both very uncivil. Also call on Kent and Son who are civil.

19: No success.

20; FRIDAY: Come down to Coventry.

21: At home with my parents.

23; MONDAY: Prince Albert buried.[37]

26: Show myself in the streets a little.

30; MONDAY: Go to Warwick to see Beamish, an old Vicar Lane acquaintance hanged, also Thompson of Birmingham. Trade in Coventry at the lowest ebb.

DEC. 31/61: Everything in Coventry looks small and insignificant compared to what it used to do. Cash's warehouse in Hertford St. looks a mere shanty. The only buildings which seem anything like what I remember are the churches.

1862

JAN. 6: I encounter John Cash by accident at the door of the Coventry Institute and tell him that I am looking for an engagement. He promises to think it over and see if he can make me an offer.

10: Weather very mild in England, but I see by the papers that the Rhine is frozen.

11: John Cash sends for me and offers me an engagement as designer at £100 a year.

13: I accept Cash's offer and begin work today. Here then after more than 6 years hard work and travel, with treble the knowledge and experience, I begin life again in Coventry on the same footing as I began it 6 years ago as designer for Cash's at £100 per year.

JAN. 14/62: Cash did not mention to me that he already had a designer at work, namely Woodward a former apprentice of theirs, a younger man than myself – so that there are two of us.

17: Am now settled down to work alongside Woodward. He seems rather jealous. Trade is very bad, the weavers have been lately working on the commons at about 6d. per day and a loaf. I saw several of my former schoolfellows amongst them.

18: Many changes have taken place at Cash's since I went away. Their cottage factory system for which they built the houses at King Fields has been a complete failure. They could obtain no rent from the tenants unless they found work for them – now at great cost they have knocked out the partition walls of the shops and converted the top of the buildings into one long factory, and filled it with looms which they have built, the houses underneath now form merely cottages for the weavers – the steam factory also which was building when I went away (and which they intended me to manage; until the trade collapsed which caused them to alter their mind) is now finished, and J. S. Beamish, who formerly managed their West Orchard factory, now manages King Fields and resides there. West Orchard is now managed by a young man named Averns.

JAN. 20/62: Cash's are making partly fancy ribbons, but a great many narrow cambric frillings, made entirely of cotton – these are made in new narrow looms which have been built in the long shops at top of the houses at King Fields.

FEB. 9; SUNDAY: Go with father to see Allans at Leamington.

11: Go and see Ratcliff's throwing mill at Brandon.

14: Ribbon trade no better yet. It is evident there is not sufficient work to employ the two of us, myself and Woodward.

20: John and Joseph Cash seem to have much changed since I was formerly with them. The collapse of trade seems to have made them arbitrary and exacting and harsher in their manner. I find that I am also much changed. I am no longer the same man. I look upon things in Coventry with very different eyes to what I did before I left England. Nature and Art are upon a very different scale in Switzerland to what they are in Coventry. 18 months travel and freedom, and seeing the world have completely altered my mind – and

'the weapon which it wields is of another temper,'

to quote Childe Harold, which was the only English author I had with me upon the continent.[38] I am also a couple of years older and can see better beneath the surface of things and I find that incessant practice of mountaineering has given me the knack of deciding instantly in difficulties where I should formerly have taken a week to consider.

MAR. 1/62: Trade but little better. I am drafting a ribbon with Prince's Feathers on it for the International Exhibition.

2nd: I cannot endure Joseph Cash. His manners are coarse and harsh and he cannot write a sentence in English without making wretched blunders in the spelling.

10: I have now been at work only 8 weeks and this morning Joseph Cash tells me that Mr. Beamish (the manager of King Fields) is going to leave, and he wants me to take his place, but he will give me no more salary than I am now having. I am to consider it. I hate factory work, especially under Joseph Cash. I saw too much of it previously when I had ample means of seeing the West Orchard factory where Joseph Cash was master and Beamish was manager. (John Cash has always managed the counting house and sale department.)

12: Having (just for the sake of appearances) taken two days to consider the matter, I this morning tell Mr. Joseph Cash that I would much prefer to remain at the designing instead of going to manage King Fields. Five minutes later they give me notice to leave, and give me a week to consider about King Fields.

MAR. 14/62: I am determined not to go to King Fields if I can avoid it. I call on Carter W. Philips, Franklin, C. Peters etc. and use every means to obtain another situation but without success.

17: As I can obtain no other situation, I disguise myself and go over by a roundabout way to King Fields at night and see Beamish and enquire of him why he is leaving, and tell him if he wishes to stay I will certainly refuse Cash's offer for he is an old friend of mine. He tells me that he has finally decided to leave Cash's, that he has had enough of factory work and cannot stand the strain any longer and intends to have a change.

19th: Tell Cash's that I will take the situation at King Fields. It is however understood that I am not to be forced to go to live there (they want me to reside there and set up house keeping again).

20: Sister Anne married today to George Carter of High Cross by Revd. J. Sheepshanks at Bablake church. Father and Helen sign as witnesses.

21: Go and make a start at King Fields this morning.

27: Am now working steadily at King Fields.

APRIL 12: Mr. Beamish leaves today.

14: I commence this morning under my own management.

APR. 18/62; GOOD FRIDAY: Go to Kenilworth.

21; EASTER MONDAY: Holiday. Go to Warwick and see the volunteer review – a man's finger blown off – 3 men fainted.

MAY 3: Go over to High Cross tonight to see Ann.

4; SUNDAY: Return today.

7: A great darkness passed over King Fields at 3 p.m. One of the workmen fainted with fright.

17: There is a young Swiss in Coventry, seeking employment, Herr Hauser.

18: It is painfully evident that the Coventry figured or fancy ribbon trade is not what it was. Although formerly we made a good many small fancies at W. H. & C. Bray's and other firms, yet S. & J. Cash had practically a monopoly of all the best part of the trade. From 1855 to 1860 their looms were always in full work, but now this trade seems to hang fire, we cannot succeed with these goods. This to my judgment is accounted for by the quantity of these goods now being imported from the continent owing to the abolition of the duty, when I was in Basel the English buyers were continually coming.[39]

23: I do not like my situation. I have to leave my father's house soon after 5 a.m. in order to walk the distance to King Fields and be there before 6 o'clock. I cannot leave the place before 6 p.m. at earliest (I have arranged to get breakfast and dinner on the spot). It is generally about 7 p.m. before I can get home. Sometimes it is later for Cash's are still building looms, and they have got into a squabble with a loom builder at St. Etienne about some battants, and I have to do the correspondence, and there is no other than myself connected with the firm sufficiently competent at French – and as I have not a moment to spare in the daytime, I occasionally have to stay later at night to attend to this. The long hours, the incessant harrass, and the impossibility of obtaining sleep owing to the fear of being too late in the mornings are beginning to affect my health, I am gradually becoming unwell.

24th: We are making narrow goods now at King Fields – wides will no longer sell.[40]

29th: We are making whites now, we dye a lot of shoot for them. Mr. Joseph sends it back today to the dye house as the colour is not to his satisfaction.

30th: Time being thus lost, some looms have to stand for want of white shoot.[41]

31st: Mr. Joseph Cash complains today about the looms standing for white – we quarrel. He at once gives me a month's notice to leave. I am not sorry. My only regret is that I did not at once put on my hat and coat and leave the premises. How glad I shall be when the time is expired, the present is worse than slavery.

JUNE 20TH, 1862; FRIDAY: Coventry Fair begins today.

21: King Fields is to be closed all next week and as my time expires on Monday 30th, Mr. Joseph Cash tells me that I need not come after today. I pay the hands, balance my accounts, put tickets on all the silk, close the establishment at the proper time, and send the key of (the) desk to Mr. John Cash (head of the firm) in an envelope.

23; MONDAY: A Godiva procession.

28: I call at Hertford St. and settle with Messrs. Cash. We part very friendly. Mr. John hopes I may find another and more suitable place. My own feeling is that whatever may be my fate in future, I trust that I may never again be the servant of the Messrs. Cash. I have a sincere respect for Mr. John, but as for Mr. Joseph – – – – – – – –. I have been privately informed that Cash's intend to remove their factory from West Orchard and to concentrate the whole of their manufacture at King Fields and to place Mr. Averns (the present manager of West Orchard) as manager. I do not know Mr Averns personally. Although for the last three months I have been in almost hourly correspondence with him about the business, I have not seen him.

30; MONDAY: Mr. Averns begins his management of K.F. today.

JULY 1, 1862: Being now free again and it being summer, I resolve to take a fortnight's holiday. I will visit London for a week and see the International Exhibition, and then I will once more shoulder my knapsack and go for a week's tramp in south of England. I have seen a good deal of the continent but now I want to see England.

5TH: Coventry to London. Visit South Kensington Museum.

6: To Kew Gardens with sister Helen.

7: Royal Academy Exhibition.

8: Wimbledon shooting, see the Queen's prize shot for, afternoon International Exhibition.

9: Exhibition.

JULY 10/62: International Exhibition. I meet two foreign friends there whom I knew on the continent.

11: Temple Church, Westminster Abbey, Houses of Parliament.

12: Woolwich dockyard. Wimbledon Review.

13; SUNDAY: London to Brighton. Brighton to Southwick by rail.

14: Southwick to Chichester } rail
Chichester to Havant }

Havant over Portsdown on foot where I see them building the new forts, then to Portsmouth Pier on foot. Cross to Ryde by boat.

15: On foot to Brading, Bonchurch, Ventnor, and St. Catherine's Point. Sleep at Buddle Inn.

16: On foot from Buddle to top of St. Catherine's, down then along the cliffs to Freshwater Gate and to Yarmouth. Cross to Lymington by boat – stay at Ship Inn.

17; THURSDAY: To Lyndhurst by rail, then on foot to Minstead, Rufus' stone and Romsey – Romsey to Salisbury by rail – leave Salisbury by the road to the north in the evening – pass by Old Sarum. Get benighted on Salisbury Plain, reach Amesbury at 9½ p.m., stay at King's Arms. Weather dark and stormy with heavy rain.

18: Walk by Stonehenge to Wylye station, then to Gloucester by rail, stopping at Westbury, Bath and Bristol.

19; SATURDAY: Gloucester to Eckington. Rail, Eckington to Evesham. Walk. Evesham to Millcote. Rail. Millcote to Stratford. Walk. Stratford to Hatton. Rail. Hatton to Kenilworth. Walk. Kenilworth to Coventry. Rail. The expenses of my holiday were £7. 8. 0.

JULY 20; SUNDAY: At home again. My health is recovered. I am in good trim.

21; MONDAY: A friend who knows informs me that the firm of Dalton and Barton are about to lose their manager and recommends me to apply for the situation, he thinks it will suit both parties. Their present manager is J. Iliffe my old fellow apprentice, the man to whom Cash's let my house in Draper's Fields. This firm is not one of the largest, it is not equal in size to Hart, Franklin, H. Spencer, W. Spencer or Carter and Philips, etc., etc., but their trade is a fancy trade and an outdoor trade in the main (although they have a few looms in a small factory). I therefore write a note to the firm stating that I have heard that they are about to lose their manager and informing them that I am looking for an engagement.

22ND: Mr Dalton (the head of the firm) calls on me this morning. We come to an engagement. He instructs me to go at 9 a.m. next Monday. £100 per year.

25TH; FRIDAY: Am further instructed that J. Iliffe is to stay another week with Dalton and Barton in order to set his books straight.

AUG. 4; MONDAY: Commence at D. & B.'s today.

9: See a comet tonight near the pole-star. It is very faint and just coming into view.

21: The comet continues. It is not very bright.

23: Sister Helen comes home from London.

AUG. 29/62: Ribbon trade still but middling. Shaded goods appear to be wanted.[42]

SEP. 11: Hear that J. Iliffe has not yet obtained anything to do.

12: I am charged with income tax today, £100 at 6d = £2-10-0d. I give notice to appeal against it.

23: Appeal against the Income Tax and get exempted.

27: Ribbon trade still flat.

OCT. 21: Ribbon trade at a dead stand still.

31: Ribbon trade no better.

NOV. 6: We have just obtained an order for a new set of whites for spring from Leaf. We are dyeing the silk.

15: We are putting in a good many whites for spring on account of the coming marriage of the Prince of Wales.

DEC. 10TH: Mr. Wiberley dies today aged 61.

12: Ribbon trade still very bad, we are selling nothing but most of our hands have their warps in now.

23: Sister Anne has a daughter at 2 a.m.

31: Iliffe has not yet obtained a situation.

1863

JAN. 1: Attended the midnight service at St. Michael's last night. Mr. Widdrington preached.

JAN. 8: Mr. W. H. Bray dies this evening, aged 55.

JAN. 10: Trade slack. We are making a good many whites on account of the approaching royal wedding.

JAN. 29: Trade not much better. We are putting in cheap whites fast. We now pay for weaving: 8 @ 1/3, 24 @ 2/3, 30 @ 3/-, 40 @ 4/-, 60 @ 6/-.[43]

JAN. 31: 132 persons leave Coventry this morning for Queensland, including 4 of D. & B.'s weavers with their families: Rollason, Stanley, Hewson, Horsfall.[44]

FEB. 2: Raise our price today to 20 @ 1/6, 30 @ 3/3, 40 @ 4/3. Other widths as before.

FEB. 12: Dislocate my right shoulder again this evening when at work at Dalton and Barton's. I was handling a heavy box at the moment. Dr. Bicknell set it half an hour later.

FEB. 13: I think my shoulder was *damaged* last night, as when replaced it seemed to be gradually lifted instead of going in with a jump.

FEB. 23: We raise our prices for 40 to 4/6.

MAR. 2: Prices today 8 @ 1/6, 24 @ 2/6, 30 @ 3/6, 40 @ 4/6, 60 @ 6/6.

MAR. 7: Princess Alexandra lands today from Denmark.

MAR. 10: Prince of Wales married, festivities in Coventry.

16TH: Receive a telegram today at 1.30 from High Cross, that Carter is going to sell all and is beating Ann. Take a van and go over with father. Find Carter mad drunk and Ann at neighbour Scotten's. We visit a magistrate and decide that Ann shall take out a warrant against him for assault.

17TH: Ann takes out a warrant. Late this night Carter's father drives him to the Rugby station after which he is not seen.

18TH: Two constables search the house at High Cross but without finding Carter. Ann comes home to Coventry today.

19TH: Carter's mother is left in possession of the house.

20TH: Carter is said to be gone to France.

MAR. 21ST: Carter's mother goes to Nixon, the auctioneer, and postpones the sale.

23RD: Ann and one of Mr. Davis's clerks go and take forcible possession of the house at High Cross and drive out Sarah and Wm. Carter. The sale is arranged to take place next Monday.

26TH: George Carter suddenly reappears at High Cross and turns out the man in possession. Ann happens to be at home in Coventry.

30TH: The sale at High Cross takes place today. Carter has put in bail to appear on Thursday.

31ST: G. Carter makes his appearance in Coventry this evening.

APRIL 1ST: G. C. knocks at our house at 12h. 15m. this morning, and demands his wife. Father threatens to give him in charge, on which he goes off. G. C. hanging round the neighbourhood this morning and annoying the family. He is given in charge, but let off by the superintendent on promising not to repeat it.

AP. 2: Father, Ann, and Mr. Davis go over to Lutterworth. The case is compromised. A deed of separation is drawn up. G. C. is to allow 2/6 per week for the child, and his father becomes responsible for the payment of the £20 money lent.

AP. 11: Ribbon trade still but middling.

23: Buy a 16 shuttle, 750 machine figure loom for £4/12/6d. This loom was left behind by one of the train load (Rollason) who started for Australia on Jan. 31st.

27: I am at work about an hour every morning and evening taking the loom down.

MAY 1ST: G. Carter sends an advertisement to the Coventry Standard that he will not be responsible for his wife's debts. At our suggestion they send it back to him.

MAY 6: Fetch the loom away and stow it away in Fleet St. as best I can.

7TH: Trade very bad. Spring trade all over.

20TH: Go by trip to Epsom to see the Derby run. Rained all day. Cremorne at night.

21ST: Spend the day with Mr. Wirz of Basel who is now living in London.

22ND: There has not been a drop of rain in Coventry.

28TH: Buy the house, No. 1 Gosford Green tonight by auction for £230. Clarke of Foleshill bid against me.

30TH: Begin dark colours today, principally shades.

JUNE 25: Warping dark colours fast, principally shades.

JULY 3: Take legal possession of the house, No. 1 Gosford Green today.

AUG. 10: Repairs at Gosford Green are now begun.

11TH: We are exceedingly busy at D. & B.'s principally with shades. The trade elsewhere in the city is generally flat.

12TH: Gather the pears at Gosford Green.

13TH: Now that I have a house of my own with a shop I am determined, sooner or later to go into business on my own account, and make a commencement today by quietly purchasing a warping frame and some fixtures at Hammerton's sale. The prospect is not an encouraging one seeing such a collapse in the trade during the last 4 years and half the manufacturers wrecked. However, I am determined to make an effort not to be a servant all my life.

SEP. 8TH: Ribbon trade very good with us, shades, tones, and tartans.[45]

12TH: Repairs at house approaching completion.

18TH: Home finished today. Pay Makepiece.

19TH: Trade good, tartans, satins and shades wanted.

SEP. 24TH: Remove from lodging at my father's house, 15 Fleet St., to my house at Gosford Green. Sister Ann being without occupation, goes to keep house for me.

OCT. 5TH: Mr. Dalton a few days ago mentioned to me that he was desirious of placing me at the factory to manage it, and engaging another in my present place. I was rather surprised at this, considering that since I have been their manager, their business has very much improved and extended. However, I instantly made up my mind and at once declined.

6TH: There was an earthquake throughout England at 3h. 20m. this morning, but I was asleep.

8TH: Coventry election consequent upon the death of Ellice. Morgan Treherne at last gets in defeating Peel.

10TH: Hear today that J. Iliffe (who has been in a situation at Derby and left it and returned to Coventry) is stating that he is going to supercede me in my present situation.

12TH: I enquire of Mr. Dalton today about the truth of the above. He acknowledges that some time ago he sent for Iliffe and made a positive engagement with him. Considering all circumstances I positively decline to accept the place at the factory. I tell him that if I went there, I certainly should not stay and that if I am to lose my situation, I prefer to go at once. I also tell him that I shall have one satisfaction in leaving him: namely that I leave his business in a very different position to that in which I found it, it being so much improved and extended. Mr. D. then offers me £20 more per year as an inducement and persuades me to think it over. For the sake of appearances I consent.

16: I finally decline Mr. Dalton's offer.

17: Mr. Dalton argues with me for an hour this evening and endeavours to change my mind. He exhausts every argument, but I am inflexible.

19TH: Mr. Dalton this evening tells me not to take any further steps about another situation. He will see if he can induce Iliffe to go to the factory. He commends my firmness and wishes he were as firm himself.

OCT. 20: Iliffe has no choice but to take Mr. Dalton's recommendation about the factory. It is therefore settled that he is to go there, and I am to remain where I am, and to have £110 per year or £10 increase.

21ST: The above circumstances have made considerable sensation in the ribbon trade.

22ND: Iliffe commenced at his new situation yesterday.

NOV. 16TH: D. and B. have taken stock and I believe have found it very satisfactory. Nearly every piece we have made has been sold at a profit.

17TH: We have made 5,000 pieces of shade this season and sold every piece at a profit.

23RD: Examine my well at Gosford Green and find it 35 feet deep and 30 feet of water in it, water smells abominably.

27TH: The goods we are making for spring are principally shades and tones.

30TH: G. Carter has been prowling about my premises. I send him a written notice to keep away.

DEC. 14TH: We are very busy at D. & B.'s, shades etc.

26: Prune my pear tree.

1864

Exceedingly busy at D. & B.'s, having already taken orders for more than 4,000 pieces of fancy goods. Attended midnight service last night at St. Michael's.

25TH: Very busy at D. & B.'s.

FEB. 13: Trade is rather flatter in the town, but D. & B. are still very busy.

26: Trade very flat. Shipping trade seems to be over and home trade not yet begun.

MAR. 7: Trade very flat, warpers on short time – the first time for 9 months.

14: Trade very flat.

19TH: A lot of country buyers have been in this week. We have got rid of a lot of goods.

28TH: Trade better. Mais and Leghorn goods wanted.

AP. 14: Trade flat. Fancy goods cannot now be sold at any price.

30: Spring trade already finished.

MAY 4: We have only 700 pieces in the looms, nearly all plain goods.

23RD: Commence to warp dark goods, tones and shades.

30: Leave Coventry by trip to Rhyl with Burbridge and Ryley. Rhyl Sands, Rhuddlan Castle, stay at Rhyl.

MAY 31: First train to Llandudno. Gt. Orme's head, dinner at Llandudno, Conway, tea at Llandudno, round Gt. Orme's Head, stay at Llandudno.

JUNE 1: First train to Rhyl, Rhyl sands, dinner, train home.

27TH: Have already warped 1200 pieces of side shades for the Autumn season.

JULY 2: Stierlin arrives on a visit from Manchester this evening.

4TH: Stierlin returns. Mr. Dalton raises my salary from £110 to £120 this morning unasked for.

AUG. 20; SATURDAY: Weighted in this week 400 pieces shades, $\frac{800}{1200}$ other goods, and 1,000 pieces last week and week before.

SEP. 1: Have warped 5,400 pieces of shades to present date.

SEP. 18; SUNDAY: Go to Edge Hill, Fenny Compton at noon, cross-roads near Arlescote at 1 o'clock, Edge Hill Tower at 2 o'clock, Sun Rising 2h. 20m. where I dine, walk back in two hours to Fenny Compton.

21ST: We have warped 6,000 pieces of shades this season.

23RD: Tartans much wanted.

OCT. 8: Very busy with Tartans.

20: Just beginning Spring colours.

24: Trying spun silk for shooting the spring goods.

NOV. 11TH: George Carter leaves High Cross about this date with his woman, said to be gone to Canada.

12TH: Mr. Dalton informs me that the stocktaking is satisfactory and that my salary is raised from £120 to £130.

17TH: Trade flat.

DEC. 3: The magistrates send for me this morning. I go, find they have two Frenchmen, Pierre Malaise and Charles Castetx charged with stealing coats etc. I have to interpret. They are committed to the sessions for trial.

DEC. 11TH: Dr. Payne comes today and sounds my chest. He says I am quite sound.

21ST: Trade flat.

23RD: Stierlin has obtained a situation in Birmingham at £70 per year.

25TH; SUNDAY: Stierlin visits me today and tomorrow.

29TH: Warehouseman's party at Mr. Dalton's house.

31: Labrey finishes his apprenticeship.

1865

JAN. 5: Am subpoened to attend at Quarter Sessions today to interpret in the case of Pierre Malaise, charged with stealing a coat. He is found guilty and sentenced to a month's imprisonment with hard labour. The other prisoner Charles Castetx is ill of consumption and did not appear. His trial is adjourned to the assizes when I am bound to appear.

19: Trade flat.

FEB. 4: Ditto, very.

11TH: Trade exceedingly flat. Mr. Dalton has been ill at home three weeks.

MAR. 1: Go to Warwick assizes to interpret at the trial of Charles Castetx. He is found guilty and sentenced to 2 months imprisonment.

4TH: Trade flat.

11TH: I was taken with a violent attack of illness in the night, lasted about half an hour, skin raised in lumps.

21ST: Trade exceedingly flat. Weighed in only 280 pieces last week.

27TH: The city club opens today.

31ST: Trade flat as ever.

APR. 1: Mr. Dalton's brother Edward buried today.

10TH: The firm of Ratcliff and Son stop payment. This firm is the oldest house in the ribbon trade.

APR. 13: Trade still very flat.

22: Ditto.

28: Mrs. Tyndall my next door neighbour died early this morning. I spoke to her on Tuesday evening at my front gate.

JUNE 1: We are now at work on dark colours. Trade rather better.

9TH: Obtain leave and start on a trip to Devon this afternoon at 3h. 40m., arrive at Bristol at 10 p.m., stay at Andean's White Swan.

10: Leave Bristol at 8h. 45m. by steam-boat for Ilfracombe, arrive at 1.30 p.m.

11TH; SUNDAY: Remain at Ilfracombe, attend service in Parish Church.

12TH: Trip to Clovelly and back by steamboat.

13TH: Coach to Barnstaple, rail to Eggesford, walk to South Tawton.

14TH: Leave South Tawton on foot at 6 a.m., eat my breakfast on summit of Cawsand Beacon at 7. Steer due south across the desert, arrive at Post Bridge at 1 o'clock, Tavistock at 7 p.m. rail to Plymouth.

15TH: Dockyard, Keyham Yard, Victualling Yard, night excursion round Eddystone, leave at 8.50, back at 11.30. Stay at Millbay Hotel.

JUNE 16: Rail to Torquay and then to Paignton, stay at Crown and Anchor.

17TH: Rail to Torquay and then to Exeter, stay at Tiges Commercial Inn.

18TH: Rail to Leamington and to Coventry.

20: Election in place of Paxton. Eaton defeats Jones.

JULY 1: Trade brisk.

2ND: General election. Treherne and Eaton defeat Flower and Jones.

27: Trade very brisk, black grounds, brocades and pads.

AUG. 17: Trade the same.

18TH: Receive a note this morning from Mr. Hands requesting to see me at his house. I go and am informed that Green, Slater & Green have dissolved partnership and that Slater wants a manager. Hands has recommended me to him. Slater has made enquiries about me which are satisfactory.

21ST: Receive a note from Mr. Hands requesting to see me. I go at 9 o'clock. He informs me that Slater will give me £200 per year and tells me that Slater will see me at 7 this evening at his house. I go and have a long conversation with him. Question is deferred till he has asked Mr. John Cash about me.

AUG. 24TH: Slater come to see me at Gosford Green this evening. He made enquiries of Messrs. Cash concerning me, which were answered very satisfactory, especially from Mr. Joseph Cash. Mr. S. seemed offended when I told him that it was just possible I might decline his offer. I promise him an answer on Saturday, Aug. 26th.

AUG. 25TH: I inform Messrs. D. & B. this morning that a berth at £200 a year awaits my acceptance. They at once raise my salary to the same amount, telling me they do not do it grudgingly but with pleasure.

26: Go to Mr. Hands this morning and tell him that I have decided to decline Slater's offer with thanks. Go to Slater this evening and tell him the same. Found him very civil.

SEP. 9: Trade brisk as ever. Pads wanted.[46] Black ground ribbons.

16: Trade still busy.

20TH: Take the front shutters off my house this week.

21ST: Had one bunch of grapes last year on my outdoor vine, but have a larger one this year. Vine is 6½ feet high.

SEP. 22: Commence to get my house ready for going into business on my own account. Begin today by putting skylights into the coal house so as to convert it into a pantry, in order to set the present pantry at liberty and convert it into a weaver's warehouse.

23RD: Trade still very busy. The demand for pads very brisk.

24TH: Purchase today at F. Iliffe's sale (which firm has broken up), scales, counter, 2 warping frames etc., etc. Intend to set them up at my house.

OCT. 2: Trade still very busy. Pads much in demand.

3RD: Go to Nottingham by trip today.

8TH: My bunch of grapes, quite ripe, weighs 5¼ oz.

14TH: We have now three weighing departments in D. & B.'s this week, a total of 2,000 pieces of ribbons and pads has been weighed in. Estimated average profit 3/- per piece.

28TH: Trade still keeps up.

30TH: Stock-taking today.

NOV. 1ST: The profits of D. & B. for the year's trade are believed to be about £5,000.

NOV. 18TH: Still warping a few dark goods, black and scarlet.

DEC. 7: Have a doorway put in today out of kitchen into the old coal house to convert it to be a pantry.

1866

JAN. 1: Crocuses 1 inch above ground.

6TH: This week I have put a wooden floor in the pantry and papered the walls, and am converting it into a room to wait on weavers.

20: Owing to the mildness of the season a few crocuses are in full bloom.

31: Yellow crocuses in full bloom.

FEB. 24: Factory ribbon trade flat.

MAR. 4: Yellow crocuses still in full bloom.

18: Ditto.

19: Ribbon trade flat. My warping frames are now all fixed, gas laid on and everything ready to start. The weavers warehouse is also finished, gas fixed and scales put up. I wonder when the time for a start will come.

APRIL 2: Fancy ribbon trade very flat.

14TH: Ditto.

21ST: Ditto.

30TH: News arrives today of the death of my uncle Hay Andrews on Saturday night at Dalkeith.

MAY 11TH: Trade is excessively bad.

12TH: Mr. Dalton gives me notice to leave today, giving as a reason for selecting me my much higher salary than Iliffe or Penn, who manage the other two departments. I think his object is merely to reduce my salary as trade is so bad, but I at once accept his notice and tell him that my mind is made up to go into business on my own account. When I became manager in 1862, they had only one department for weighing out work. Trade increasing, two other departments were added under my general control as head manager. Iliffe managed one and Penn the other. The firm now does one of the largest trades in the city, whilst Messrs. Cash (my former masters) have lost nearly the whole of their ribbon trade and now make little but cotton frillings.[47]

13TH: Have recently bought of Solomans & Co. London a 3 inch astronomical telescope. It turns out satisfactory and defines well.

18TH: Am looking for premises in High Street or Earl St. for a sale room. There are two eligible, the one at corner of St. Mary's St., the other at Bank Chambers.

21ST: Bill and Dresser the silk merchants doubt my wisdom in going into business considering what a wreck the trade has become and what a number of firms have broken up. They tell me that the post of manager at Bridgett & Co. at Derby (Sarsonet manufacturers) is vacant and that they have spoken to the head of the firm (Mr. Lewis) about me. This firm has 350 looms in factory. At recommendation of B. & D. I have an interview with Mr. Lewis today at their warehouse about it. He offers me the post of manager. He is, I believe, a director of the Midland Railway. I give him but little hope but tell him that I will think it over.

JUNE 1: I write to Lewis and decline his offer with thanks.

2ND: Mr. Whitten declines to let me have the rooms at corner of St. Mary's St.

4TH: Godiva procession.

5TH: Go to London and have a talk to Mr. Madle, the buyer for Leaf, Sons and Co. I think he will probably be a customer to me.

6TH: Engage a sale room at Bank Chambers at £6 per annum, no rates.

9TH: Leave Messrs. Dalton and Barton. We part friendly. I entered the service of this firm on Aug. 4/62. The amounts which they paid for wages for *weaving* have been as follows: 1860 about £5,000, 1861 about £5,000, 1862 about £5,000, 1863 about £6,000, 1864 about £9,500, 1865 about £14,000. The full amount of wages paid including weaving, winding, warping etc. was as follows: 1862 Aug. 12 – Dec. 27 £2,389, 1863 £7,206, 1864 £11,950, 1865 £16,435, 1866 to Ap. 14th £4,815.

In my own department only, not including the two sub-departments of Iliffe and Penn, I have manufactured for D. & B. the following number of pieces of goods (36 yds. each): 1862 9,100½ pieces, 1863 26,619½ pieces, 1864 37,296½ pieces, 1865 21,421½ pieces, 1866 6,015½ pieces. Weeks 198, 100,453½ pieces. Nearly all these goods were sold at a large profit. 507½ average per week.

The business of D. & B. has increased to three times the size during the time I have been their manager.

JUNE 12: I buy some silk of Bill and Dresser to make a start with.
JULY 2ND: I open my sale room at Bank Chambers and am at last in business on my own account. I send out a few pattern cards of belts to customers.

3RD: Go to Alton Towers excursion.

4TH: Receive my first order for 10 pieces of goods from H. Bannerman & Sons of Manchester. Mr. Woodcock is the buyer.

7TH: End of my first week have delivered 17 pieces of goods.

AUG. 23RD: When I started in business, I had £220 in ready cash. Have since delivered goods in value £410 and have still £40 in bank.

SEP. 22: Trade in plain coloured pads falls off this week.

25TH: Visit Oxford today by trip.

29: Black pads still in demand.

OCT. 6: Demand for black pads over, fancy ribbons wanted.[48]

NOV. 13: See the November shower of meteors this night. It lasted until 2 a.m. They were most numerous at 1.15, when there were about 200 per minute.

DEC. 31ST: Upon taking stock I find that my trading has been successful and I am now well established in business.

Notes on the Diary of William Andrews

1. The Baptist movement had been established at Longford since 1759.
2. The Coventry, Bedworth and Nuneaton railway was begun in 1847.
3. The School of Art had been founded in 1842. Like the School of Design, it was intended to remedy the inferiority of design in English as opposed to Continental silk manufactures.
4. The Roman Catholic Church in Coventry was evidently flourishing in spite of opposition. A new church was begun in 1843 when the number of worshippers became too great for the chapel then in use.
5. The Great Exhibition of 1851 contained fine exhibits from French silk manufacturers. Coventry and London manufacturers also displayed their products, but they were generally adjudged to be of inferior quality.
6. The Brays were a well-known local family. Charles Bray, the philosopher and friend of George Eliot, was also a member of it.
7. Processions were revived in 1678 in honour of Godiva, the wife of the Saxon Earl Leofric of Mercia. By 1842, when the part of Godiva was played by a drunken prostitute who rode semi-clothed through the town, they had become ribald affairs, the subject of adverse comment. Later processions were more respectable, being an occasion for the parade of the various societies and organisations of the city.
8. The Congregational Chapel at Vicar Lane, which Andrews attended, had been founded in 1723.
9. All freemen had right of pasture over Lammas lands from Lammas Day until early February, and exercised it by seeing that no fences were erected to prevent animals grazing freely.
10. Gaveston's Mount (Blacklow Hill) was reputedly the site of the execution of Edward II's favourite in 1312. It rises near the house built on the traditional site of the hermitage of Guy of Warwick.
11. An official programme of the procession and ceremonies in St Paul's Cathedral is preserved in one of Andrews' scrapbooks.
12. The Coventry Mechanics Institute was founded in 1828 to spread useful and scientific knowledge among the working classes. The Religious and Useful Knowledge Society, founded in 1835, was more avowedly Christian in aim. However, a merger between the two groups was effected in 1855.

13. Following the Exhibition of 1851, the Department of Science and Art, still part of the Board of Trade, gave grants to encourage improvements in design, etc.
14. Sir Joseph Paxton, the designer of the Crystal Palace, had been elected M.P. for Coventry in 1854.
15. Napoleon III and the Empress Eugenie were then at the height of their popularity.
16. Guilia Grisi, the Italian soprano, was the most famous exponent of her day in the title role in Bellini's 'Norma.'
17. Prince Eugene, Napoleon III's only son.
18. The peace conference which ended the Crimean War had been in session in Paris since February 25th.
19. The building which had housed the Great Exhibition of 1851 was removed to Sydenham Hill where it was reopened as the Crystal Palace in 1854.
20. The Liberal, Edward Ellice, was first elected M.P. for Coventry in 1818 and represented the city continuously from 1830 until his death in 1863. He fought for the protection of the silk industry on several occasions, though the general policy of his party was for Free Trade.
21. The Indian mutiny had begun in January 1857 and forces were marching to the relief of Delhi and Lucknow by the autumn of that year.
22. The spelling of 'King Fields' is standardised throughout the diary. Andrews more often spells it with the final 's', but sometimes without.
23. Ribbon with a narrow satin strip along to the edge which was generally corded was known as an 'oriental'. A piece was thirty-six yards. The figure 24 refers to the width of the ribbon, in this case $3\frac{1}{12}$ inches.
24. The agreed list of prices was designed to prevent wages being forced down in time of depression and surplus of labour.
25. The shaft referred to carried steam power to the looms in the various weavers' houses.
26. Queen Victoria combined visits to Coventry and Stoneleigh Abbey on this occasion.
27. 'Singles' refer to raw silk twisted to give more firmness to its texture, while 'tram' was two or more threads twisted together. Both were used for 'shoot', as the weft or cross-thread was called.
28. War began on April 26th, when Napoleon III sought to support Piedmont and the cause of Italian unity against Austria.
29. Incomes below £100 were free of tax at this period.
30. The Volunteer Movement began in 1859 as a result of fears of the apparent power of France under Napoleon III. It was encouraged by Lord Palmerston.

31. The timing of this announcement of the terms of the Cobden Treaty was particularly unfortunate for the English silk industry. The ribbons already made for the coming season found little sale since the generally superior products of France came in duty-free for the Spring. A severe loss of capital to English manufacturers resulted.
32. The Silk Manufacturers' Association was sending deputations abroad at this period to study Continental methods. They received back reports that the French and Swiss were ahead, especially as regards machinery and training of skilled labour.
33. The strike had begun on July 17th, and was called off at the end of August when both sides accepted the device of a committee of arbitration to judge the terms of offers of employment in the future. In two respects Andrews' verdict on events appears correct: the weavers' list operated no longer, and the Swiss did take the opportunity to expand their exports of substantial plain goods to England while the Coventry silk trade was idle.
34. Count Cavour, the Prime Minister of Piedmont, had been the architect of Italian unity.
35. 'Les Soyeux' of Lyons operated an effective closed shop, so Andrews' failure to obtain work there is not surprising.
36. Blondin, an acrobat and tight-rope walker, had achieved the feat of crossing Niagra Falls on a tight-rope in 1859.
37. The Prince Consort had died on December 14th.
38. The theme of Lord Byron's *Childe Harold's Pilgrimage* obviously appealed to Andrews as he set out on his lonely travels, though he shows few of the characteristics of the true Byronic hero.
39. Other reasons for the decline of the silk trade were the move in fashion away from ribbons to feathers, and a disease among silk-worms. Moreover, the loss of the American market owing to the imposition of a tariff and the onset of the Civil War added to the depression.
40. Narrow goods consisted of ribbons. Wides were broad silks; trade in these had flourished earlier in the century.
41. It was the custom to give the shoot (weft thread) to the weavers in hanks enough for a whole set of warps at a time.
42. Shades were ribbons of diverse colouring.
43. The figures here refer to penny widths (dy), an English measurement of the width of ribbon. Thus $8=1\frac{1}{12}$ inches, $20=2\frac{7}{12}$ inches, $30=3\frac{10}{12}$ inches, and $40=4\frac{7}{12}$ inches, etc.
44. Other workers emigrated to the United States or the more prosperous areas of England.
45. The revival in trade was aided by the fact that several leading wholesalers

kept 'Coventry Departments' and so maintained a steady demand for the traditional, plain ribbon which the city produced.

46. 'Pads' were thick ribbon used for waist-bands, being produced from cotton with a silk facing.
47. Messrs Cash are still in business as makers of woven labels and name-tapes, etc.
48. The trade in brighter ribbons revived in the period 1865–74.

THE AUTOBIOGRAPHY OF JOSEPH GUTTERIDGE

Preface

AMID the growing luxury of our age and the over estimate of mere surroundings as necessary to happiness, it is of inestimable service to humanity to be, from time to time, recalled to the truer pleasures of plain living and high thinking. The chief of such reminders are the lives of men who, in spite of adversity and penury, have proved that the higher joys of life are mainly independent of circumstances. We cannot have too many of such records, provided they are worthy; and the present is another of these that deserves this rank. It is the more to be welcomed that it is the story of an English workman; for England has had fewer such histories than its smaller and poorer sister, Scotland.

This narrative differs from those of most others of the kind in that it is written by the man himself, unadorned by the pen of another, a fact that lends it interest. Had it been elaborated by being set in its local, scenic, and historical relations, like others of public note, it would have taken rank with the more popular of these biographies. But the man is greater than his book. A visit to his snug home in Coventry, with its tasteful adornments, its varied scientific collections, and, still more, his own uncommon personality, is a rare experience and a happy memory.

The tale deserves to be generally known, as another proof, unobtrusive and telling, that true manhood is superior to external condition; that the love and study of nature, science, and art may be successfully and happily pursued under the most untoward circumstances even in the heart of a city; and that, with all the decadence of much of modern life, we have still among us some of 'the noble, silent men scattered here and there each in his department, whom no morning newspaper makes mention of, but who are the salt of the earth, and with none or few of whom,' as Carlyle says, 'a country is in a bad way.'

WILLIAM JOLLY

Contents

I

Boyhood

My Ancestors – My father and his brothers at the Wars – State of Coventry on their return – The Silk and Watch Trades in Coventry – The City hemmed in by Lammas lands – Riding the Lammas – Breakdown of the custom – Enclosure of the Lammas lands – A Paradise – My birth and early schooling – Novel aids to education – First acquaintance with Nature – Visits to Berkswell – The beauties of Hearsall Common and the Schoolmaster's Garden – Birds as pets – House duties – My mother – Musical treats – Illness – Loss of memory for music – Early mechanical skill – A brutal schoolmaster and his tender wife – My mother's death – Swanswell, Harnall Lane, Primrose Hill and Hill Fields – New schoolmasters – Favourite walks – Early efforts at collecting – Non-resistance.

BEFORE giving an account of my past life with its incidents and events, it will perhaps be as well very briefly to refer to those from whom our family traces its descent. The earliest authentic information I can obtain from our family registers is of Thomas Gutteridge, a Fellmonger and Woolcomber, who came from Austrey, a small township on the borders of Leicestershire, about five or six miles from Tamworth. This was about the year 1676. At that time the wool trade was a very prosperous one, and formed one of the chief staples of commerce in Coventry. Coventry was also noted for its permanent dyes used for this fibre, hence the proverb 'True as Coventry blue.'

Thomas Gutteridge appears to have been a man in good circumstances. His eldest son, Thomas, continued his father's business. But the sons of this second Thomas embarked in the Silk trade, a new branch of commerce then just beginning to be established in Coventry. The Wool trade at this time was rapidly being absorbed by the Yorkshire capitalists, who by the aid of steam and water power for working their improved machinery, soon put an end to the hand trade of Coventry. I can just recollect the last Woolcomber in this city; his name was William Eburne, and he lived in Gosford Street.

From William, one of the sons of the second Thomas, came my father, Joseph. He was the third of six brothers. Another of these brothers named William enlisted when quite young in the 11th Regiment of Foot, and went through some hard service during the Peninsula war under Wellington. While serving in Portugal he married, and became the father of eleven children, all born in the Regiment. His company formed part of the forlorn hope to assault the breach in the second storming of Badajoz, for which he obtained the Brevet of Sergeant Major. I believe that neither he nor any of his family ever returned to England. He died, I believe, at Malta, one of the Ionian Islands, but what became of his wife and family I am uncertain. If they did not return to England, they probably settled in Spain, for the name of 'Gutterieze' is frequently met with in the later annals of that country, and I have often wondered whether it is identical with the English 'Gutteridge.'

These were, indeed, troublous times for the young people, my father and his brothers. The fearful drafts made upon the country to sustain our forces in the Peninsula and America where they were struggling for their independence, drained Coventry terribly of its able-bodied young men. The consequence was that five of the six brothers were compelled to serve either in the regular army or militia. My father was drafted into the Tower Hamlets regiment; his period of service was spent chiefly in Ireland, then in a most disturbed state. The people were driven to a state of anarchy by poverty, misrule and neglect, and their feelings towards the English non-resident landowners were embittered a thousand-fold by the military rule under which they were kept. At indefinite periods my father would visit his home on furlough.

All the brothers had received what was at that time considered a good education, and soon rose from the ranks, the eldest attaining the rank of Sergeant-Major, and the others were Sergeants in the various corps to which they belonged.

About the close of the year 1814, while my father was recruiting in Warwickshire, he was taken with an illness which prevented him from re-joining his regiment, and, being near Coventry, he was allowed to come home to be nursed by his wife. His regiment was disbanded immediately after the Battle of Waterloo, and his discharge was sent down to him while he was staying in his native city. The only recompense he received for this long service was a certificate of good conduct; pensions not being awarded to such as him.

After the peace, his brothers obtained their discharge and returned home. They found their native city in a most fearful state of collapse, provisions at famine prices, the various trades at a complete standstill, their former comfortable homes a wreck, and their wives and children in great poverty and distress. The brothers worked as journeymen at the trades in which at one time they hoped to have been masters. After a time, as national affairs became more settled, matters at home improved, and trade and commerce resumed their normal position. Coventry slowly recovered from its losses, and a time of prosperity set in, which lasted many years. This arose chiefly from the great demand for silken ribbons, and Coventry became the principal seat of the manufacture. The single-hand loom, which had hitherto been the only means of production, gave place largely to the engine loom, which made many breadths at the same time, and enabled manufacturers to meet the demand more readily than by the single-hand loom. After the wars, Coventry became famous for two staple trades, the manufacture of ribbons and watches, and rapidly increased in population.

Coventry would at this time have become one of the most important towns of the midland counties but for one circumstance which more than any other crippled its growth. It was hemmed in on all sides by Lammas lands and commons that really left no room for extension. These lands were claimed by the freemen for pasturage during a certain part of the year and could not be used for building purposes unless the two interests – the interests of the *bonâ fide* owners and of the freemen – could be separated. The freemen – men who had gained the freedom of the city by serving an apprenticeship of seven years to a trade in Coventry – had received by charter and the wills of donors the right of herbage over these lands 'for ever from the feast of Lammas unto the Purification of our Lady,' or from Michaelmas till the Purification. The evident intention of the donors was to benefit the community, but the common right over these lands, owing to the conditions attaching to the freedom of the city, ultimately became restricted to comparatively very few people, who regarded their privileges with a very jealous eye. Every year on the 13th of August, it was the custom of the chamberlains, pinners, and such of the freemen as cared to join them, all mounted on horseback, to assert their rights by riding over the lands. Any gates or obstructions to free access to them not previously removed were unceremoniously broken down.

Circumstances occurred, however, which dispelled the delusion that the

Lammas lands were sacred against all interference. About the year 1828, land was required for the improvement of the turnpike or coach road to Holyhead, and later, about the year 1843, the London and Birmingham – now the London and North Western – Railway Co., required land for their railway; but the freemen would not give up their rights over the only land that was available until compelled to do so by Act of Parliament. The money received as compensation, amounting to £2,476 4s. was invested for the benefit of the freemen, and the interest arising from it forms what is now known as the Freemen's Seniority Fund, from which a certain number of old freemen receive six shillings a week. It was not long before other portions of the Lammas lands were enclosed. After a severe struggle the freemen, in 1860, consented to accept absolutely and in perpetuity a given proportion of the lands in exchange for their right of herbage over the whole. With the sanction of the Inclosure Commissioners a scheme agreeable both to the real owners of the land, and to the freemen was carried out. The proportion of land awarded to the freemen was seven twenty-fourths of the Lammas lands, and one-fifth of the Michaelmas lands, the freemen's share amounting to about 273 acres. The management of these lands was vested in trustees known as the Freemen's Trustees, and the revenue arising from the land is now devoted to the benefit of the freemen, being distributed in small sums weekly amongst some of the oldest of their number.

These Lammas lands, prior to their enclosure, were to me in my youth a veritable paradise. I would roam over them without let or hindrance, and my earliest feelings of pleasure in wild flowers, insects, and birds were acquired upon these wastes.

I was born March 23, 1816, and from birth was weak and delicate. At five I was sent to a dame school kept by a Quakeress, where I soon acquired all the knowledge, educationally, that the old lady could impart. Being of a practical turn of mind, she not only taught us her limited stock of general knowledge, but instructed us – boys and girls alike – in the arts of sewing and knitting, and many others of a peculiarly feminine character. Even now as age advances I recall her gentle, placid face and her motherly kindness in dealing with the rough untutored natures committed to her care, her repugnance of physical force and her facile and winning mode of attracting attention. I am afraid my highly excitable and nervous temperament might have been warped and rendered intractable by any ruder mode of teaching. She was just the woman to soften down the rough asperities of human nature. At seven I had so far profited by her teaching as to be able to make out the contents of the local papers, and I derived much pleasure and knowledge from their perusal. Another means of learning that I made use of was the sign board literature of public-houses and shops, so that I soon became acquainted not only with the names of the streets but of the resident shopkeepers of the town. I found here the advantage of having parents who could read and write well, as sometimes words and names would occur that I could not pronounce properly. These I would either write down or carry in my mind for correction. My father always cheerfully helped me and encouraged me in this mode of gaining knowledge.

When I left the dame school, my father put me under a Mr Holland, an itinerant preacher among the Wesleyans, who had the reputation of being a passable scholar and a good teacher. He was a kind, gentle, large-hearted, charitable man, and it is pleasurable to recall the progress I made under his teaching. I am afraid, however, that I did not take so much advantage of this opportunity as I ought to have done. Whether this was due to my physical weakness, or to a restless desire to be in the fields and lanes culling the flowers, chasing butterflies, hunting after birds' nests, sitting by the brooksides watching the waterflies, or angling for minnows that glanced in the sunlight like streaks of burnished silver, I cannot say, but I think I must have derived much of this desire to look at nature in its varied moods from this gentleman's method of teaching. He would show his pupils picture-books illustrating the animal and vegetable kingdoms, which were full of wonders to my youthful imagination. It was his nature to help all with whom he came in contact. He was very kind to me personally, and his face and form are still vividly impressed on my memory.

At the outset of my endeavours to become acquainted with nature, I was beset with difficulties in regard to the common and the technical names of plants and animals. They were beyond me and foreign to my former experiences, and rather unsettled me for a time in my lessons. At that time perhaps not ten persons in a hundred could read or write; books upon science were very expensive and altogether beyond the limited means of the artisan. This, too, was a great drawback.

A source of extreme pleasure to me at this time was the permission that was given me to accompany my father upon his visits to his brother Thomas, a schoolmaster at Berkswell, a small village about six miles from Coventry. The early summer was generally chosen for these visits. We had to cross an extensive piece of waste land called Hearsall Common, one of the tracts over which the freemen had herbage rights. It was used but very little, however, at that time for grazing purposes. Indeed the place was unsuitable. Excepting the highway that passed over it and a few patches of grass here and there, it was a mass of gorse and bracken. To me it was a very paradise. I loved to stray among its gorse bushes redundant with vivid yellow blossoms. The tall strong ribbed fronds of its brake ferns almost hid one amid their luxuriant growth; and there were great patches of broom, magnificent masses of yellow blossom, at frequent intervals about the Common. Upon the barer pieces the delicate harebell was strikingly prominent with its azure blue flower; the erica, or heath plant, with its spikes of deep purple, and the wood betony with its erect stem and light purple flowers peeped everywhere among the bushes. On the edges of these clumps of vegetation, dotted here and there, were the cruciform pale yellow flowers of the tormentel scattered about like crosses of gold. The wild thyme, too, scented the air with its delicate fragrance. To me at that time they were simply flowers and plants that I had never seen before, but their forms and the particular spots in which they grew – their habitat, as I afterwards learned to say – lingered in my memory.

Thus the monotony of school was relieved. I loved also to get into the schoolmaster's garden at the back of his house, though this was forbidden ground to the boys on account of the damage that it was feared would result. One end of the garden was bounded by the remains of the old town wall, about nine feet thick and twelve feet high. The square facing stones had been removed for building purposes, leaving the cemented rubble of the interior of the old wall exposed. Up the rugged face thus formed I used to climb to gather the wallflower and the wild snap-dragon which grew in the crevices or on the top, interspersed with delicate ferns. If discovered, I would be punished by excess of task or by being kept in after school hours. In time, however, I think the master must have noticed my peculiar proclivities, for towards the latter end of my time with him he often gave me liberty to go with his son into the garden.

Climbing too, was a mania with me, and I have often wondered, since, how I managed to escape serious accident when ascending the tall and stately elms that were so common in the neighbourhood. The sight of a crows' nest, no matter how tall the tree that contained it, was sure to provoke in me an irresistible desire to become possessed of the eggs. Many a buffet have I had with birds before securing the prize. Once I fell a considerable distance and had a narrow escape. I never wantonly took the young birds, except sometimes a young magpie perhaps, which I would take home and rear as a pet. My pets, however, caused trouble to the neighbours and at home by their thievish propensities. Their cunning was most extraordinary. Nothing seemed to escape their keen observation or their inordinate curiosity, and many a lost domestic article belonging to my mother or to neighbours has been found among the litter of their cage. My magpie pets generally came to an untimely end in the pursuit of their natural instincts, being either killed by cats or lamed by boys throwing stones at them. After many failures with magpies and jays, I turned my attention to starlings with better success, but could not get them to articulate words so well as I should have liked. Their beauty and vivacity were all I could wish, but their guttural and harsh discordant notes were in marked contrast with the sweet plaintive notes of the linnet, or the gushing full melodious strains of the sky-lark. The nests of these birds – the sky-larks – I had frequently found, but could not succeed in rearing their young owing to my having to be away at school. The mortality among my pets was so great that my father at last forbade me bringing any more home.

My mother was a confirmed invalid. Her illness – rheumatic fever – which left her a helpless cripple, was caused by going too soon into a newly-built house. After a fashion, we lads – three in number – had to do what we could under her guidance to keep the house in order. I was the eldest of three, and had, before going to school, to prepare for dinner, and upon leaving school at twelve, to complete the preparations against my father's return at one o'clock. I recall with painful recollections many little things that I left undone, which, if done, would have added much to my mother's comfort. This did not arise from wilfulness, but from my inherent intense desire to be in the fields and lanes. I must confess, too, that I did not receive so much correction as I deserved for these youthful failings. My parents considered that my health very much depended upon exercise and freedom, and this was the advice of the various doctors that my father had taken me to. I well recollect one old physician, a Quaker, named Dr Southam, refusing to prescribe for me, remarking that the money in my case would be wasted. He recommended that which suited my tastes and habits much better, namely, as much exercise in the open air as I could take. The consequence was that I took more liberty than perhaps I ought to have taken. I would sometimes take my brothers with me, much to the inconvenience of my poor mother, who could not move from the place in which she was left. Whenever I transgressed in this manner, I received only a gentle reproof from my mother. She was most kind and considerate to her children, and would often screen our faults rather than that they should come to the knowledge of our father, who would often, with his military notions of discipline, treat us occasionally to a little rope's end. True, it was not so frequently applied as we deserved, but whenever we did taste it, the remembrance of it kept us within bounds for some considerable time to come.

My father and his brothers were in the habit of meeting together on holidays or festive occasions with their musical instruments, for all were members of the bands of the regiments to which they belonged. These times I count amongst the happiest experiences of my youth. I would sit almost entranced while they played the pieces of music then most in vogue – quick and slow marches, set pieces, and ofttimes compositions of their own. I imagine this love of music had been transmitted to me by heredity, and it was fostered by my being so often within hearing of it at home. My father laid a strict injunction upon me not to use any of his instruments – he played the flute in its various keys, the eight-keyed flute not having then been invented – believing probably that some injury might result. However, I surreptitiously learned the rudiments on the octave flute and piccolo, and when my father discovered this, he expressed his surprise at my facility in fingering, but was still determined not to let me learn the flute. For a considerable time he kept them locked up. I rummaged over his music books, a liberty which he considerately allowed, and I tried to unravel the mystery of musical notation. After some time spent in learning the names of the notes and their durations, I began to see my way more clearly, and was soon able to follow him as he played from copy. My memory at this time was very retentive, and a lesson once understood was seldom forgotten. A strolling street band would irresistibly draw me as far as I dare go away from home. Glee parties, too, then so common in England, would also lead me far astray listening to their singing. At these times I seemed to forget everything in the enjoyment of the moment, and even in these later days when I hear music played by a master hand I am spellbound.

About this time I was utterly prostrated by a severe illness – a malignant fever – and when I reached a state of convalescence afterwards, I found my knowledge of musical notation almost gone, but not so the love of music nor the aptitude to distinguish accurately musical sounds. I lost the faculty for reading a piece at first sight, and since then the reading of musical notes has always been a labour to me, rather than an intuitive perception. I was left by this illness as weak as a little child, and several months elapsed before I could gain strength enough to indulge even in a ramble or any ordinary amusement. I feel and realise now how much I owe to the tender care and solicitude of my parents, who by the mercy of God were the means of snatching me as it were from the very jaws of death. It is only when we arrive at adult age that we can fully appreciate the anxieties and troubles that children bring to parents in the cultivation of their minds and the keeping of their bodies in health so as to equip them for the battle of life. The return to my normal condition of health was a slow and tedious process, and at no time have I regained that perfect memory that once enabled me to retain whatever came under my notice or ministered to my youthful pleasures. During my enforced physical inactivity, I amused myself by rudely carving various devices in soft wood, and with the aid of a chisel, fashioned from a watchmaker's flat file, I passed a great deal of time constructing little boxes, small bird cages, and other useful – and useless – articles, for the mere love of construction. This desire for mechanical construction increased as years advanced, and from these early efforts I trace the skill in this direction which I possessed in after years, and which proved so helpful in keeping the wolf from the door at times when work was scarce.

After recovery, I was placed in Baker, Billing and Crowe's charity school, where by examination I soon graduated into the first class, a position retained as long as I remained on the foundation. I look back to my first year in this school with anything but a pleasurable feeling. To the school lately left I was much attached, for, as I have said, the master was one who won the love and respect of all under him; but here the long and massive ebony ruler and the birch rod were the principal monitors. Trembling with dread lest I should make some mistake, I have often gone up to the master's desk to repeat my lesson, and notwithstanding that, as I thought, I had it indelibly fixed upon my memory, the sight of those instruments of torture would make me forget everything. I have seen lads struck so severely as to draw blood. The master's wife was a kind, bustling little woman, and would often by her interposition in cases of extremely severe punishment cause a scene in the school. Many a time has she taken a boy into the house to attend to his wounds, rating and scolding her husband for his brutality. The lads were not long in discovering this kindly disposition on her part, and many a one has shouted louder than his punishment warranted in order to attract her attention. Punishment by means of the birch rod was a brutal and disgusting exhibition. The culprit was stripped and hoisted on the back of the tallest boy in the school, the master standing by his side with a rod of stout twigs. The first blow would extort a scream of agony, and if a dozen were given, as was often the case, the power of crying out would be almost taken away. Then would occur a scene between the master and his wife, who would come upon the scene attracted by the boy's screams. Many thanks to the brave little woman for her intervention! The boys would have done anything they could for her; she won their sincere affection by her kindly disposition. I do not recollect being chastised myself by the master, but it is a great wonder that I, above all others, should have escaped. He died at the end of my first year, and the lads were jubilant at the thought of a change, which certainly could not be any worse for us, but which might be a good deal better.

About this time too, my mother died, and a great and serious loss we found it, for we were turned over to the tender mercies of an old lady who was engaged as house-keeper. Although she looked after the affairs of the household as well as might have been expected of a stranger, she was not to us what our mother had been. There was on her part a great lack of sympathy for us and our peculiar proclivities, and we sadly missed the tender care and solicitude which only a mother can exhibit towards her children. No doubt we could have agreed much better with her if we could have fallen in with her mode of management, but it was so entirely different from that to which we had been used, that we thought we were too hardly dealt with, and we seemed to labour under the impression that she, a stranger to our ways and wants had no moral right to restrain us in our youthful pleasures. Home under these circumstances had but few attractions, and whenever an opportunity occurred, either in the early morning or after school hours, we were in the fields and lanes of the neighbourhood collecting bird eggs, insects, and flowers. The old lady would complain bitterly of the 'litter' we made by what we regarded as valuable treasures.

By this time I became well acquainted with the locality in which we lived and for miles round, and also knew the common names and habits of the birds that frequented the neighbourhood. Even now I watch with as much interest as then for the first appearance of the swallow and the swift; but many a bird have I missed in these later times that was very common then. The wood-lark seems all but extinct in this locality, as does also the goldfinch, the brown linnet and the golden-crested wren are scarce. In fact, many of the small birds, both stationary and migratory, have disappeared, and we have now to travel some miles from the town before we can see their well-remembered forms or hear their well-known songs. A rather large pool of water still remains, called Swanswell Pool, upon the borders of the old city and the New Town – as it was for a long time afterwards called – of Hill Fields. At the time to which I am referring, this now thickly populated district was a wild and romantic place. The low ground immediately surrounding the pool was covered with extensive osier and reed beds. This place was the favourite resort and breeding place of several kinds of water fowl. The wild duck, the widgeon, the dipper, and the water hen were constant visitors, and the reeds and osier beds were enlivened by the songs of the warblers that abounded. The water itself teemed with fish, as it does to this day. Pike, perch, roach, tench and eels afforded fine sport for anglers. Before the new town of Hill Fields encroached upon the pool it was a wild and weird place. The water was bordered with fine old pollard willows, and on two sides the ground gradually rose from the edge of the water into Hill Fields. The view of the pool was almost obscured in the narrow causeway by the willows and clusters of tall elms, oaks, chestnuts and maples that surrounded it. These now add to the picturesqueness of the ornamental recreation ground into which the place has since been converted, and handed over to the town by the trustees of Sir Thomas White's charity.

A very ancient stone-built mansion formerly stood on the site of the present flour mills of Mr Powers. It certainly, in my early days, was much dilapidated and converted into tenements. It adjoined the old Water Works and Baths, for the use of that part of the town. The entrance to it on the North side was through a massive stone porch, with seats of the same material on either side. This front nearest the Pool was two stories in height. On the South side facing the meadows it was three stories; it seemed to be the principal front, and was reached by two flights of stone steps. It must have been a fine pile of building in its normal condition, seemingly dating back to the Tudor times, most elaborate in its ornamentation and sculpture, and presenting a most imposing appearance from the meadows, which no doubt were the gardens attached to this grand old residence. The current report in my early days was that it was the country residence of the Bishop of Coventry. It was within a short distance of the Priory Gate, and the porch entrance was easily reached from the Cook Street Gate and from

Bishop Street Gate by the old Leicester Causeway, that joined the Fosse road just outside that town.

The path across the fields that bounded the pool on one side led into a lane called Harnall Lane, which in olden time was the highway from Coventry to Leicester. This lane was reached by turning sharply to the right at the termination of the field path. Harnall Lane, which is nearly a mile and a quarter long, still bears the same name. It ends at the point where Coventry joins Stoke, the Stoke end being called Swan Lane. It was a rugged but beautiful place in bygone times, so narrow in parts that farmers' carts almost touched the fences on either side. In other parts there were broad stretches of waste land bordering the roadway, the furze and brambles upon which made them a veritable paradise in my eyes. Ferns grew in rich profusion in the more sheltered parts. There were the male fern (filix mas), the female fern (filix femina), the bird's nest fern (filix nidus), the polypody (polypodum vulgare), the hart's tongue (scolopendrium commins), with pretty specimens of smaller species in the hedge bottoms and on the banks. In a secluded lane like this, one may be sure there was no lack of birds, butterflies, or wild flowers. There we could find the primrose, the blue bell, many species of cranesbill (geranium sanguineum and others), stellaria (stellaria holostia, graminea and glauca), St John's wort (hyperieum calicinum), alehoof (glectioma hederacea), two or three species of epilobium (epilobium angustifolium), the large yellow toad flax (linaria vulgaris), avens (geum urbanum), the wild horehound (marubium nigra), and wood sage (tencrium scoradium), and many other plants that were used in the household for their medicinal properties. During one of my rambles in these lanes, I met with an accident which almost deprived me of the sight of one eye. A stone thrown at a bird by another boy struck me with its full force in the eye, and it was a long time before I recovered from the effects of the blow.

The highest part of Hill Fields is called Primrose Hill, from which a path runs across two fields into Swan Lane. This hill is beautifully wooded with stately elms of two species, the common and wych elm (ulmus montana), maples of two or three species (acer), and pines of several kinds (pinus sylvestus, pinus pendula, black larch, pinus alba, white spruce). One part of this hill had been quarried very extensively and to a great depth for the valuable sandstone it contained. The stone was used in the construction of the city walls and gates about six hundred years ago. In the deep holes made by the excavations, forest trees now grow, towering by straight stems to a height of thirty or forty feet, their heads making one umbrageous mass of foliage almost impenetrable to the sun's rays. The sides of the excavations are terraced in all directions under the shade of the trees and at the more open parts. It well deserved the name it bore, for in my early recollection it was a mass of primroses (primula vulgare) and daffodils (pseudo narcissus), while the lower and damper parts were yellow with the flowers of the lesser pile wort (ranunculus ficaria). It was a most romantic, wild, and beautiful place, and although it is now shorn of much of its grandeur, it has for me, on account of its happy associations, no less than on account of its beauty, many attractions still. The mansion called Primrose Hill House was embowered among these stately trees. Interspersed among the other trees and nearer the fields were clusters of birch (betulus alba) strikingly prominent by their white bark and pendulous branches clothed in light green, contrasting delicately with the sombre back-ground. Here was the home of the nightingale. the thrush, the blackbird, and the various kinds of finches; and many migratory birds here found ample shelter and protection during the brooding season. These pictures of sylvan beauty are as strongly impressed upon my memory now as when first I saw them. The rich verdure of the fields, the exuberant foliage of the tall stately elm vied with the majestic oak (quereus rober), and the lowly and graceful birch. This spot, most beautiful in the summer time, when enlivened by the songs of birds that swarmed thither, will never be forgotten.

But I must return to my school days. The next master was of a very different type to his predecessor. His mode of teaching, too, was different, but the boys soon acquired a strong dislike for him. He lacked his predecessor's stern unflinching character and dominant will, and he lacked also the essential quality in a schoolmaster – the realisation that boys' capacities for learning differ as widely as their other characteristics. He was an able scholar, but he imagined that all boys could come up to his standard of teaching. He regarded the school as a piece of mechanism which could be actuated by only one kind of motive power, instead of looking upon it as a conglomeration of units actuated by an infinite variety of personal interests which it was his duty to understand, to control, and to make the best of. As a sample of his dealing with us, I may instance his method of enforcing discipline. For good conduct and effiicency, he gave us metal discs which bore numbers denoting the number of good conduct marks to which each boy was entitled. At the end of the week we totalled up our marks from the checks in our possession, and each boy was supposed to have checks to total at least fifty marks, otherwise he would be reduced to a lower class or be kept in after school hours. To the great astonishment of the master, this system soon resulted in the almost utter extinction of the first and second classes, a great proportion of the best boys being defaulters. The master was puzzled as well as astonished, but a stringent investigation disclosed the fact that some of the boys did not produce the number of checks they earned, while others who had been notoriously indolent, produced tokens to show that they had been working remarkably well. By cajoling and threatening some of the boys, the master found out that there was in the school a system of currency by which a fixed quantity of sweets or fruit, or a certain number of marbles, or even a certain sum of money, was fair and just exchange for a certain number of metal tokens. The boys had put into practical use one of the master's favourite themes, that of traffic and barter. The boy who brought to school the most plentiful supply of sweets, fruit, marbles or money, was able at the end of the week to produce the greatest number of tokens, and was thus practically able to purchase preferment in the school. Once a month we had a half holiday, which depended upon tickets. During the week in which this holiday occurred we kept our own tickets, so that we might not miss the holiday. After school hours, we amused ourselves by concocting schemes for the annoyance of the master, telling impromptu tales, or laying plans for the spending of our monthly half holiday. When the weather was favourable, we usually took a long ramble over the commons and heaths or along the lanes that were easily accessible from the city. A favourite walk was through Radford, Coundon, and Brownshill Green to Allesley. Another was to Radford, and by the lane which branches off to the left by the old Radford toll gate house, across fields and along to Coundon, back to the top of Hill Street. The termination of this lane is called Barker's Butts, from the fact of its being an old practice ground for the bowmen of the city. The site of the ancient butts is now occupied by the new reservoirs for holding the water supply of the city. To the right of the toll gate is another interesting lane called Coundon Lane which runs through the Whitmore Park estate to the Holbrooks, Foleshill, and on through Lockhurst Lane to the main road from Coventry to Leicester. These lanes, not being much frequented, were richly stored with plants, many of them useful as herbal remedies, and all of them very interesting to the botanist. Plants, ferns and mosses were there in great profusion, some of the finest specimens I have – especially the hypnums – were found in these lanes.

At the end of the second year the schoolmaster resigned, having lost all control over the boys, who cared but little for his punishments, indeed rather courting them than otherwise. The new master, Mr Couldrey, introduced a new system, which was more congenial to the scholars. The school had removed to more commodious premises, and under the new régime the boys settled down to work in accordance with the will of the master, who by his reasonable and kind treatment of them soon won their respect and esteem. Except for a few escapades on the part of some boys who were slow to break with the past, the work of the school went on with remarkable smoothness, and the last year of my school days was the happiest I had seen. The master was firm but gentle, and sought to improve the boys by encouraging a spirit of emulation among them rather than by corporal punishment. The practice of staying in after school hours was abolished, allowing us more leisure for outdoor exercises and recreation. My leisure was not now given up to promiscuous rambling; there was more method in my walks. My father gave me an old edition of Culpepper, with coloured plates. By the aid of this book I soon found out not only the common names of plants but their uses and medical properties. The boys of the first and second forms were allowed by the master to sketch in pencil and to use water colours, and availing myself of this privilege, I experienced great delight in delineating the forms and colours of plants and flowers. The ability to do this proved to me in after times a ready means of fixing in my mind the peculiar characteristics of plants that otherwise might slip my memory. Another means of obtaining accurate representations of botanical specimens was to take an impression of the leaf or flower between two sheets of manifold paper. An exact reproduction of both sides of a leaf could in this way be preserved showing the veinings down to the minutest details. I made quite a collection of these leaf impressions with the name attached to each and a record of the locality where it was found – its habitat.

I was growing very fast, and was physically rather weak and unable to mingle with other boys in their robust amusements; I had to be a passive on-looker, while my heart was in their pleasures. I could never endure much rough play, and therefore had to keep aloof from their petty quarrels and conflicts for physical supremacy, and at times, on that account, was subjected to many insults from bullies. This feeling of incapacity to cope successfully with others in trials of mere brute force, was the first step towards implanting within me the principle of non-resistance, to which no doubt may be attributed many of the hardships which I afterwards endured.

As an outcome of this state of mind, I dreaded trespassing when rambling, and have missed many a gratification in my pursuit of insects or search after plants. For the sake of peace and to secure the goodwill of others, I endured much, having to live as it were in a little world of my own, and finding so few congenial spirits with whom to associate in my peculiar pursuits.

II

Youth

Apprenticed to the ribbon weaving – Early experiences of factory life – Incipient pleasures – Hard times – A termagant step-mother – Weavers' riot – Mr Beck's factory burned down – Three rioters transported – One returns a wealthy man – My father's death – Ill-treated by our step-mother – A horrible night – Leaving home.

BETWEEN the age of thirteen and fourteen, I came out of the school to be apprenticed to my father to learn the art of ribbon weaving. This was a most unwise selection on his part, as my youthful practices were more in favour of a mechanical trade. The very monotony of the business produced in me an aversion, and I was a long time becoming reconciled to it. Although the trade was light at that time, the changes of a few years soon made it a most heavy and laborious one. Jacquard looms for the manufacture of fancy ribbons had just been introduced. As my father worked in a factory, I had to learn the trade under his supervision, paying the owner of the factory one-half of my net earnings for the use of machinery and the advantage of an experienced foreman.

At the back of the factory there was a large and beautiful garden well stocked with fruit and other trees, and near one end was a spring of water of very ancient date, lined and arched over with cut stone. This was the old St. Agnes's well of monastic times, belonging to the old Priory. The spring of water had more attractions for me than the factory had, with its continual din and clatter of shuttles and machinery. Many a pleasant hour I passed watching the copious flow of water, and the birds that visited it, either for a bath or a drink. I was down at this place so often that complaints were made to my father about my loss of time, and I had to attend more to my business.

I commenced work by helping others to change their patterns, and doing odd jobs about the shop. This variety of occupation began to interest me, and I strove hard to excel the other boys or 'helps' as we were called. Very soon I began to feel my place among them by dint of application and willingness to help in various ways the journeymen, who in return would, practically, show me how to manage things that I might have asked the foreman in vain to instruct me in.

The foreman, by the way, was more given to drinking than to teaching, and ultimately fell a victim at an early age to his intemperate habits. He was a talented and capable workman, but this failing made him extremely unfit, either by precept or example, to have the care of young people.

I would do anything I possibly could for the simple love of doing it if I could gain the approbation of those I helped. But here as everywhere there were those who would order me to do things that were neither justifiable nor reasonable, and although young in the ways of the world I had peculiar ideas. To force me to do a thing against my reason and inclination would be like trying to drive a wooden peg into an iron anvil, and no punishment would alter my determination. The factory held about sixty looms, nearly half of which were worked by journeymen, the others by apprentices.

Factory life was very demoralising to youths with any pretensions to refinement. There was one custom in particular against which my whole nature revolted. Every newcomer was expected to pay for a gallon of ale, each of the other men in the factory adding a pint. The men would either strike or at any rate prevent the new hand from going on with his work until he had complied with this custom, so that it was morally impossible to resist. Sometimes the men would adjourn to a public-house to drink the beer, but oftener it would be brought into the shop. The older apprentices were allowed to share in these orgies, and the younger ones – lounging about – would get an odd drink now and then. These indulgences were the prelude in many instances to young men becoming habitual drunkards in after life. Several within my own knowledge, through giving way to these temptations, have been cut off in the prime of life. Some amongst them were prudent enough to keep aloof, as far as they possibly dare, without giving offence to those above them.

The tyranny and persecution that the more thoughtful youths were subjected to who refused to join in these carousals can scarcely be realised by outsiders. These practices sometimes ended in riot and mischief. I had my share of trouble and annoyance, but my firm determination and sometimes gentle reproofs convinced the leaders that it would be best to let me alone. Though not devoid of appreciation for innocent fun, I hated practical joking which would injure a man or subject him to personal inconvenience or loss. Being of a mechanical turn of mind and able therefore to help the men at their work, I gained the confidence and good will even of the wildest amongst them by little acts of kindness and assistance. Although I never joined my companions in their more reckless pastimes, they had no scruple about unfolding their plans in my presence, for they began to have confidence in me that I would not betray them. Many a reward has been offered for the discovery of offenders, but no one was ever found to accept it. I twice forfeited part of my earnings rather than give information within my knowledge. In this, however, I am sorry to add that a virtue was made of necessity, for none dare tell under fear of the consequences.

Thus passed two or three years, in which, much against my proclivities, I mechanically made headway with the art of weaving, but the machinery interested me more than the mere act of weaving. Some relief to the *ennui* of sitting in the loom all day was found in taking jobs to the loom carpenter, and I would spend a good deal of time in watching his operations. I gained much practical information in this way, which was useful in after life, and it would have been more to my advantage both on the score of health and of success in life had I been at that time turned over to the business of loom making. After mastering the difficulties of the then undeveloped Jacquard machine, the rest of the business was mere monotony.

The hours of work in the summer were from six to eight, and in winter from eight to eight or nine o'clock, so that the only time I could get in the fields was in the early summer mornings from four to five. I suffered very much in health from the close confinement, and not feeling any inclination to join the others in their pot-house pleasures, I generally amused myself with bits of incipient carpentering, wood-carving, or reading. Still, whatever time could be made available, was spent in the fields or on the common lands around the city; Sunday being usually devoted to long walks of this sort.

Even this pleasure was soon curtailed. My father – finding his household going to rack and ruin under the management of a housekeeper – married again, and his choice fell upon a young woman but few years older than myself. About this time we had long intervals without employment, and some of our experiences were bitter indeed, particularly in the severe winter, with bread at famine prices, and potatoes spoiled by the frost so as to be almost uneatable.

These were times of suffering not easily forgotten. My father had been out of work about sixteen weeks, and we lads were earning but little, and scarcely knew where to look for the means to satisfy our hunger. One day on coming home I picked up from a heap of rubbish a piece of paper, which was at once recognised to be a One Pound note. I hurried home gleefully with my prize, thinking it would be received with delight as a means of buying food, or at least paying for what we had already had on credit from a little shop in the neighbourhood. My father sent me and a brother to the shop, not however to pay off the old score, but to solicit credit for another week's provisions. When the shopkeeper heard our appeal, told in language that only hungry lads could use, he filled our basket and bade us come again for what we wanted until times improved. This was just before Christmas, and on Christmas Eve the shopkeeper sent us as a present some grocery and a quart of home-brewed ale with which to keep the festival. The One Pound note was not claimed by any one, although we had made it well known that we had found it. It was kept for three weeks, and was then handed over to the shopkeeper who had so kindly befriended us in our time of need. After Christmas trade revived somewhat, and we found ourselves in work again.

My father's second marriage must have been in the early part of my apprenticeship. It was a most unfortunate circumstance for us, for the young woman soon alienated from us whatever affection we might have felt for her as our father's wife by her imperious and tyrannical conduct. We soon began to feel ourselves as strangers and interlopers in our once happy home. All our little enjoyments were curtailed, and an iron hand was laid upon us. Little things that had cost me much labour, and had given me much pleasure to construct, were destroyed, and plants and other natural objects I had with so much patience and toil collected were treated as 'litter' and cleared away. We had but little music now of an instrumental kind, for my uncle's visits had ceased, but this loss was partly compensated for by the vocal music of a little sister who made her appearance and to whom we were much attached. The presence of this child was like a gleam of sunshine in the intervals of storm. We had never known what a boy's love for a sister was, and while the child lived we seemed in a manner to forget our own troubles and inconveniences in the pleasure of ministering to its wants. It died at an early age, and although another took its place, the mother's conduct towards us, and the child's own perversity, seemed to break the link that ought to have bound us to this as to the first. Frequent altercations took place between us and our new mother, and these invariably ended in fits of hysteria on her part that would sometimes last for hours. The only opportunity I had of following the bent of my inclination in mechanical construction was by stealth in the house of a neighbour who pitied our miserable condition.

When I had served about three years of my apprenticeship, a serious riot occurred among the weavers during a strike. A loom, very much larger than the ordinary one, had been invented by Mr Josiah Beck, to be worked with steam power. He had already fitted a large building with these looms, and employed young women at weekly wages to manage them. This was entirely against the usages of the trade, as the weavers had always opposed female labour in the actual making of ribbons, and only employed women as subsidiary helps. The proposed reduction in the price of labour, and the introduction of steam power and female labour, incensed the weavers to such an extent that the town was soon in a state of ferment and uproar. Mass meetings of the discontented weavers were held, who after violent denunciations from the leaders, formed themselves into procession and perambulated the town. The attitude of the men became more threatening every day, and the civil power was almost helpless against the outbreak. The Magistrates called in the aid of the military to disperse the people. The massacre by the yeomanry cavalry at a mass meeting of weavers in a field at Peterloo, near Manchester, was fresh in the memory of the people, and the appeal to the military so increased the excitement that the worst results were anticipated. After one of their indignation meetings, the weavers proceeded in a body to Mr Beck's factory, with the determination of subjecting the proprietor to the indignity of riding on a donkey through the streets face tailwards. Mr Beck, becoming aware of this intention – a common punishment for those who had transgressed any usage of the various trades in Coventry – made his escape. An entrance was forced into the factory and soon a cry was raised that he was climbing over a wall at the back to take refuge in a neighbour's house. He was dragged forth, and without ceremony set on the ass backwards admidst the yells and execrations of the crowd, and was also subjected to much brutal and rough treatment. Others of the roughs dismantled Mr Beck's house, cut out the warps from the looms in the factory and threw them into the mill dam, a filthy piece of water on the site now occupied by the Smithfield. I was an eyewitness of these doings. Having an intense desire to see the new machinery which dispensed with manual labour, I went to the ill-fated factory with one of the men employed there, and it was while I was inspecting the looms, absorbed with the beauty and simplicity of their arrangement, that the rioters commenced to demolish them, to pile the broken pieces on a heap of shavings, and deliberately set fire to them. At such a sacrilegious proceeding I stood aghast and felt my strength of body and mind failing, and would certainly have collapsed and been trodden to death by the mob, had I not been at that moment seized roughly by the arm and dragged forcibly through the dense crowd to a place of safety. I found then that I had been rescued from the crowd by my father, who risking his own safety in order to save me.

My father–missing me from amongst the hands at the factory where we were employed, which was separated from Mr Beck's only by the sheet of water to which I have referred – suspected my whereabouts, and mad with alarm at the supposed danger I was in, rushed out in search of me and found me on the point of swooning. I only recollect very dimly the difficulty we had in forcing our way through the crowd. The cavalry from the barracks were driving the people before them, and completely blocking up the narrow lane that led to our place of refuge – the factory where we worked. From the windows of this building we could see the fire. It spread through the factory with lightning rapidity, the materials being of such a highly inflammable nature. The factory and looms were completely destroyed, and nothing remained in a few hours but the blackened walls. The Riot Act was read, and many arrests were made. Three young men, whose names were Toogood, Burbery, and Sparkes, were at the ensuing assizes condemned to be hung. By the intervention of Mr Edward Ellice and his colleague in the representation of Coventry in Parliament, the death sentence was commuted to transportation for life. Subsequently one of these convicts, Mr Toogood, re-visited his native city a comparatively rich man. He brought with him a quantity of natural curiosities – skins of birds and animals, planks of various valuable woods, native implements and weapons of warfare and of the chase, besides a varied assortment of curios from different parts of the vast continent of Australia. For the accommodation of these curiosities I, at the recommendation of one of his friends, made him some show cases. During his visits to my house the subject of the riot was frequently discussed, and he narrated his experiences of convict life, to which the death penalty – it seemed to me – would have been far preferable. By steady perseverance and a fixed determination to work his way up again in the social scale to his former status, he succeeded, after a few years of convict life, in regaining his independence. He was soon able to work on his own account, and began to be known as a thriving and prosperous man, a man who could be trusted in matters of business

After staying in England for a short time, he returned to Australia, the country of his adoption, taking back with him his wife and children from whom he had been so long parted. I have heard nothing of him since.

After the riot the St. Agnes Lane factory was continually watched and protected day and night by relays of the hands employed there. My father of course had to take his turn. It was towards the end of November, and the winds were bitterly cold and raw with dense and chilling fogs. My father's constitution had been rudely shaken by his long and protracted military service in foreign countries. He was also unhappy at home, and suffered in no small degree from the neglect of his thriftless wife. He was obviously therefore not in a fit and proper condition to resist successfully the attacks made upon his health by these repeated exposures; but he nevertheless regarded it as part of his duty to share in these vigils. He paid the penalty by catching a severe cold which brought on an attack of inflammation of the lungs. During a violent fit of coughing he ruptured a blood vessel. Medical aid was immediately summoned, and under skilful treatment he was after about six months' illness able again to walk about. As soon as he possibly could he insisted upon going to work again, being in a manner compelled to take this step by the fact that the Benefit Society to which he belonged had for some time past suspended payment for sickness; he thus courted death in his efforts to sustain life. He had only resumed work a few weeks when he had a relapse much worse in character than the first attack. Medical aid was of no avail, and after lingering through a year and a half of intense suffering, he died of pulmonary consumption. We were thus left without a natural father or mother, but with a most terrible termagant for a step-mother, who subjected us to all manner of makeshifts in the matter of obtaining the necessaries of life, notwithstanding that we brought her in a weekly income which with prudent management would have placed us above want. If there had been any sympathy for us on her part, we might have had a much happier home, but we suffered terribly at her hands.

At the time of my father's death, I had about about two years and a half of my apprenticeship to serve. I had been apprenticed to him, and I was now transferred to the firm for whom we had both hitherto worked. By the terms of my new indenture, one of my uncles was bound to see that I was provided with proper and sufficient food, clothing, and lodging. This part of the agreement, however, soon became a dead letter. My step-mother took possession of our entire earnings, and our lives became daily more and more miserable. Besides having scanty food of the poorest description, we were very badly off for decent – not to say substantial – clothing. Appeals to my friends were in vain, and I began seriously to think that it would be much better that life should end than that it should continue under such irksome conditions. We children were in a complete state of bondage, both of mind and body, with no prospect of improvement. It was my father's dread before he died that this state of things would happen after his death, and he made me promise that I would stay at home to look after the interests of my younger brothers and protect them as long as I could.

Under these trials I became emaciated in body, and was fast drifting into a mood of careless indifference with regard to everything; a morbid feeling of melancholia was absorbing my whole nature, crowding my imagination constantly with wicked and desperate thoughts. On one occasion, provoked beyond my power of endurance, a violent altercation took place between us. She would have struck me down with a heavy stick had I not averted the descending blow, wrested the stick from her, and broken it. I was ordered to leave the house immediately, but remembering my father's injunction to stay and look after my younger brothers, I did not obey.

I had foreseen this for some time as the probable result of her conduct, and I was determined not to be driven forth thus unjustly from the home of my childhood; I took a night's reflection on the courses that were seemingly open to me. Throughout the night I was in a complete state of unrest. Of course I could not sleep, but lay, my imagination darkened by the events of the previous day, mentally picturing to myself what my future would be. At one time I would fancy myself a waif, a castaway, in the midst of an ocean illimitable in extent, with no prospect of help or a haven in view, and the darkness of unutterable despair in my heart, when lo! just as I would feel myself sinking into an unfathomable abyss, the scene would change, and I would find myself – by my own unaided efforts – building up for the future a structure that seemed to fulfil all that I could conceive as being required to fill up the measure of a man's earthly happiness. Then again the scene would change, and when it appeared that I had attained the summit of my desires, a dark and impenetrable mist would hide from view the seeming labour of years, and on its disappearance the hopes of a life would fade, leaving me in a barren waste of sand with not a blade of grass or an atom of verdure to enliven the dreary scene, the pangs of hunger and thirst almost unbearable, until oblivion or apparently death closed the scene. I am utterly unable to convey in words the faintest idea of the mental horrors of that eventful night. Years passed in the course of those few sleepless hours; I distinctly heard the boom of the great bell that tolled out the passing hours, and yet it actually appeared that I passed through a lifetime. I rose to go to work, but was almost broken down by the reflections or rather visions of the night. I could do but little work because of the thought, which would weigh upon me, of where I should lay my head that night. I told my troubles to a man who some time previously had lived next door to us, and he at once offered me shelter until I could make other arrangements. Having lived near us so long he knew all the circumstances of our position. Though he was a low black-guard, he was hospitable and kind to me in extremity. I stayed with him one week, sleeping at his house at night, but buying what little food I needed and eating it at the factory. Young as I was, I was proof against the temptations that were presented even during the brief period I was with them.

My next brother left home a few weeks afterwards. He had a rough boisterous temperament, which, without a gentle restraining influence from outside, would break out into violent exhibitions of passion whenever he was crossed or coerced wrongfully. He had a strong and healthy physique, and an energetic and dominant will, was a hard worker, but had no pleasure in books; education was wasted upon him. His strong will, an intuitive feeling of self-respect, and a desire to cut a respectable figure in society, together with the remembrance of the paternal injunction never to disgrace himself or his family by doing a mean action, kept him somewhat within the bounds when released from the restraint of home. My third and youngest brother remained at home longer, but was very uncomfortable. He was a quiet and steady youth, always a favourite with his elders; skilful and industrious at his trade of ribbon weaving, but declined to extend his studies beyond the limits of his business. After leaving home he boarded with an uncle, of whom more anon.

III

Courtship and Marriage

Sceptical tendencies and reading – Doubt and enquiry – A romantic living picture – Love at first sight – A presentiment of coming happiness – The second meeting – Match-making in the Spring-time – Opposition and persecution from relatives – Kindness of friends – Thoughts of marriage – The event frustrated – Successful – A good wife.

LET me now hark back a few years to narrate an incident that greatly influenced my after life – an incident which might almost be regarded as prophetic, or in which Fate apparently played a conspicuous part. No believer in Fatalism, with but little faith then, indeed, in what is ordinarily known as Providence – the event I have to relate nevertheless impressed me with the fact that there is 'a Divinity that shapes our ends, rough hew them how we will.' The so-called Providence of God seemed to me utterly inscrutable. It was a gordian knot, the unravelling of which I left to the future, when perhaps a key might be forthcoming to unlock the mystery. Fond of Bible History, especially that contained in the Apocryphal Books of the Old Testament, and the Acts of the Apostles in the New, and having read through the Books repeatedly, so as to be able without trouble to find any passage at will, I yet was often in doubt as to the validity of these ancient writings. In this sceptical mood, Voltaire's 'Dictionary of Philosophy' had a fascination, but I was not at all pleased with his unphilosophical mode of dealing with the subject, his bitter sarcasm respecting religious subjects, or what seemed to me his utter abnegation of the idea that there was any Ruling Principle which by general consent and for want of a better term we call 'God.' I next read Volney, whose arguments seemed more natural and reasonable. The bold arguments of Tom Paine, as expressed in his 'Age of Reason,' took more forcible hold of my imagination, for while he believed in 'one God and no more,' he also hoped for 'salvation in another and a better world.' This I could follow, but his exposure of the contradictions, mistranslations and interpolations of the Scriptures jarred upon the feeling of respect and reverence I had always been taught to entertain towards these writings. His idea that we are all children of one All-creative Principle, and that with our finite powers of reasoning we can only faintly realise the nature, character, or attributes of such an All-pervading Power, harmonised somewhat conflicting ideas. Tom Paine's 'Common Sense' seemed unassailable, and in this I regarded him as the champion of man's civil, religious, and moral liberties. These, and works with a similar tendency, I eagerly devoured, and they exercised a great influence over me. All these writers, however, were of an extreme type, and I felt the need of works of a more impartial character from a mind capable of solving the mysteries which life is permeated. Such a writer I could not find, and I wandered farther and farther into the wilderness of Scepticism.

Some three or four years before the commencement of these days of doubt and earnest enquiry, I found myself with a companion of a similar turn of mind, one Sunday afternoon before the palisading of a house, at the doorway of which stood a young lass blooming with health, her cheeks vieing in colour with the roses that blossomed in the garden before the door. I was struck with the beauty of this living picture. On either side of the doorway the luxuriant foliage of creepers formed a rich frame which enclosed the lovely picture. I stepped up to the gate, and asked the young lady to give me a rose. She hesitated for a moment, and then said, 'I don't think I dare give you one, as they are not mine to give, and my master is not at home.' I awkwardly excused myself as best I could, and, thanking her, I was turning away with my companion when impulsively she called out 'Stop a moment, and I will give you one, but I must let the master know what I have done.' She gave me one, and bashfully disappeared into the house. Although I had to pass the house constantly I never saw that picture within that frame again. I could not forget the form of the face, and both became enshrined in the memories of that Sunday afternoon.

Some time afterwards I found out that she had left that house, and had gone to more lucrative employment. I well recollect the observation I made to my companion, that if I grew to manhood that girl would be my wife. I knew nothing of her, not even her name, and I was too diffident to make enquiries about her. Several years afterwards – just before I was turned away from home by my step-mother – one Easter Monday, I and some others took a walk to the Red House Inn, Stoney Stanton Road, Foleshill, a mile or so from the town, a place which was much frequented as a holiday resort by visitors from Coventry.

At that time the spring was much earlier and more genial in its aspect than it is now. The winters were more severe, it is true, but they did not last so long, commencing with the close of November or beginning of December with heavy falls of snow and intense frost – a Christmas without skating was a novelty – and ending about February, when the ice and snow would disappear, and the earth resume its mantle of green. The hedgerows would show their bursting buds, and would be enlivened by early songsters. The gardens were already full of rich clusters of early spring flowers; the snowdrop, polyanthus, and primrose were bright and gay, the buds of the trees were appearing to view under the genial influence of the sunshine, and the mezereom was redundant with pale lilac blossoms, which appear before the leaves. The purple and white lilac were already covered with the buds of early foliage which would soon become flowers. The daffodil, too, was much earlier then than now, and the rich clusters of flowers in the spring-[time were as refreshing to the sense of sight as they were grateful to the sense of smell. This Easter Monday morning was particularly fine and sunny, and when we arrived at this popular resort the house and rooms were crowded with visitors. The scene inside was not so much to my taste as the nicely kept garden. After looking round it we left the crowd and took a ramble in the neighbourhood. Upon returning to the inn, as we were ready to depart I cast my eyes around, and who should look into them but the very girl, now a fine young woman, who had given me the rose some years before. For some few seconds I seemed nonplussed, but collecting myself I reminded her of the flower she had given me. She, too, remembered the incident, and after some little conversation we thoroughly understood each other. We walked and talked in confidence together and sympathy, and the past and present conditions of our lives seemed to fit us the one for the other. I discovered that like me she was fatherless. She was the principal support of an ailing mother who could do but little for herself, much less for her children, of whom she had four, three younger than the one I had become acquainted with so strangely. I learned from the mother afterwards that she had contracted a second marriage, a most unfortunate one for herself, with a worthless man, who was not only lazy but a confirmed drunkard. This vice, as is usually the case, carried with it that of brutality both to wife and children. The family was reduced ofttimes to the direst poverty, and when I first became acquainted with the mother, her constitution was almost broken down with the misery, privation, and ill-usage to which she had been subjected. Some few years before this, while drunk, the husband turned her and her infant, scarcely a fortnight old, into the street, cruelly beating her, selling the home to a broker, and then absconding. He was never afterwards heard of. The wife did not grieve at his loss. She was a high-spirited woman, who would rather starve than beg. With her first husband she was happy and comfortable, and the changed conditions which came with the second, preyed heavily upon her mind and body; from chronic asthma she was fast drifting into consumption and the grave.

After parting from the young woman on that memorable Easter Monday afternoon I began to think that for the love of so sweet a girl I could cheerfully forget all the hardships and misery I had passed through. That one day of happiness was like a gleam of sunshine flitting its radiant beauty across the dreary wilderness of my life, and I went home at the close of the day with a lighter heart and brighter hopes than I had dared to entertain for a long time past. The contrast, however, was keenly felt when I had to descend again from this blissful heaven to the dull monotony of life; but the dull monotony itself now seemed sanctified and tolerable gilded by the sweet thought of love. It would have taken much more than that night's trouble to have ruffled my temper in the slightest degree. I had found the one above all others whose image had been constantly present to my mind ever since that pleasant Sunday afternoon when I received the rose from her hands. All at home, upon my return, wondered what had happened to produce in me so marked a change. I seemed now to have found something to live for, and each evening would find me in the company of the lass I loved, and who exercised such a benign influence over my disposition.

Soon discovering that my passion had not overrun my discretion, I found the girl true, trustful, and loving. Our love for each other strengthened day by day. Of course the step I had taken soon came to the knowledge of my step-mother, but she was ignorant of the object of my affections. She made strenuous efforts to find out who the girl was and to gain some knowledge of her status in society. A family conclave was convened upon this important question, the result of which was that I was cautioned and rated severely by one of my uncles – the man to whose guardianship I was committed by the indentures of apprenticeship already referred to. He gave me a lecture upon the impropriety, not to use a coarser term, of the step I had taken, and dilated, as I thought, in too dictatorial a manner upon this affair to one in whom he or his family had hitherto taken so little interest. On many occasions we had appealed to him in our distress, but he had taken no heed. I had also often complained to him of the ill-usage we suffered at the hands of our step-mother, and asked for his interference when things had reached such a pass that it seemed impossible for them to get worse, but he repelled our advances. His present action, therefore, seemed all the more unwarrantable. He taunted me with the lowly condition of the young woman. As if her condition could have been worse than my own! My step-mother joined in these taunts, and it was during one of these daily occurrences that I taxed her with irregularities and her cruel conduct towards us, with the result, as previously stated, that I was ordered to leave home.

Not being able to stay at the first place I went to after leaving home I made my case known to the mother of the young woman to whom I was engaged. She listened patiently to my tale of woe, and then gave me a lesson from her own unfortunate experience, and bade me be honest and true to myself, carefully weighing every step that I might not fall into error or be misled into wrong doing. She had a kind and considerate heart, almost hidden away on a first glance by an incrustation of reverse produced by the cruelty, privation, and suffering she had undergone. She recommended a place where I could board and lodge for ten shillings a week, but after that sum was paid weekly out of my earnings very little remained for clothes or luxuries. I was still an apprentice, and had no money to spare. Of this my step-mother was fully aware, and she had promised to make me suffer whenever she had a chance. I therefore naturally expected some rough treatment, designed to 'bring me back to my senses,' as she termed it. I very soon found my fears realised, being kept short of work while others were doing well. The weekly payments for board and lodging soon begain to fall into arrear, and I was obliged to do odd jobs apart from my trade to get enough money to live. The people I lodged with did not suit me. Their tastes and habits were ofttimes very repugnant to my feelings, and I determined to get away at the first opportunity.

Thus things went on for nearly a year. I had no relatives to take council with or to aid me, but was thrust out into the world to sink or swim as chance might befall. Almost at my wit's end to provide the means of keeping up a respectable exterior, I made application to my guardian uncle, telling him of the wrongs that we had to endure at the hands of the heartless woman who, as our father's widow, had assumed authority over us. I spoke of the persecution to which I was subjected in being deprived of regular employment when I might have plenty of work, and informed him of my fixed determination, if nothing could be done to alter this state of things, to leave the town and seek the means of living elsewhere. I was listened to coldly and threatened with imprisonment if I dared to leave before my term of apprenticeship had expired. I left him with a saddened heart and bitter thoughts, and from this time the breach between us became wider. We passed each other daily in the street without recognition. In after years the sore was happily healed. It came about in this way. His wife died, domestic troubles overtook him, when I was able to repay him good for evil. He met with an accident, or rather sustained a brutal assault at an election riot, being thereby incapacitated from following his employment, and obliged to break up his home. By a strange coincidence he took a small house next door to the one in which we were living. Then it was that I was able to repay him, not in his own coin, but in coin of truer metal. I once more sought his confidence, which, now that he was himself in distress, he did not refuse. From sources, which were easily available, seeing that he lived in the neighbourhood where his brother (my father) had spent so many years of his life and where he had died, he soon learned the facts in regard to our case. He acknowledged freely that his mind had been poisoned against us by our step-mother. When he saw that we were not so black as we had been painted he was sorry for his former hostility, and seemed as though he could not do enough to assure us of his altered feeling. We were very grateful that one who had been so bitter should come in his latter days to know, and consequently to love us rather than to hate us on account of the calumny that had been poured into his ears by others. Towards the close of his life we were constant in our attentions to him, and his end was not embittered by any ill-feeling towards us. Although we much regretted his death so soon after this reconciliation it was a great consolation to know that we parted in amity and peace.

To return from this digression. The rebuff from my uncle almost maddened me. I had come to the definite decision to go away from them all as far as possible; but procrastination, the thief of time, was in this case the thief of opportunity. It often happens that results of the most important kind, whether for good or evil, are frustrated by the merest accident. My lass and her mother noticed the alteration in my demeanour, my extreme restlessness, and they very naturally enquired the cause. I had intended keeping the matter entirely secret, and disappearing without any explanation. Confronted by their pertinent enquiry, I fairly broke down. The reasoning of the mother, and the clinging affection of her daughter, overcame me, and I left their house that night happier in mind, with the determination to stay in Coventry, my native place, to battle with the cruel world, and tread the difficulties of the rugged uphill road which lay before me a little longer. My lady-love's home was poor and scantily furnished, compared even with the one I had been accustomed to, but it was clean and neat. The resources of her and her mother were very limited, but by keeping well within their means they were free from debt, although the state of the mother's health precluded the possibility of her doing any work to augment the small pittance that her daughter earned. Still, notwithstanding their straitened circumstances, they showed nothing but kindness and sympathy to me in my distress. This was a source of happiness that I had long been a stranger to, and it had a wonderful effect in relieving the morbid and misanthropic feelings to which I had so long been a prey. I was fast merging into a careless and indifferent frame of mind, and should surely have come to no good had I not been rescued by the saving grace of these two loving souls. I shudder to think of the consequences that might have ensued had nothing occurred to break the spell of the thraldom to which I was being subjected by those whose duty it was to encourage rather than to hinder me in the earnest endeavours I was trying to make to improve my position. This passage in my life's history is indelibly imprinted upon the very texture of my nature, and I still retain the diffidence and lack of energy that resulted from these experiences. They formed a cloud upon my existence that has never yet been, and in this world, I fear, never will be, dissipated. The days, weeks, and months passed, their monotony varied only occasionally, but lit up always by the light of sincere affection. Increased hopes arose only to be rudely dashed to the ground, or snatched from me by new troubles which I seemed to have lost the courage to resist, or the resolution to overcome. Utterly irresolute I felt quite at a loss what to do. To retaliate for wrongs done to me was impossible. I had not the resolution, though sometimes, it must be confessed, I had the inclination. Reflection would furnish a passable excuse for non-retaliation by reminding me that retaliation may for a time gratify the spirit of revenge, but two wrongs do not make a right.

Amidst these conflicting elements I began to think very seriously of tightening the bond of affection by matrimony. I was willing, and the young woman was willing, but her mother hesitated. This was quite natural. She had had a bitter experience of married life with her second husband and could not honestly recommend matrimony, and was rather reluctant to assent to a union that offered such a poor outlook materially. Though not having quite completed my apprenticeship there was not long to serve. I argued my case with the girl's mother with an energy that seemed almost beyond me. Something desperate must be done to stave off a crisis which appeared inevitable. We might, I argued, do better for our united efforts than either of us could do singly. The step might also be the means of bringing about a better understanding with my relatives, who might be induced to hold out a friendly hand to us should need arise. It was with much reluctance that the mother at last consented. The banns were published, without delay, at the parish church. This proceeding, however, gave the intimation of our intentions to my relatives and employers who attended the church, with the result that the further progress of the event was stopped by their interference. It is almost impossible to describe the state of mind that this further opposition engendered. Though exceeding the bounds of legality in thus contemplating matrimony before I had been released from my indentures, I yet considered myself morally entitled to choose and to follow that course which appeared most certain to lead to happiness. I was now aroused, and was equally determined to carry out my plans as others were to frustrate them. Shortly afterwards, when I thought the commotion which the first attempt aroused had abated, we tried again. The banns were published at two churches simultaneously, at one of which we were again refused on the ground of living outside the parish and being under age, but at the other church no objection was raised; and on Monday, January 5th, 1835, we were married at the church of St. John the Baptist, Coventry. Our witnesses were an aged uncle and aunt of my wife's, who had generously placed at our disposal a tolerably well-furnished room at a nominal rent until we could produce a home of our own.

Even at the last moment an incident occurred which almost prevented the ceremony taking place, or, at all events, postponing it for a time. I had been striving to get some extra work done in view of this occasion, but did not finish it until the very morning of the wedding. I had to wait so long before I could get paid for it that the time for the wedding had nearly expired before I could start for the church where the bride was waiting for me. I arrived at the altar, however, a few minutes before the expiration of the time they had allowed, and the ceremony was completed that bound us together for a life of happiness or misery. I never had occasion to repent the choice I made, for as long as she lived my wife proved good and kind, true and faithful, and patient under the many difficulties that beset us in after life.

IV

Hard Times

Opposition of relatives – Short of work – Carpentering – Primitive tools – Botanical and Entomological studies – A bonny little son – Economies in the home – Keeping a night school – Removal – The Carmelite and Carthusian Monasteries – Completion of apprenticeship – Freedom or slavery? – Stamp duties on Freemen – The evils of 'Individualism' – Poverty – Unorthodox views – A short improvement – Down again – In work and out – Semi-starvation – Friends in need – A loving brother – Step-mother again – An accident – A clergyman and the Four Pound Gift – Independence of mind.

IT was some time before my friends became acquainted with the step I had taken, but when it came to their knowledge they threw every obstacle in the way of advancement. I had hoped that my wife would have been allowed to help me at the factory by doing work that she was well able to do, and which indeed she had been accustomed to do before being married, but she was not allowed to go, owing, as I believed, to representations on the part of relatives. For a time, therefore, I had to pay out of too limited earnings for assistance which she could easily have rendered. It is impossible to give an adequate idea of the contumely, scorn, and persecution to which we were subjected during the first year or so of married life. I could have borne it patiently had it only been directed against myself, but the total abnegation and denial of recognition to wife was unbearable. To be utterly cast off from the intercourse and friendship of relatives whom one had been taught to regard with feelings of affection, notwithstanding that I did everything in my power to remove their scruples, seemed like being severed from all that was worth living for. I hardly dare allow my mind to recall the events, and look back to these times with a feeling of horror at the cruelties we suffered, and amazement that we should have passed through them unscathed. I made up my mind for the worst, and when work was short, which was only too often the case, I turned my hands to other means of earning money, such as odd jobs of carpentering, wood carving, &c. I put up a small work bench, and with the rude tools I possessed made better ones. My first plane was made at this time; a small tenon saw I constructed from a steel busk, and also made bevelled and right-angled squares. Chisels were too costly to buy, and, living in the watchmaking district, I made them out of watchmakers' worn-out flat files. It is the sight of these primitive tools that brings back the memory of the past, with its struggles to obtain knowledge and the means to live under such extreme difficulties.

Scarcity of work afforded opportunities for pursuing botanical studies. I lived near Hearsall Common, the scene of my childhood's delightful rambles amongst the wild flowers. Many a stroll I had over it in leisure hours, of which unfortunately there were too many. By this time I had got a smattering of botany, and began after a fashion, as best I could without a tutor, to arrange specimens of flowers by the aid of an original copy of Dr. Withering's work, published in 1776, obtained from an old bookstall.

There is no book of the present time by which to find a native plant more readily than this, and although the words 'empalement,' 'blossom,' 'chives,' 'pointals,' 'seed vessels,' &c., sound very obsolete, yet they are easily transposed into more modern phraseology. The greatest difficulty was in the change of name and order of many species, and their re-arrangement into different classes by modern investigators according to a more natural system. The systems of Jussieu, Candolle, and Blainville, still retained in France and on the Continent generally their peculiar arrangement, while the labours of the old English botanists, Gerard, Ray, Parkinson, Culpepper and others were closely followed until the Linnæan system, about 1760, began to make headway in England. Then followed many changes by the talented but cumbrous classification of Linnæus. The science has been much simplified since, and names more in harmony with the natural structure of plants have been adopted by modern writers. Had means allowed, I should have studied the science more closely and systematically, if only for the love of flowers. Withering had always been a favourite with me, because of the facilities his work affords for the study of entomology. Along with his description of trees, shrubs and herbaceous plants, he describes the moths, butterflies, beetles, and other insects that feed upon or infest them. By this means I naturally was led to take an interest in the study and collection of insects. Very often in botanical excursions I would come across broods of caterpillars, or it might be isolated specimens of strange form and colour upon the particular plants, trees, or shrubs described in the work. Taking these home, I made a large frame with coarse canvas sides and top to allow of free ventilation, and placed them in it, supplying them with the leaves of the plant I found them feeding upon, in many instances supplying them with a heap of soil in which to burrow for their change into chrysalis. By rearing insects in this way I obtained the finest specimens, as catching them by means of a net would frequently damage their wings, rendering them unfit for preservation as entomological specimens. I could not make very much progress in entomology, because of the amount of time necessary to be spent in hunting after particular species in localities wide apart, and on account of the fact that some of the insects or caterpillars could only be found at times when it was inconvenient to hunt for them. So I had to content myself with such specimens as could be found when searching for plants.

The beginning of the second year of married life found us with another life to provide for – a bonny little son – and although his presence brought joy to our hearts, a cloud still hung heavily over our prospects. I was receiving only two-thirds of the net sum my work came to, so that my wages as an apprentice were very scanty, and it was hard work sometimes to keep the wolf from the door. My wife had been reared in the school of adversity, and was careless of the luxuries of life. She was frugal, thrifty, and handy in her household management, and by dint of care and forethought we gradually accumulated many little necessaries of an unpretentious character such as no home, however humble, can very well dispense with. By exchanging labour for useful articles – I had no spare cash with which to make purchases in the usual way – I contrived to furnish our home with some degree of completeness.

To eke out my earnings still further I taught at night to some few friends the rudiments of reading and writing, but this mode of raising money was more pleasure than profit. It at least kept me from worse company, and was the means of increasing my circle of friends.

I was very anxious to get a home together before the completion of my term of apprenticeship, as it appeared probable, judging from what had happened, that I might not be allowed to continue to work for the same firm afterwards as a journeyman. If I could have stayed in that part of the town – Spon End – which was exclusively a watch manufacturing district, I might, being still young, have engaged myself for a term of years to some branch of that trade in which supernumerary help was required apart from regular apprenticeship. Watchmakers were very jealous of any one learning the more finished branches of the trade without going through the usual routine of a seven years' apprenticeship. The object of serving an apprenticeship of seven years was to gain the freedom of the city, one of the privileges of which was the Parliamentary Franchise. At that time this was the only means, practically speaking, by which a working man in Coventry could gain the right to vote for a Member of Parliament. Just before completing my apprenticeship we were obliged to leave Spon End, the property – in which some people had resided for over fifty years – being required to make room for modern improvements. We removed to a house near the end of Gosford Street up a back yard overlooking the workhouse, but with a glorious and extensive view of fields. The prospect included the old Carthusian Monastry called the Charterhouse, in which Parliaments have met. The workhouse was once the old Carmelite or White Friars' Monastery, which shared the fate of others of a similar kind during the reign of Henry VIII. The beautiful cloister with a roof of finely wrought stone, is still well preserved, and is now the dining room of the inmates of the workhouse. The dormitories, too, of the White Friars are still in a good state of preservation, and are used for the same purpose. An ancient staircase leading from the dormitories to the church is also well preserved. Not a mile from the Charter-house is Whitley Abbey, standing on rising ground from the banks of the river Sherbourne, and believed to be the place that Charles I occupied, when in 1642 he vainly summoned the city to surrender. The estate connected with the abbey is about three thousand acres in extent, and is separated from the Charter-house by the extensive piece of waste land known as Whitley Common, over which the freemen have herbage rights.

While living in Gosford Street I finished my apprenticeship, but could not take up the freedom of the city because of the heavy stamp duties which attended the swearing in. The amount, I believe, was £1 3s. 6d.; I thought it such a monstrous wrong to have to pay this after serving seven years to obtain the freedom, that I vowed never to claim the freedom until the obnoxious duty was repealed.

Either of the political parties would have paid the money – this being, as previously stated, the only means by which any Coventry men could secure the franchise – and have had me sworn in without a fraction of expense to myself. Repeated applications were made to me to be sworn in, and the offer was made to relieve me of the expense, but I could not absolve myself from the vow made, nor conceal the indifference, not to say disgust, I had for both parties in their attempts to traffic with my conscience. To have acceded to their entreaties would have destroyed rather than have gained my freedom, for I should not have felt free to choose who to vote for, but should have considered myself bound to the party who had thus given the bribe, whether its principles accorded with my own or not.

The freemen, as already pointed out, had herbage rights over extensive tracts of common and lammas land, privileges which they jealously guarded. The sale subsequently of some portions of these lammas lands and the rents of large and valuable tracts that the freemen now hold as *bonâ fide* property, ceded to them by Act of Parliament for the cession of their lammas right over the whole, have enabled the Freemen's Trustees and the Seniority Fund Committee to pay to a considerable number of senior freemen six shillings and to others four shillings weekly. It was seven years before the stamp duties were abolished. I was then sworn in, but had I taken up my freedom upon completing my indentures, I should now at this advanced age, when able to earn so little, have been in receipt of an allowance weekly from the revenues of the freemen's estate, not as a charity but as a right. Though not able to foresee the course events would take, I do not regret the vow, and feel that I could come to the same resolve now with all the advantages in view rather than submit to an unjust tax.

It was as expected, my employers would not keep me long at work after my term of apprenticeship had expired. Having no loom of my own I was in great straits, but felt reluctant to work in a private factory where the expenses of loom hire and other incidentals would have eaten up half my wages, and left a less margin of profit even than apprenticeship wages. I had looked forward to being able to work at full wages, but at every place where application was made, it was a question of what was the lowest sum I would take the work out for, not a question of paying the standard rate of wages. Being disgusted at the uncivil, not to say brutal, treatment received while searching for work, I very unwisely perhaps preferred starvation to the low terms offered. It was the custom of the trade for an apprentice to be allowed, after having completed his indentures, to purchase a loom and pay his employers for it by weekly instalments, or to hire one at a reasonable sum per week. Although I had served faithfully and, with the exception of getting married, to the entire satisfaction of my employers, the usual offer was not made to me, and under the weight of real or imaginary wrongs I felt too independent to ask favours, not realising the fact that no one can be independent, but that all are reciprocally dependent upon each other. I had hitherto trusted too implicitly in my own individuality and to my own unaided efforts in the race of life, and as a consequence soon found myself too heavily weighted even to run, let alone to win the prize. Had I possessed a loom, I could have had work at trade prices from manufacturers who gave work out, and many a year of hardship would have been spared.

We still lived in full view of the workhouse, and were very severely reduced in circumstances. Christmas came and brought with it another life to provide for – a girl. So low had our exchequer become, that for the first time we knew the want of a morsel of bread. It was the custom at this time of the year for employers to distribute beef to heads of families in their employ. The cost was defrayed by the accumulated fines of the year supplemented by donations from visitors, or if there was still insufficient, the employer himself would make up the deficiency. Although I had left the factory, I was considered entitled to a share in this distribution, and on Christmas Day found myself in possession of a joint of meat with no bread or vegetables to eat with it. How the life of my wife and children were preserved under these trying circumstances I cannot, nay dare not, think, and feel thankful that the harrowing details have passed from memory.

Notwithstanding the efforts made to conceal our poverty, it soon came to the knowledge of my wife's mother, who insisted upon our going to her house as soon as my wife could be safely removed, and we were to stay until our circumstances brightened.

I tried many times to get back to my old place of work, but could not succeed, and my health would not permit me to follow any very laborious employment. The mode of life and thought I had adopted were also a hindrance rather than a benefit to me; I began to be known as a very 'Free Thinker.'

Our little world was strictly orthodox, and it required a large amount of moral courage to publicly acknowledge oneself to be out of agreement with accepted religious beliefs. I associated with a band of advanced thinkers whom the professing religious communities branded with the names, Atheist and Infidel. I must say to their credit, however, that the moral status of these so-called Infidels and Atheists would have put to shame the characters of many of the professing Christians who derided them. Though mixing up with these people, attracted by their breadth and liberality of thought, I never found myself in danger of merging into such a state of mind as to deny the existence of a Supreme Being. Everything in Nature, from the single grain of sand to the mighty mountain, from the simplest living organism to the most complex, everything in the vegetable and animal kingdoms contains that within itself that is a sufficient assurance of a Power behind Nature which for lack of a better term has been designated 'God.' The Economy of Nature is ruled by something more intelligent than mere chance–

> 'All are but parts of one stupendous whole,
> Whose body Nature is, and God the soul.'

The position seemed to me unassailable that there must be a Prime Cause of all things, from the smallest speck of dust to the mighty orbs, with their attendant infinite variety of planets and satellites, that roll ceaselessly in countless numbers through illimitable space.

To return from this digression, we lived happily together through these distressing times, though often inconvenienced by the lack of material comforts which tend to make a home what it should be. It was a long time before permanent employment came, and our means of existence depended again upon odd jobs of carpentry, repairing household furniture, or even making new articles in cabinet or veneered work. For this kind of work I even gained some sort of a reputation within a limited radius, and our income was slowly but surely improving, no doubt with a little business tact – a quality of which I was lamentably deficient – I might have earned a fair living. As on so many previous occasions, our intentions were thwarted. We were beginning to feel the effects of a material change for the better in our circumstances and were looking forward to the future with brighter hopes, when my wife's mother, with whom we were still living, died from the effects of the illness previously referred to. The home was broken up, and before we had sufficiently recovered our financial position to be able to carry on an establishment of our own, we were obliged to leave. Not being able to get a house in this locality suited to our limited means, we removed to another district – the new town of Hill Fields, where I was comparatively unknown. This was a most unfortunate change, for before we could settle down, or become known, one article after another from our home had to be sold to raise money to provide the necessaries of life. True I was in the midst of the weaving district, but from false notions of pride I felt a decided repugnance to working in the capacity of a weaver's journeyman. Having acquired a complete knowledge of the mechanism of the Jacquard loom, I felt that it would be rather *infra dig* to take a subordinate position. After a short stay in this neighbourhood, we left for a partly furnished room in a court in Well Street, the rent of which was two shillings and sixpence a week. This was a most miserable hole in a very low neighbourhood – the worst change I had made. There was a public-house adjoining the court with a bowling-alley facing our window, the resort of the reckless and the improvident, and the scene of frequent gambling quarrels. This was not a very pleasant prospect truly, and quite out of harmony with my tastes and feelings. With a natural dislike for gambling, the woeful effects of it upon some of my fellow apprentices had given me an utter detestation and loathing for the practice.

The new factory of Mr. John Day for the weaving of ribbons, was completed about this time, and our family being personally known to him, I obtained employment. The wages were very low, but adversity compelled me to accept work as a journeyman. I might have had work at Mr. Day's old factory, in Gosford Street, had I condescended to apply for it, but with a dislike for factory life on account of the low moral status, generally speaking, of those employed there, it was my ambition to become a home worker with looms of my own. This consummation being very remote, I was forced by circumstances to take whatever presented itself. After working for the firm for about six months, it was proposed that I should be articled by the year, at twenty shillings a week. I accepted the terms but after the engagement had lasted about three months, the firm suddenly and without warning collapsed. Our improved conditions therefore did not last long. The factory was closed during the bankruptcy proceedings, and I was again deprived of the means of living. We had been very economical during our time of comparative affluence, but had not been able to save any money because of having to buy so many articles for the household, and to replenish worn out garments. Had there been the slightest suspicion that the employment would so soon have terminated, we should have been a good deal more careful even than we were, and kept back a small reserve for contingencies. The scenes witnessed at this factory were of so demoralising a character that nothing short of absolute want would have induced me to work in such a place again.

We made the last week's wages last a fortnight, and then came the thought of where or how to find food for ourselves and our two children. Our furniture that we had only so recently purchased, went one article after another, at a heavy discount, to procure rent, bread, and oatmeal for porridge; but there was a limit even to these scanty means and the time soon came when we had disposed of the last article that we could raise money upon. I was severely blamed that I did not apply to the parish for relief, but I would rather have died from sheer starvation than, being so young, have degraded myself by making such an application. I feel thankful that I have never in all my troubles made an application to the Guardians. An unprecedently severe winter set in, and from lack of food and fire we suffered very severely. One night we thought our youngest child was dying from the unavoidable exposure to cold and want, and we had to break up an article of furniture in the dead of the night as fuel, to warm the child back to life. For two days not a particle of food had passed our lips, and for nearly a fortnight, in this bitterly cold weather, we had slept on the bare boards huddled together to keep as warm as we could. How bitter my thoughts were no tongue can tell. I was maddened almost to suicide, until the thought of wife and children would recall me to myself. One morning I stood in front of a baker's shop where the loaves were temptingly exposed, and never in my life was I so near becoming a thief. The impulse to procure a bit of bread for my starving wife and children was so strong that I could scarcely resist. Hesitation is fatal to action in most enterprises, and by hesitating a moment the opportunity in this instance passed. That inward monitor, Conscience, which, it must be confessed, was somewhat abnormally developed, exercising its restraining influence. 'Conscience does make cowards of us all,' and on this occasion I was really too cowardly to steal, walking away from the temptation honest in act if not in purpose. With trembling limbs, almost fainting owing to the excitement of the temptation, I wended my way towards the desolate home which I had left only a few minutes before with such desperate resolves. On turning down the court I met the landlord of the public-house adjoining, who perhaps struck with my pallid face and uncertain gait, asked me if I was ill, and whether he should help me home. Not willing that he should be an eye-witness of the straits I was reduced to, I excused myself as best I could. He earnestly pressed to be allowed to give some assistance, but with thanks I declined. He, however, gave me threepence, as he said, to get a pint of ale at his house. I did not buy ale, but hurried back to the baker's shop that had presented such a formidable temptation, and purchased a loaf with the money. Never was a meal so sweet as this.

We could have consumed much more, but it was perhaps as well that in our famished condition we had not an unlimited supply, or after such a prolonged fast we might have received permanent injury. So far from satisfying our hunger, one loaf only served to whet our appetites. At night an old lady who used to nurse our children while we were at work paid us a visit to ask if we required her services again, and was shocked to find us in such a pitiable condition. Under a rough exterior was concealed a gem of the first water – charity without ostentation. She entered into conversation respecting our circumstances and then left, to return shortly afterwards with a man pushing a handcart, in which was a bed, bed clothes, and bedding. The articles were quite new. She had gone from our house to purchase them at her own risk without consulting us in the matter, and we were to pay for them by weekly instalments when we got work. We soon fixed up the bed, and had a more comfortable night than we had experienced for a long time. Before this kind benefactor left, however, she provided us with the means of obtaining another frugal but ample meal and fuel for a fire. Words could not express the feeling of gratitude that we entertained towards that kind-hearted lady, or the reverence still felt for the memory both of her and the generous publican who was the means of supplying our wants earlier that day. The old nurse's large-heartedness was all the more notable when it is remembered that she herself was very poor and needed help. Surely such acts as these can never go unrewarded! These occurrences are still fresh in my memory, although more than forty years have elapsed since they took place, and I hope I may always retain them *in memoriam* of kind friends who have since passed away.

My next brother lived in the same court, but was not on speaking terms in consequence of my remonstrance with him in respect to a young woman with whom he kept company. He was entirely under her influence, and she kept him from entering our house or even speaking to us. In our adversity it was a sore trouble to have no one with whom to converse. The transition from cold bare boards to warm comfortable blankets was like a transformation from the cold plodding earth to the bright scenes of fairyland. The next morning brought good news. Work was offered at the shop where I had been apprenticed. My old employers – having found out the true character of my step-mother, whose influence with them doubtless prevented my getting work there – sent for me. The first week's wages – twenty-four shillings – seemed a little fortune in itself, and as we had not incurred many liabilities through living, or rather starving, on our limited means, we soon recuperated our fallen fortunes.

Another circumstance which still further improved our position was this. My youngest brother, George, who since leaving the old home had lived with his uncle – the man to whom I have already referred as having tried to prevent my marriage – expressed a wish to come and live with us, not withstanding our limited accommodation. He came, and the uncle and other members of the family taxed me with having enticed him away from a comfortable home to a 'poverty-stricken hole,' as they pompously designated our humble abode. The breach between me and my relatives by this incident was widened, but the love I felt for this young brother – the one whom my father on his death-bed had asked me to care for – was so intense that for his sake I could have suffered more calumny and vituperation than I actually endured. I had endeavoured as well as I could to carry out my father's injunction; we enjoyed each other's confidence, and he only left us for a home of his own.

Our circumstances again improved under these more favourable conditions. My brother paid us a small sum for his maintenance, and this combined with my own earnings, enabled us to quit this low neighbourhood where we had suffered so much privation, contumely, and misery. Even now on passing through the street, recollections of these hard times crowd thickly and vividly upon me and cause a chill of horror to run through my frame. Our next house was in the row where my father had lived, and in which my youth was spent to the age of seventeen or eighteen years. Many friends and neighbours still remained to welcome us to the old spot. My step-mother was still living in the vicinity, having sold up the old home and kept the proceeds. There were many little articles amongst our father's things that we, as children, prized very highly, and would have liked to have kept as mementoes, but they were sold, we knew not where. Some time previously, however, I managed to secure my father's regimental sword, his flutes and music books, and one or two other things he set great store by, which it was tacitly understood before my father died I should have. Living so near my step-mother, I was frequently called in to render assistance whenever she was seized with fits, to which she had been subject for many years. I used the means to restore her that were effective during my father's lifetime, until she showed signs of recovery, and then leaving instructions, would quietly retire before being recognised.

It is a source of satisfaction now to feel that I was able to minister in some small degree to her comfort, notwithstanding the harsh treatment I had received at her hands. With our improved fortunes we succeeded again in getting a comfortable home together. My younger brother still lived with us in peace and concord, and throughout the vicissitudes of life we clung affectionately together.

The desire to leave the weaving and take to carpentry and joinery grew upon me, but owing to physical weakness, accentuated by recent privations, the realization of that desire was quite impracticable. The grim hand of starvation had also left its imprint upon my wife's frame. From being a plump rosy-cheeked young woman she had become pale and emaciated. The suffering we endured was so severe that the effects did not pass off lightly, and she was never afterwards the woman she used to be. The desire to adopt wood working as a trade received a further check by an unfortunate accident which befel me. While repairing a Jacquard machine on the top of a loom, I fell a distance of about twelve feet to the ground. The result of the accident was a permanent injury, which quite incapacitated me from following any robust employment. I was therefore fettered more closely than ever to the weaving. Notwithstanding these drawbacks and disappointments, fortune on the whole favoured us more than ever before.

No doubt I could have progressed much better had it not been for the sturdy but ofttimes mistaken notion of independence that frequently kept me back from receiving help. Not realising how thoroughly dependent human beings are upon each other, I was in a manner, by mental conceptions, cut off from exterior sources of supply. Ultra in politics as heterodox in religion, it naturally followed that I could not conscientiously seek the aid of those from whom I so widely differed without, as I thought, sacrificing the principles of self-help and individuality which were then so dear to me. All grades of society were intensely Conservative, and to differ from them was to be branded with the opprobrious name of 'Revolutionist' or 'Radical' in a political sense, and by the sectarians with the equally odious names of 'Infidel' and 'Atheist.' An instance of this want of charity came within my personal experience. A member of the firm for whom I worked, in a friendly way, insisted upon my making application for Sir Thomas White's Four Pound gift, which was then only given to freemen. The trustee to whom I was recommended to apply was a clergyman of the Church of England, and on account of the strong and earnest recommendation of my employers, he expressed great pleasure in being able to oblige them. I passed the ordeal of a searching examination as to my habits of life and character, and I thanked the benevolent gentleman for his promise that I should receive the Four Pounds. I had, however, barely stepped off the threshold of his house after bidding him 'Good morning,' when I was called back to answer the important question – What church do you attend? In reply, I truthfully stated my disbelief in the doctrines of modern Christianity, which I believed to be not in accordance with simple truths laid down by Christ for man's guidance and rule of life. Without being allowed to complete my statement I was shown the door, but on the threshold I told him that I was more sorry for him than for myself; that he had morally no right to put any question as to my religious belief, which was a matter that concerned only myself and the Author of my being. It was with much reluctance that I had consented to make the application, for I felt certain of the result should any question be asked as to religious belief. I again bade the reverend gentleman 'Good morning' and departed, feeling some little satisfaction in having stood firm in defence of my opinions. Of course I did not get the promised Four Pound gift. A note came to my employers next day, complaining of the insult they had given this clergyman in having recommended an infidel and an atheist to his Christian charity. The note was shown to me, and I was asked for an explanation. I related what passed, and added that I thought I was the insulted person. I lost nothing in the estimation of my employers by this incident. An application by my employers next year to a trustee not so closely fettered by religious scruples was more successful. In the strict sense of the term this Four Pound Gift was not considered a charity, but a right belonging to the freemen. The many thousands of pounds which these trustees had at their disposal were too often prostituted to the basest purposes of political and religious propagandism. Many of those who received the Four Pounds would spend every farthing of it in drink before doing another stroke of work, but to the thrifty it was a boon. At this time the ruling power of the town was a close Corporation, in a manner self-elected, the voice of the people in the election being so nominal as to amount practically to their disfranchisement. From the same source as the Four Pound Gift sums of fifty and a hundred pounds were lent out free of interest for ten or twelve years to start young men in business. As the money could be had on personal security, the loans often brought those concerned into difficulties, but the Charity Commissioners interfered, and it has now become necessary that a *bonâ fide* security for the full amount should be deposited. Fewer applications have, as a result, been made for the loans, and an immense sum of money now lies idle awaiting some future scheme for its administration. A large portion of it has been expended in the erection of commodious buildings, including a school, for the education and training of orphan girls being children of freemen. This institution has proved of great benefit to many families who but for its existence would have had to fall back on the parish to defray the cost of the education of their children. Sir Thomas

White's Orphanage is a fine building admirably suited for the purpose for which it was erected, occupying a considerable frontage to Leicester Street and the Stoney Stanton Road, very near to the Coventry and Warwickshire Hospital. The whole question of the Coventry Charities and their disposal and administration demands serious attention.

V

Mental Struggles

Three brothers – The adaptation of the Jacquard machine to various purposes – Pleasures of reading – Vaccination and its effects – Heavy expenses – Home treatment of disease – More trouble – Unexpected help – Materialistic tendencies – Mental struggles with religious doubts – Early Christian ideas of the Trinity – The Coventry Mutual Improvement Class – John Yardley, a disinterested mechanic – The mystery of the future – Constructing a microscope – Opening up a new world – The Great Problem – At what point does life commence ? – A new order of thought.

THE receipt of the Four Pound Gift recorded in the last chapter marked another turning-point in my life. Every farthing of the money was spent in the home. The gradual increase in our family, together with the fact that my younger brother still lived with us, rendered the house too small for our comfort, but we felt very reluctant to leave because of the memories connected with it as being near to the home of my childhood, and also next to the house in which I became reconciled to my uncle, who at his death left us his blessing. Our youngest child died at this juncture, and after that we had no desire to remain. We went to a house with a weaver's shop over, large enough to hold two looms, which my employers offered to let me have on hire. My next eldest brother having freed himself from amorous toils, settled down to a more staid course of life, and also came to live with us, so that there were three brothers living together.

In the shop I fixed up a work bench at which to do carpentry, and cabinet and inlaid work. More profitable employment, however, was the repairing of Jacquard machines for figure looms. At this early period in the history of the ribbon trade, the designs and patterns woven were somewhat crude and simple, being chiefly confined to goods known as 'gauzes' and 'figured lute strings.' In the Manchester district Jacquard machines were used for producing figured designs upon hitherto plain surfaced dress materials, thus giving a wonderful impetus to the trade in wollen goods. Yorkshire had a monopoly in the manufacture of these machines, and supplied the world from its busy workshops. Paisley soon became famous for the adaptation of the Jacquard machine to the manufacture of elaborately patterned shawls, and at Nottingham quite a revolution was effected in the lace trade by the adaptation of the machine to that industry.

During the early years of married life I gave myself up to extensive reading upon all subjects that came within reach, but my greatest pleasure was in ancient history and the mythologies of past ages. Favourite books were Gibbon's 'Decline and Fall of the Roman Empire,' Volney's 'Ruins of Empires' and 'Laws of Nature,' Rollin's 'Ancient History,' and Mosheim's 'Ecclesiastical History.' With these I was highly delighted, and a great part of the matter contained in them was committed to memory. From the Utopian reasoning and theoretical disquisitions of some of these writers I turned with great pleasure to the practical illustrations of the theory of communal life in the experiences of Robert Owen the elder, whose works were being published at a price that brought them within my limited means. Robert Owen's efforts to benefit, elevate, and ennoble the working classes, are now matters of history. Very few of those who branded him with the names of Socialist and Atheist could understand the intense earnestness that prompted him in his experiments to better the moral and educational condition of the toiling classes, who at that time were little better than serfs under the control of the political and ecclesiastical powers. His great specific for the regeneration of the wealth-producing classes was Education; and he claimed that these people had an absolute right to live in comfort by their labour. He taught the equality of man, and showed that the Creator had provided abundance for all, if it were but properly distributed. Although he failed fully to carry out his noble and philanthropic intentions, his labours of love and self abnegation have not been lost to the world. His efforts have helped on the cause of National Education, and through him many who sat in darkness have seen a great light – the hope of improvement in their material conditions. His talented son, Robert Dale Owen, followed closely in his footsteps. The writings of both in the cause of humanity deeply impressed me, and I cannot but feel a reverence for these early pioneers who strove to redeem from mental and material slavery the poor working bees of the human hive.

The fall from the top of a loom to which I referred, not only prevented me from seeking employment that involved hard work, but even rendered weaving irksome and fatiguing. Above all it made me incapable of following the natural bent of my inclinations, and deprived me of the pleasure of taking long excursions into the country. This enforced confinement produced irritability, which annoyed my wife and brothers. It was as a relief from the monotony that I took so voraciously to reading.

My material circumstances would not improve. Strive how I might we could only just manage to keep our heads above water. This was due in great measure to the expenses incurred through sickness amongst the children. In the absence of dispensary or hospital, the doctor's charges made a serious inroad upon the weekly income of the family. My eldest son, a fine healthy lad, after being vaccinated, was attacked with virulent ophthalmia of a terribly severe type, which lasted for years. During the whole time he had to be kept in semi-darkness. When at last the swelling subsided and showed the eyes, the pupils were covered with a thick white opaque film which rendered sight impossible. We procured the best medical aid from Southam and the Birmingham Eye Infirmary, but without avail, until, from sheer inability to meet the expenses, we were obliged to fall back upon our own resources. To succeed in this I procured by loan or purchase all the medical and physiological works I possibly could, especially books treating on the eyes, including Fyfe's 'Anatomy,' Grainger's 'Elements of Anatomy,' Southwood Smith's 'Philosophy of Health,' and two or three Dictionaries of Medicine, but the work most suited to my wants was Gray's 'Supplement to the Pharmacopea.' It is said that 'A little knowledge is a dangerous thing.' The sentiment would perhaps be more accurate if it read '*Too* little knowledge, or knowledge mis-applied, is a dangerous thing.' Certainly, in my own case, the study of these works laid the foundation for a more intimate knowledge in succeeding years of those abstruse questions relating to chemical affinities and to natural cause and effect, which in these more modern times have revolutionised the world. It was a great drawback that I could not – owing to illness when young – commit to memory the details of matters of importance, but could only remember general results. It became a necessity therefore, especially in regard to the mixture of powerful and active substances used in medicine, to keep a fair supply of books of reference upon these subjects. I did not feel at liberty to use this knowledge as a means of profit, though great demands were made upon it by sufferers amongst our friends and neighbours. It was a source of pleasure to be able, by relieving pain and suffering, and sometimes even curing deep-rooted diseases, to earn the gratitude of those benefitted.

We were scarcely ever free from difficulties, owing to my want of employment or the inability to do such laborious work as presented itself. Thus events moved on for several years. My brothers left me to start homes of their own. My own family increased to five. The fourth child became afflicted after vaccination in much the same way as his elder brother. The care, anxiety and trouble of attending to the children, produced a marked change in the health of their kind and patient mother, who spared neither time nor trouble in ministering to their wants. The child was also attacked by small-pox of a most virulent kind, and notwithstanding vaccination, fell a victim to the disease. This was perhaps one of the most trying events of my life; it happened at the close of the year when trade was invariably slack. We had been without work for many weeks, but I had made up my mind that come what might, I would not appeal to the parish for relief. Help came at last from an unexpected quarter. On New Year's Day, 1845, while acting as door-keeper at a ball given by the 'Philanthropic Lodge of the Manchester Unity of Odd Fellows' at St Mary's Hall, my despondency attracted the attention of two of the senior officers of the lodge, Thomas Barnes and James Rushton. I had cause to be down-hearted; my boy lay at home dead, and I had not the means to bury him. The two gentlemen enquired the cause of my grief, and on learning my story they expressed their sympathy, and when the ball broke up at about two o'clock in the morning, they bade me stay awhile and presented me with a sum of money obtained from friends, which enabled me to bury the child decently. Fortunately no other member of the family contracted the disease, though we were prevented by circumstances from properly isolating the case, indeed we had to sleep in the same room even after death had taken place. The study of chemistry had armed me with the means of preventing infection. No other case occurred in the neighbourhood, though a week elapsed before the boy's funeral.

Fast merging into the materialistic tendencies of the age, the struggle for existence was a stern lesson. Others got on in the world without any seeming effort, whilst I struggled and strove with honest intention to make headway without avail. It seemed that God was very unjust and partial in keeping from me the means to sustain the life He had given. Conceiving myself to be a creature of circumstances, I was fast losing the power of free agency and falling into a state of unbelief in the Providence of God. Casting aside all previous theories of life and adopting the attitude of Free Thought, I endeavoured to strengthen my position by culling from the Old and New Testaments whatever glaring contradictions or apparent interpolations could be found. I read Archbishop Wake's Translation of the Apocryphal Books of the New Testament in the hope of finding something to elucidate matters. The narratives in the Book of Mary, the Protevangelion and the Infancy of Jesus were of so unnatural and extravagant a character that the myths of Greece and Rome seemed to pale into insignificance before them. There seemed little doubt that these books were compiled in the second and third centuries, when the simple but grand teachings of Jesus of Nazareth were fast merging into sacerdotalism and absolute Church government, and when the various sections of the so-called Christian Church were engrafting upon the simple truths of the Gospel the theories and practices of polytheism. The pure stream of Christian doctrine was polluted, and upon the simple idea of one God the polytheistic notion of three Persons to constitute a Godhead was introduced. One of the earlier Fathers of the Christian Church, Clement of Rome, who is supposed to have held the office of Bishop of that city about the end of the first century, taught that Christ was a distinct being from God and subordinate to Him. Hermas, who is said to have been the brother of Pius, Bishop of Rome, about A.D. 142, asserted the pre-existence of Jesus, but denied his possession of superhuman power. Ignatius was decidedly not Trinitarian, nor was Barnabas the companion of Paul and others of apostolic times immediately succeeding the death of their Teacher and Leader. In the narratives of these times, we find that there was a tendency among the leaders of the various Christian sects (at this early time they were not all of one accord) to enhance the character of Christ's work and teaching and to regard it as Divine. Through these early times the Christians believed only in one God. Justinus was the first to intimate approximately the doctrine of the Trinity. He used the term 'Logos', as representing the Word or Wisdom of God in which all things centred and from which all things were derived. The Logos then began to assume a personality, and was converted into a Being, but, as was argued, not from all eternity. Then came Tatian the Syrian, and Theophilus of Antioch, in whose time the term 'Trinity' was first used. Athenagoras, about the year A.D. 177, preserves the supremacy of the Father. Irenæus separates the Son from the Father, and regards Him as subordinate. Tertullian, a Latin Father (A.D. 200), makes the Godhead and the Son two Beings, Christ being decidedly inferior. Clement, of Alexandria (A.D. 193-217), denies the co-equality of Christ with God, and strongly asserts Christ's inferiority. Origen, who was ordained in Palestine, taught the inferiority of the Son to the Father, but held the doctrine that all souls were pre-existent, and at the consummation of all things would be restored to light and happiness, and that matter itself would become spiritualised. Sabellius, who wrote about A.D. 255-57; Paul of Samosata (A.D. 260), the teacher of Zenobia, Queen of Palmyra, who was much inclined to the Arian doctrine; Cyprian, Archbishop of Carthage, who suffered martyrdom A.D. 258, all strove earnestly to preserve the belief in One God. Novatian, the contemporary of Cyprian, was perhaps the most eloquent and learned man of his age, and he was an able defender of the Unity of the Godhead. He wrote a copious and exhaustive treatise on this subject which has come down to us almost intact. No doubt the theology of Clement and Tertullian had a great influence on their successors. Tertullian taught that whatever is born of God is God, for he says that God is Spirit, and from Spirit is produced Spirit, from God God, as from light light. Thus he supposes the Son to be in some sort divine and absolutely of one substance with the Father as being derived from Him, but still the inferiority of the Son is insisted upon, the One being the Giver and the Other the Gift, yet so as not to make two Gods, for in his 'Apology' he says – 'Hence it is that a Spirit of a Spirit, or a God from a God, makes Another, the Second of two, not in number but made of subsistence in order of nature but not in identity, as the Son is subordinate to the Father, as he comes from Him as the Principle but yet not separated from Him.'

There were in these early times differences of opinion respecting the character and attributes of the Deity and the various claims to consider Jesus as a supra-mundane Being co-equal with God the Father. In course of time the monotheism of the Early Fathers gave way to, or became absorbed into, the impirical influences of creed and dogma enunciated by the Eastern and Western Churches that God was not Unity but Triune, and that each part while perfectly distinct was indissolubly united to form a simple Unity.

These subtle distinctions were at that time a source of great mental uneasiness. I wished to know more, but could not step across the line of demarkation that, like an impassable barrier, separated the physical from the purely spiritual. The arguments of the disputants appeared unreal, intangible, and unsupported by proof or such evidence as would be admissable upon any ordinary subject of controversy. The only evidence that could seem allowable, acceptable, or even understandable, was such as was acquired by the scientific methods applied to the investigation of Nature. The miraculous birth, pure life, and cruel death of Jesus seemed to follow the same lines as the life and death of Buddha nearly a thousand years previously, or the various incarnations of the Chrishna of the Hindoo mythology with its triune deity of far more ancient date. The analogy between them seems so close that it is difficult to arrive at any other conclusion than that the Christian system is but an outgrowth or copy of the systems that preceded it.

For several years prior to 1845 I had been gradually merging into this sceptical frame of mind, doubting the ability of orthodox teaching to offer sufficient proof of the continuation of life after the dissolution of the body. It was not a total denial of the possibility of a future life, but a consciousness that the certainty of it was not proven. It seemed improbable that there could be such a change, or that the physical atoms of the human structure could be dispensed with, and a new form built up of such ethereal and impalpable atoms that only the term 'spiritual' could convey an approximate idea of its reality.

For several years succeeding 1845 I experienced a most severe trial. My mind was so much exercised with these doubts and fears respecting the great mystery of a life hereafter, that existence itself became a torment almost unbearable, and I often longed that I might drink of the water of Lethe to drown in oblivion the memory both of the past and present. Such a state of mind could not have continued much longer without merging into madness. The direful effect produced in my home and on the health of my faithful and loving wife no words can express. Were it in my power I would cheerfully give up ten years from my life to compensate for the misery wrought in my home circle by this state of semi-madness and uncertainty.

Towards the close of this time I joined a class of Free Thinkers called the 'Coventry Mutual Improvement Class,' of which Charles Bray, John Farn, and Charles Shufflebotham were prominent members, and from this association I derived much mental relief.

My connection with this Class was an agreeable change, because its members could give free expression to their thoughts upon any subject whatsoever. It was not to be expected that followers of such teachers as Robert Dale Owen, Robert Southwell, George Jacob Holyoake, and Thomas Cooper, the Author of the 'Purgatory of Suicides,' could do otherwise than ignore orthodox teachings upon the probability of a conscious existence for man after the dissolution of the body. But strange as it may appear, although I had been in the main so long in agreement with these people – not having sufficient positive evidence to the contrary – yet whenever it was my lot to prepare an essay upon any topic of this kind, I often found myself intuitively opposing the doctrines of annihilation and non-responsibility which found favour with most of them. It very often happened that after writing hurriedly in preparation for 'the night,' I have used arguments which upon reading them over afterwards I found to be quite contrary to preconceived notions upon the subject.

A turn was given to my youthful prepossession by the perusal of a new serial called '*The Magazine of Science and School of Arts*.' My thoughts were directed into a new channel – the exploration of physical science. The Magazine contained articles upon the various departments of natural science, and upon the use and structure of the telescope and microscope. These latter particularly interested me, as did also articles upon the polarization of light.

About this time I became acquainted with a friend, by name John Yardley, a watch case maker, one of the most remarkable mechanics I had ever met. Inventiveness was with him an intuitive faculty, and he was able to carry to a successful issue whatever he set himself to produce. From him I gained my first practical lesson in the art of grinding and polishing lenses for telescopes and microscopes. Never have I found a man more diffident of the powers he possessed. There is no one whose memory I can recall with greater pleasure than this simple-hearted, but talented friend. In his business as a gold and silver watch case maker he had no superior. He had the practical knowledge not only of alloying his metals to a certainty, but the chemical skill to assay them, and to regain from the soot and cinders of the furnace flue the gold and siver lost by sublimation. He was one who thought but little of his own time where the spending of it would be the means of helping others.

He was a prodigal of his time and labour for the benefit of others as he was provident of the precious metals with which he worked. But for this circumstance he might have become possessed of an ample fortune. I revere his memory because of his self-abnegation and the readiness with which he ministered to the wants of others without thought of pecuniary recompense. He taught to some the art of electro-plating and gilding, to others photography, to others he elucidated technical and trade difficulties where he saw the lack of this knowledge curtailed the means of living. He died August 28, 1863, aged 52 years. His life and death often brought into my mind many thoughts respecting a probable future.

I ofttimes found myself wondering whether he would be lost to me for ever. He himself could give no clue, being 'without the pale' of what the orthodox call 'religious convictions.' He never attended a place of worship, and descanted freely on the extravagant expenditure incident to a State Church as not warranted by the life or teachings of Him whom they set up as an Example. This elaborate religious system seemed to him a complete contradiction of the precepts and example of the meek and lowly Nazarene.

A study of human nature as exemplified in the characters of people met with in every-day life gave no assistance in solving the problem of a future life. In the operations of physical and chemical science – the combination of intangible, impalpable atoms and molecules to form tangible physical forms – it struck me that there might be some analogy. But even chemists were beginning to doubt whether there was in reality such a thing in Nature as a simple element. I had hitherto looked for static forms or conditions from which there could be no deviation, but here were constant changes, dissimilar atomic elements having the power to assume new forms under new conditions. All thought of absolute entities must be put aside, and the nature and character of atoms of matter composing organic or inorganic structures traced back by experiment or analogical reasoning as far as possible. This would lead to the point where they would be lost to view. An atom of matter once in existence is always so. Nothing in nature is lost or annihilated. To properly investigate nature in view of these speculations a microscope was necessary. To purchase one was out of the question. I made one, but it was more of a compound than an achromatic form, though I tried to approach as nearly as possible to the latter. The eye-piece was of the huygean form or plano-convex, the curvatures being as one to three placed together at the exact focus of each of the lenses, with a stop between to shut off divergent rays of light, each lens having the plane side to the eye. The object glass was a double convex, the curve of which had a quarter of an inch radius. Although its magnifying power was high, its defining and penetrating powers were very feeble, especially when a large aperture was necessary to increase the field of view. The object then became distorted by spherical aberration, or fringed with colour by refraction of light. Upon stating these difficulties to my friend John Yardley, he smiled in his usually quiet way, because we had both been stopped by the same difficulty – the difficulty of obtaining a distinct image of an object free from spherical and chromatic aberration. He then showed me an objective microscope that he had just made, composed of three plano-convex lenses the curves of which were one-fifth, one-tenth, and one-fifteenth of an inch in diameter respectively, fitted in separate cells with their surfaces almost touching. I was delighted with this instrument, under it animalcules which by means of the old arrangement were indistinct, now unfolded their hidden beauties of structure in the finer parts. Lines upon the scales of butterflies and moths were no longer simple lines, but splendidly sculptured and beaded designs. Not slow in taking advantage of this to me new and beautiful idea so splendidly worked out by my friend, I set to work to make an instrument upon this model, and even improved upon it by adopting a series of doublets of higher power, a combination of three making a powerful objective of less than one quarter of an inch focus. It gave, with its greater angular aperture, a flatter and more extensive field of view, with greater penetrating power and clearer definition of the object, than either my first microscope or that of my friend.

By dint of perseverance and under many difficulties, therefore, I at last succeeded in making a powerful achromatic microscope with one-eighth inch, quarter inch, and half inch doublet objectives, buying nothing but the raw material from which to construct it, and also making all the tools for the purpose. I think of it now with much pleasure as the greatest triumph I ever achieved towards helping me to understand the various phases of matter and the myriad forms and functions of animalcular existence. It opened up a new world. It passed the utmost stretch of imagination to conceive that the mass of green filaments, which I had always conceived belonged to the Vegetable Kingdom, was endowed with life and motion, and with the power of procreating its kind.

These simple-looking animalcules, viewed through a quarter inch objective, are found to contain within themselves a remarkable cellular structure most beautiful to behold, in some instances splitting up into seams, in others budding off into squares of an oblong form, or assuming various other curious and wonderful forms. The rotifera, vorticellidæ, diatoms, and desmids were favourite objects of scrutiny. The two last were easily procurable, the siliceous envelope being proof against all acids except the fluoric. Whether examined in their living forms or as preserved frustules of pure silicon, their endless variety, notwithstanding their extreme minuteness, was almost bewildering. It was a great joy to contemplate these wonderful and exquisitely beautiful structures concealed from the normal powers of vision. Another strange animal inhabiting the water is the amœba, a creature without any defined static form or apparent cohesion of particles, in a state of rest seemingly a spat of protoplasm with no mouth, and yet possessing the ability to absorb food. Its mode of reproduction seems to be by means of minute cells. Portions of sarcode with cells attached bud off from the parent to lead the same kind of life in endless variety of form.

The study of plants had always been a source of delight, and I had ofttimes produced hybrids of a favourite flower by innoculating it with the pollen of an allied species, but could never conceive the processes involved until the microscope revealed the secret. The simple-looking pollen grain was found to be a compound body consisting of three parts, the innermost being the nucleus containing the impregnating principle of life and the power of reproduction. When a pollen grain comes into contact with the mouth of the stigma or pistil, it is retained there by a viscid fluid secreted for that purpose, and also in many flowers by a minute fringe that holds and closes over the pollen grain. A most remarkable change then takes place in the pollen grain so retained. The two outer envelopes burst, and an extremely fine and delicate filament penetrates the style of the stigma to the flower cup, and upon the ovaries there deposits the central contents of the pollen grain which it has carried down upon its tip, and with it impregnates the ovaries with the life principle that enables the plant to reproduce its kind.

It would be almost impossible to describe the intense pleasure or the valuable instruction received from these examinations of the structure and functions of plant life. The wonders unfolded by this instrument enabled me to form more rational conclusions as to cause and effect, and I could with greater confidence realise that a Power existed behind Nature unknown to physical law. Still the great problem was unsolved – At what point or under what conditions is inorganic matter converted into organic forms of life? The aggregation of inorganic atoms to compose the immense variety of beautiful crystals each with its absolute, definite, and invariable form was equally perplexing. In regard to animal life, too, the same problem presented itself – At what point is food converted into living tissue? Scientists trace the chemical change from chyme into chyle, but cannot tell at what point it is endowed with the principle of life. They trace the absorption of the chyle by the lacteals, and follow it through the mesentric ducts into a reservoir called the receptaculum chilii, and through a valved duct into the left jugular and subclavian veins to mix with the dark venous blood of the system at a point where the venous torrent is making quick haste through the liver to the right side of the heart. Dr Southwood Smith says that 'before the chyle has reached this stage, it has passed through several changes, each increasing its life principle until it reaches its highest point of vitality in the lungs, and then from the left side of the heart it is distributed through the system for its support and to build up a new structure, and that continuously from in a great measure the waste of the old.' The great and important problem was – At what stage of these wonderful transformations does life commence? The scientist answers that life begins in the chyle, and that through all its processes it becomes more highly animalised, especially in its passage through the messentry, where it mixes with the lymph of the glands which was once considered an excrementitious or waste product, until at the termination of these complex processes it is converted into living arterial blood.

Although I could not with my limited knowledge of cause and effect solve this Mystery of Life, still these researches left the mind more receptive and open to the evidences of scientific research in anthropology, biology, animal and vegetable physiology, and physical science in general. This new world was a beautiful region to revel in, and though it lowered my pride and egotism considerably, it more than compensated for the loss by the thought, the conscious and inherent feeling, that beyond all these seeming wonders there must be, although beyond human comprehension, a Power, a Causative Source of all existence.

The years that succeeded were momentous ones. A new order of thought was slowly but surely impinging upon the domains of the Materialistic notions which for eighteen years of the best part of life had enveloped me in the mists of its cold, plodding, austere morality. About this time the phenomena of Modern Spiritualism began to attract attention. Though sceptically inclined towards it at first, yet on more thorough examination I was satisfied that there was an intelligent force with which it was possible to hold communication, and which pointed to the existence of a realm called (for the sake of a better term) the Spiritual, and which also proved the reality of a life after the change called Death. But more of this in another chapter.

VI

Pleasures of Science

Interruptions to the study of Spiritualism – Re-examination of negative position – The Exhibition of 1851 at the Crystal Palace – A clue wanted to the ultimate cause – Illness – Dread of the Surgeon's knife – A risky experiment – Michael Coulcher – A kindred spirit – Wife's illness and death – Pecuniary difficulties – The cold, plodding, austere morality of the sceptic – A beacon light to nobler things – Geological studies and collecting – Whitley Common – The Sherbourne and its valley – A Holiday in Leicestershire – Abundance of Fossils – Astonishing the natives – Antiquities of Leicester – Dissolution of Coventry's religious houses – Returning home laden with spoils – Benefits of the Holiday.

THE investigation of Spiritualism referred to at the close of the last chapter extended over many years, and was several times discontinued for long intervals owing to pressing matters relating to the affairs of mundane existence. First they had to be put aside on account of my having obtained a situation as foreman in the factory of the late Mr R. A. Dalton. I continued there till the concern was disposed of to Mr Hennell, and then came home again to work at a loom which the firm built, and which I paid for by weekly deductions from wages. This was an improved loom, much larger than the ordinary old form of hand loom, adapted for either steam or hand power, and was technically known as an 'a-la-bar' loom, on account of the bar or pole in front for the purpose of setting it in motion. The bar was dispensed with to give place to a motion of my own which reduced the labour to a minimum.

As a Free Thinker I had only looked on the physical, and had clung so tenaciously to a physical cause for every effect, natural or mechanical, that my mind seemed bewildered by having obtained a clue in Spiritualism that might connect immateriality with material existence. The question – 'If a man die shall he live again?' was constantly present, and in the light of this new revelation it was necessary to re-examine the negative position which for the past eighteen years had left me no hope except in the present.

The great Exhibition of 1851 was opened at the Crystal Palace during the time I worked for Mr Dalton, and a week's holiday was allowed me to visit it. This was then the longest journey I had ever undertaken, and the delight and pleasure of seeing this varied collection of products from every part of the world was unbounded. However much the wonderful structure of glass and iron in which the exhibition was contained might have been admired – it seemed almost a realisation of one of the gorgeous pictures of the Arabian Nights – the treasures it contained interested me most. They surpassed anything previously conceived or read about, and they kept my mind in a state of continual excitement for some time. Amongst other things, I realised how little I knew of botany, for although possessed of a fair knowledge of British plants, I was lamentably deficient in a knowledge of the vegetable products of other countries. In the peculiarly grotesque forms and strange colouring of orchids, the airy lightness and wondrous frondage of ferns, some of which were so large as to afford shelter to the wayfarer, I was particularly interested, and was inspired with an earnest desire to visit the climes in which they grew. Never had mind been so much engaged or reason so much at fault to find a clue connecting previous negative convictions with the evidences of design and purpose which by this collection of natural products was so strongly emphasised. Robert Chambers's 'Vestiges of Creation' had not then come under my notice, nor had the early works of Charles Darwin, nor 'The Malay Archipelago' of Alfred Russell Wallace. My mind under the influence of the dawning light of Spiritualism was in a continual state of unrest, ardently longing for the remotest clue that would connect physical structure with its ultimate Cause.

While in this state of doubt and uncertainty, an illness that baffled the skill of the 'faculty' took hold of me. The doctors were even unable to agree as to its nature. There seemed but little hope of recovery, seeing that the disease rendered the assimilation of food impossible. Dr Laxon, who at that time was esteemed the most skilful medical practitioner in Coventry, undertook the case, and consulted with another medical gentleman. Having executed for Dr Laxon several odd jobs that required delicate manipulation, we were on intimate terms. We talked together of the nature of the illness. After listening patiently to my notions, he decided to call in two other medical men, and to subject me to a careful examination. Next day the doctors agreed that only in an operation was there any hope of life being spared. From their professional conversation I gathered that there was acute inflammation of the intestines, which threatened mortification. The expression on their faces showed that they were doubtful of the issue. I had a fearful dread of being cut and slashed with the surgeon's knife, lest it should result in total disablement. After they had left I tried a very risky experiment upon myself with half a pint of fresh barm. The effect was magical, although it caused a night of fearful agony. The doctors next day brought their instruments to perform the operation, and were astonished at my improved condition. They severely reprimanded me for having relieved myself by means so dangerous, and expressed surprise that they had not proved fatal. Their scolding was quite tolerable in the relief of having escaped the terrors of the surgeon's knife.

It was then winter, and I was not able to go to work again before midsummer. Our exchequer consequently became very low, and it was a sore struggle to sustain life. To make things worse, our eldest son had got into bad company, and was fast drifting to degradation. He died in the prime of life, and this was a sore trial, especially to his mother, who clung affectionately to the lad, notwithstanding his faults. During my illness I received ten shillings a week from the Manchester Unity of Oddfellows, of which I was a member.

Some time prior to this I had become intimately acquainted with the House Surgeon of the Hospital, which was then in the building now occupied as the Girls' Reformatory, in Little Park Street. His name was Michael Coulcher, a very clever surgeon and anatomist. His father was an intimate friend of Dr. Mantell, whose works on the geology of the Isle of Wight, etc., had induced so many to study this interesting science. Dr. Coulcher, as one of his disciples, was an earnest student of geology. At the instance of a medical friend he called upon me to examine my little collection of fossils of the Warwickshire coal field, and was much interested, and equally so with the microscope I had constructed. From this time he was a frequent visitor, and as our tastes were congenial, we became intimate friends. I derived a vast amount of information and knowledge from this intimacy. Whatever he could do to help me in my pursuit after knowledge he did willingly and without reserve. I had access to his rooms, and whenever he was at liberty he would reach down his microscope and explain to me the use of the instrument in pathology and in physiology. It was, I believe, through his instrumentality that the attention of Dr Laxon was directed to my case, for the cure of which he gave medicine and attendance free of charge until I was convalescent. During my illness ministers of religion called upon me to offer what consolation was in their power. I could not do otherwise than thank them for their intended kindness, but still retained my independence. I felt ready to take up the slightest clue that would lead me to a knowledge of a life to come, but they had none to offer.

From this time the health of my wife declined. She wasted away, and a hectic flush would often mantle on her cheeks, strongly contrasting with the pallid hue her face was permanently beginning to assume. She had overtaxed her strength in ministering so patiently and faithfully to the needs of her partner in life. I endeavoured to convince myself that there was no immediate danger, and that when this reaction had worn off she would assume her normal condition. She was, however, fast merging into tubercular consumption, having never since my recovery regained her former condition, and although I obtained the best medical advice possible, none of the doctors were able to arrest the progress of the disease, and for over two years she was unable to attend to her domestic duties. Her condition was aggravated by the reckless life of our eldest son. She passed away, after a married life of twenty years, December, 1855.

December has been noticeably a fatal month in our family. In it can be recounted the loss of father, mother, brothers, children, and wife; it was a month, too, in which trade was invariably depressed. Under these trying circumstances I contracted many debts, some of them rather heavy for a man in my position. Friends helped me with loans, depending upon my probity to repay them when opportunity served. I had some time previously become joint security for a friend for over £20, and, in his default, was called upon to pay the money. I might easily have cleared off these liabilities by acting on the advice of a legal acquaintance, who proffered for £5 to rid me of the debts I had contracted. It was a great temptation, but what a return it would have been to those kind friends who had helped me in the bitterest time of need! I declined the offer, and in a short time obtained profitable work, so that in less than a year and a half I was able to clear off all liabilities without forfeiting the goodwill of friends who had simply trusted to my honour for repayment.

Of all troubles the death of my wife was the most severe. Although uneducated, her high moral worth and patient loving nature more than counterbalanced for this defect. Had this event happened in the hey-day of unbelief, it would no doubt have been passed over as an expected sequence in accordance with natural laws, an event of which there was no right to complain, seeing that everything possessing life is subject to the same penalty. I had hitherto looked upon the cessation of life with indifference as the end and ultimate of existence. The investigation of the occult forces however had modified my unbelief in a future life, and my wife had always held fast to the assurance of a life beyond the grave. The cold, plodding, austere morality of the sceptic, with its stoical indifference to the feelings of others had chased away the tears of pity, and I almost boasted that the bitterest calamity could not again unloose those fountains and well-springs of human sympathy. The heart could not respond in sympathy to the troubles of others; the belief in non-responsibility closed up every avenue that would lead to the belief in the Divine Fatherhood as the primal Cause of being, or even in the brotherhood of man. Who can know these trials like one who has passed through the fearful ordeal of a young and ardent life wasted in the cold chilling atmosphere of unbelief? These years with their bitter and terrible remembrances have passed, but I would not like entirely to forget them. They still hold up to view a beacon light that may guide to higher and nobler things – to the knowledge that none can live to himself alone, but that each individual acts and re-acts upon those about him.

In re-examining the evidence upon which my materialistic negative position had been based, I once more pondered over the mystery of past life on this earth. The biography of Hugh Miller and his interesting examination of the fossil remains embedded in the old red sandstones of Scotland had a great influence in determining the bent of these enquiries. From the descriptions given by English geologists, I expected to find the same kind of past life there as in the Old Devonian. The discoveries of Hugh Miller were therefore a pleasant surprise. He brought to light the connecting link between the upper beds of the Silurian and the English Devonian. It is now well understood that the limestones of England so well described by Murchison were contemporaneous with the ichthyolitic beds of Caithness and Cromarty, and therefore the discovery by Miller of the fish beds of this formation was of the utmost importance.

Having been compelled by adverse circumstances to part with my collection of British plants and coal fossils which had cost a good deal of search and labour, I was now induced to start afresh, and by perseverance and the aid of friends was ultimately enabled to get together a rather choice collection of fossil plants of the carboniferous formation, lacustrine shells and scales of fish with coprolites of the saurian.

Another source of enjoyment was found on Whitley Common, at the lower end abutting on the Sherbourne, where there was a coarse gravelly drift interspersed with large and small pebbles derived from almost every kind of primitive and succeeding formation. This gravel was worked for use in the town, the larger boulder stones for paving, and the screened residue for garden walks and other purposes. In this drift I found ferruginous nodules, which, when broken by the hammer, were found to be finely crystalized in dog tooth forms in the inner side of the cavity; also peculiar encrinic casts beautifully and sharply defined in nodules of clay ironstone formation and popularly called 'screw shells.' There was, too, an interesting section of a very compact conglomerate, which, however, was much better shown on the Foleshill side of Radford bridge which spans the Nuneaton railway, cropping out in a fine section at Corley as the lowest sub-division of the new red. The cementation is a sandy matrix which holds the same kind of pebbles as the loose drift gravel of Whitley.

Although the river Sherbourne is but an insignificant stream at this point, having but a short course in a straight line from its source in the higher lands at Corley, yet, owing to its circuitous windings, it was subject to sudden overflows after much rain, ofttimes filling the houses with mud and water in the lower levels at Spon End and other points. It can only be conjectured what it must have been in the earlier ages more than two thousand years back, when the British town was located on the higher lands adjoining Radford, and on the opposite height now called Broadgate or Cross Cheaping, while all the intervening valley through which the Sherbourne runs was an almost impassable bog or morass, doubtless the home of the great bittern and various species of waterfowl. The town, in two parts, with its intervening bog, was situated in a clearing of the great forest of Arden that surrounded it on every side, and covered nearly the whole of the northern part of the country. There is evidence of the existence of such a morass in cuttings made through solid peat several feet in thickness in these lower levels, in which were interred carbonised refuse of the vegetation of that period. The mass is made up of the remains of water plants and mosses, interspersed with fruits of the walnut, hawthorn, and hazel trees. In this deposit were found, too, the remains of the animal life of that period – the antlers and vertebra of deer, with other osseous remains, also the tusks and molars of the wild boar and other traces of animal life, of which I could not then determine the species. As the beaver was at that time no doubt a native of Britain, it is possible that this animal would have chosen such a favourable locality as this for its habitation.

This valley of the Sherbourne is best observed by beginning at Baginton, where this river joins the Sowe, the united streams falling into the Avon near Stoneleigh, the lowest level of the ground being at the bottom of Whitley Common, nearly opposite Whitley Abbey, whence the land rises gradually, and so continues through the meadows into the town, near which it attains its greatest breadth. Beyond Spon End the river was better confined to its banks, the ground rising well from that point to its source. The following are the levels of the land in the neighbourhood, taken from the ordnance survey:–

Corley Church	nearly 600 feet.
Whitley (The Sewage Works)	227 "
Station Hill, Warwick Road	315 "
Radford Road Bridge	327 "
St. John's Bridge, Burges	262 "
Reservoir, Radford Road	330 "
The Sherbourne, Gosford Street	248 "
Hill Fields	296 "
Top end of Craven Street	324 "
Barr's Hill	327 "
Primrosehill	305 "
Red Lane hill	321 "
Hearsall Common hill	331 "
Draper's Fields	328 "

The highest bench mark within the city is at Holy Trinity Vicarage, St. Nicholas Street, 336½ feet, and the lowest at Whitley, 227 feet.

These pleasurable explorations on Whitley Common were not of very long continuance, being interrupted by the illness and ultimate death of my wife as already recorded. After this sad event my own health began to give way in consequence of giving too close attention to work, of which fortunately there was at that time plenty. At this juncture an invitation came from some friends, farmers at Smeaton, a Leicestershire village, asking me to spend a few weeks with them. This change was very acceptable, and re-established my failing vitality. I left the home in charge of my eldest daughter; the younger one I took with me. On alighting from the train at Theddingworth, on the Market Harborough line, we had to walk through fields for about four miles. In my then weakened state I was much afraid I should not be able to walk so far. The first heap of stones and rubbish we came to engrossed the attention of my little girl, and she was soon hurrying me back to it, having recognised some fossil shells of the oolite gryphea, incurva, and rhynconella, with others that she could call by name. I soon found that we were in a district rich in remains of the oolitic formation where it super-imposes the lias. My dread of the distance had vanished in the excitement experienced at so unexpectedly travelling over this geological formation for the first time, and I need scarcely say that we reached the house of our friends much behind the time that we were expected. One of the farm servants was about being sent out in search of us, when we arrived heavily laden with our prizes and well-nigh exhausted, and I ofttimes think of their look of astonishment that I should have been so foolish as to encumber myself with so much rubbish, and carry it for such a distance, when I might in the pits and quarries near their house have satisfied myself to my heart's content with 'thunderbolts' and 'petrified snakes.' Their laughter and jokes were turned to wonderment when I explained that in the far distant past these curious things that they despised were living organisms with which the seas of former times teemed, and that in all probability they preceded man by millions of years, and that the spot on which their farm stood was at one time covered with the waters of a sea, in which lived and died those strange and wonderful forms of life that were now only represented by these fossil remains.

The farm house was also the village inn, at which club meetings were held. Next evening the room was crowded with visitors – the fame of my eccentricities having spread abroad – to listen to explanations of former life upon this earth in far distant epochs as shown by the strange and wonderful remains of animals preserved in the liassic deposits of Barrow-on-Soar, which were then on view in the museum at Leicester, only a few miles distant. I had with me a telescope, through which I showed them the moon, and explained that physically it was a globe similarly constituted to this earth, but upon a smaller scale, and that in the one phase that was always turned towards us we had hitherto discovered no vestige of life of any description, that it seemed devoid both of atmosphere and water, and that what once might have been sea is now dry land. The elevated parts from the level of these extensive plains rising to a height equalling our highest mountains. I further explained that this moon was constantly nearing this earth almost in the same ratio as its primary, our globe, was nearing the sun, and that a time must come when in all probability it must share the fate of others by which no doubt this earth was attended in the earlier stages of its existence, and that like others, when coming within the sphere of the earth's attraction, it must be precipitated upon its surface. 'Still they gazed and still the wonder grew' on learning what would be the probable effect of this – that the sudden impact of such a mass of matter upon the earth's surface would in a measure destroy animal and vegetable life, and for a long period of time change the climatic conditions of the earth by the sudden declination of the plane of its orbit round the sun. They listened with patience and expressed wonder that any of those brilliant specks of light dotting the heavens could compare in size with the great globe upon which they lived. Turning their attention to the brightest star then shining – Jupiter – I told them that it was nearly twelve times larger than this earth, that it was attended by four moons, that it was over four hundred millions of miles from this earth, and that even beyond that point there were three other globes – Saturn, Uranus, and Neptune – revolving with us round the sun, the last being between two and three thousand millions of miles distant; and yet vast as this distance might seem to the uninitiated, it was as nothing compared with the distance from us of the fixed stars. One of the nearest of these, which was pointed out, had been measured many times. A ray of light from that star, they were astonished to learn, travelling at the rate of 192,000 miles a second, would take over ten years to reach this earth. Most of the listeners expressed their wonder at the marvels narrated; many of them had no idea that the earth moved at all, but thought the sun, stars and moon went round it to produce the phenomena of day and night. I explained the diurnal motion of the earth upon its axis, and its annual journey round the sun of nearly three hundred millions of miles. On being told that the earth moved along its path in making this journey with a speed of no less than 68,000 miles an hour their astonishments knew no bounds; such knowledge, imparted perhaps for the first time, seemed beyond their powers of comprehension.

The days during this visit were spent rambling in the neighbourhood searching for fossils and shells. Of 'live' shells I found no new species or variety, but of fossil shells a considerable quantity, especially of ammonites, the hunting ground for which was the blue clay of the upper beds of the lias. I failed to find a single vertebræ or bone that could connect saurian life with this locality. No doubt they were to be found here as at Rugby, had the excavations been on the same scale. Here the beds in which they exist so plentifully were not reached. In a quarry of what was called cement stone were found masses composed entirely of the bivalve rhynchonella cemented in a sandy matrix strongly tinged with iron oxide. The shells themselves were in a most perfect state of preservation. The waters of the sea which once covered this spot must have literally teemed with this form of life when the event took place which entombed the myriads whose remains are embedded in this deposit.

The new railway from London to Leicester came through Kibworth, adjoining Smeaton, and there was a fine field for exploration in the cuttings and on the embankments. I found a considerable number of shells incident to both the lias and oolite; so many, that I feared I should not be able to carry them home.

A carrier, nephew to the farmer friends, took me one day to Leicester. The first attraction on arrival was of course the Museum, which contains some fine and rare specimens of the plesiosaurus, ichthyosaurus, pterodactylus, and other saurian remains found at Barrow-on-Soar, near Leicester. The rooms were richly stored with mementoes of the past history of this old town, illustrative of its successive occupation by Briton, Roman, Saxon, and Dane. I made the best use possible of the limited time at my disposal, and visited the Newarke, near the remains of the old Norman castle, of which but little is now left, and the very interesting church of St Mary, which was once within the castle domains. Thence I found my way to the massive fragment of an old Roman building now called the Old Jewry. I have little doubt that of the church of St. Nicholas, the oldest in the town, the stones used in its construction were partly cut and fashioned by Roman workmen nearly two thousand years ago. Explorations have since been made along the line of the old structure, tracing the foundations of rooms peculiar to the Roman style of architecture, with very fine tesselated pavements and other interesting remains. I also visited the site of the old Blue Boar Inn, where it is said Richard III slept the night before the battle of Bosworth, and the noted old Bow bridge over which his body is said to have been ignominiously dragged afterwards. The real place of his defeat was Redmore Plain, near Stoke Golding, about two miles from the town.

This day spent at Leicester was fatiguing but very interesting. I saw places and objects that had only been known by description, and very much regretted that time would not permit a visit to the ruins of Leicester Abbey, where Cardinal Wolsey died in 1520 while on his journey to London at the imperative commands of his tyrant master, Henry VIII, his death here saving him from the public disgrace to which he was doomed. On reaching

Smeaton, I narrated the day's experiences. To have spent the day without a guide, and without refreshment, in a strange town, excited the wonder of my friends. They could not see any pleasure in looking at such old tumble-down places that seemed to delight me so much. But on being told of the incidents and persons connected with the places, they too evinced some interest; not, however, of a very intellectual kind. I told them of the Wars of the Roses, of Wolsey, of Henry VIII, of the dissolution and dismantling of the religious houses, the Protestant Reformation, and the questionable means by which it was brought about. They were interested in hearing how severely Coventry had suffered at the dissolution of the monasteries by the destruction of the church of St. Osburg and All Saints, and the cathedral, with its fine spires, the richest in England, and the resting place of its founder and benefactress, Godiva; how soon, after its demolition the Bishopric of Coventry was merged into the see of Lichfield, while the population of the city during the next reign decreased from fifteen thousand to three thousand, and how, by reason of the loss of its religious houses, Coventry was no longer in fact what its name signified – the city of convents.

I cannot remember a time in which I so heartily enjoyed myself as during this visit to Smeaton. This was due no less to the interest attaching to geological features than to the kindness of friends. I returned home heavily laden with fossils – specimens of the remains of past life, evidences of a creation full of mystery, yet teeming with the utmost interest to the student of nature. Before leaving, I made a sketch of the farmhouse, which had now become endeared to me, and of the newly-erected church adjoining.

This change of scene was the means of bringing about a better state of health than I had enjoyed since the loss of my partner in life. With renewed health I was better prepared for the struggle incident upon becoming free and unfettered once more from social obigations involved by the distress already experienced.

VII

A Confession of Faith

The absent one – Monotony relieved – Mutual Improvement Society Programme – Abandoning a negative position – An essay on The Probabilities of a Conscious State for man after Death – Difficulties in dealing with the question – Charles Bray's Philosophy of Annihilation – Scientists and spiritual facts – Substance of the Essay – Confession of faith in immortality.

UPON becoming more and more satisfied with the proofs offered by Spiritualism of a continued individual existence after 'Death,' a happier frame of mind came. In the home my dear wife, who had so patiently and faithfully helped me through the many difficulties of our chequered life, was greatly missed. The monotony consequent upon her absence was varied by reading, by examining and arranging my collection of fossils and British plants, of which I had a large number, or in preparing for the weekly meetings of the Mutual Improvement Society. Even now the recollection of the nights spent at those meetings gives rise to pleasurable feelings. Some idea of the varied and interesting character of the discussions that took place may be gathered from the following copy of the programme of Lectures for the Winter Session of 1857-58:–

'The Past, Present, and Future of India,' by John C. Farn.
'Social Science,' by Charles Bray.
'The Poetry of Wordsworth,' by the Rev. T. Hunter.
'W. M. Thackeray,' by C. Freeman.
'The Mission of the Conqueror,' by J. S. Linwood.
'Physiology of Digestion,' by J. Gutteridge.
'The Life and Poetry of H. W. Longfellow,' by George Hall.
'Propagandism and Proselytism,' by Charles Shufflebotham.
'Consumption: its Causes, Symptoms, and Cure,' by Benjamin Haymes.
'Byron and Shelley,' by E. King.
'Intemperance: its Cause and Cure,' by W. Shufflebotham.

'Some Reasons why I believe in a God,' by Edwin Jephcoat.

The last-mentioned Essay caused a long discussion, and in further support of its arguments I purposed, when my turn came round, to read a paper on 'The probabilities of a future conscious state of existence for man after the cessation of his physical life upon earth.' A great deal of surmise was current as to what kind of arguments would be adduced in support of the affirmative, as evidence from the Christian theology was excluded. My conclusions, therefore, had to be based on stated facts and analogical deductions from them. Communications from the Unseen at this stage had been very few, but the proofs of a future state had been convincing, and I had been compelled to abandon the negative position, bordering on absolute materialism formerly occupied. This was no hardship when positive evidence was presented of a future state sufficiently strong to break down the icy barriers of scepticism which had repelled any thought or suggestion of spiritual things. The negative position was held till it was impossible to maintain it longer. Although I had never expressed an opinion respecting the continuance of life beyond the change called 'Death,' it was practically well known amongst the members of the Society that I had been ardently investigating the occult forces that assumed to prove a continuation of human life beyond the grave, and that under certain conditions, that part of man called 'Spirit,' after 'Death' still retained its identity, and could communicate with friends left behind in the body.

One is bound in seeking for truth to remain open to any change of opinion, should the evidence in support of such change be stronger than the evidence in support of one's previous convictions. The outside world knows nothing of the mental struggle within to find a resting place from the doubts and anxieties that beset us. Conviction comes gradually. Sudden conversions are unreliable. Growth and development in all things are gradual; the mind of man is no exception to the rule. To wait patiently for the removal of doubts by investigation and reading was the only course open. Every book bearing on the subject of Spiritualism that could be purchased or borrowed was eagerly devoured, and neither time nor means were spared to test the truth of supra-mundane phenomena. The result was that satisfaction came at last, that there was some foundation for a belief in a future conscious state of existence after Death.

The night at length arrived for the reading of the promised paper, which may be fitly termed my 'Confession of faith in a future life.' As its title indicated, it merely dealt with the 'probabilities' of a future life. To address an assembly consisting in a great measure of sceptics upon such a subject was no easy matter, and the nearest approach to certainty that one dare assume was to speak of probabilities. To some of their minds the probabilities, even, of a future state were very remote. Not only was evidence from the Christian theology inadmissible – it was not likely that I should bring it forward, seeing that I did not accept it myself – but the evidences afforded by Spiritualism which had satisfied me would not appeal with the same force to other minds. These evidences were therefore not adduced. The only groundwork for the arguments in favour of a future existence consisted of generally admitted facts.

Charles Bray, with his 'when-you-are-dead-you-are-done-with' theory, being a member of the Society, had many followers. His creed was annihilation, or that at death individuality is lost, and that the person becomes re-absorbed into the universe, the only immortality for man being to live hereafter in the life of the race. Though this view was held most positively, it rested on purely negative premises. He admitted the immortality of thoughts because the evidences were palpable, but denied the immortality of the thinker, holding this position because no evidence obtruded itself upon his consciousness to support personal immortality. To those who seek it, however, there is positive evidence of the immortality of the thinker. A theory resting upon negative premises must give way when another inconsistent with it is positively proved. One well-accredited fact is worth a thousand negations without proof; a negative hypothesis unsupported by facts is untenable.

Charles Bray, though a deep philosopher, was narrow in his mental range. His world was subjective – existing in the mind – the result of some 'unknown cause without called matter,' which, acting upon the senses, produces sensations within the individual consciousness. The sensations so produced formed his world. The only certainty was consciousness. The following outline of Bray's philosophy is condensed by George Willis Cooke, from an article in the *Westminster Review* for April, 1879:– 'All knowledge comes to man through the action of the external world upon the senses; all truth, all progress, come to us out of experience. Reason is dependent for its exercise upon experience, and experience is nothing more than the knowledge of the invariable order of nature, of the relations of cause and effect. All acts of men are ruled by Necessity. Pain produces our ideas of right and wrong, and happiness is the test of all moral action. There are no such things as sin and evil, only pains and pleasures. Evil is the natural and necessary limitation of our faculties, and our consequent liability to error; and pain, which we call evil, is its corrective. Nothing, under the circumstances, could have happened but that which did happen; and the actions of men, under precisely the same circumstances, must always issue in precisely the same results. Death is good and a necessary aid to progress. Society is regarded as an organism, and man is to find his highest life in the life of others. The great body of humanity (considered as an individual), with its soul, the principle of sensation, is ever fresh and vigorous and increasing in enjoyment. Death and birth, the means of renewal and succession, bear the same relation to this body of society as the system of waste and reproduction do to the human body; the old and useless and decayed material is carried out and fresh substituted, and thus the frame is renovated and rendered capable of ever-increasing happiness . . . The minds, that is to say, the ideas and feelings of which they were composed, of Socrates, Plato, Epicurus, Galileo, Bacon, Locke, Newton, are thus for ever in existence, and the immortality of the soul is preserved, not in individuals, but in the great body of humanity . . . To the race, though not to individuals, all beautiful things are preserved for ever; all that is really good and profitable is immortal. . . . All outside of us is a delusion of the senses. The senses conspire with the intellect to impose upon us. The constitution of our faculties forces us to believe in an external world, but it has no more reality than our dreams. Each creature is the creator of its own separate different world. The unity of outward things is imposed upon them by the faculty of individuality, and is a mere fiction of the mind. Matter is a creature of the imagination and is a pure assumption. It is the centre of force, as immaterial as spirit, as ethereal and as unsubstantial. As centres of force imply locality, and locality space, so space must have an extension of its own. Not so; it is a pure creation of the mind. The same holds good of time. The world of mind, the moral world as well, are our own creations. Man has no power over himself; nothing could have been otherwise than it is. Repentance and remorse are foolish regrets over what could not have been otherwise. All actions and motives are indifferent; only in their consequences can any distinction be observed between them. Such as minister to man's pleasure he calls good; such as produce pain he calls evil. There is no good but pleasure, and no evil but pain. Hence there is no distinction between moral and physical evil. Morality is the chemistry of the mind, its attractions and repulsions, likes and dislikes. God is an illusion, as are all moral conclusions based on His existence. Nor has man any reality; he is the greatest illusion and delusion of all. The faculty of individuality gives us all our ideas and feelings, and creates for us what we call our minds. A mind is an aggregate of a stream of consciousness. Ideas, feelings, states of consciousness, do not inhere in anything; each is a distinct entity. "Thinking is," is what we should say, not "I think." Here we are at the ground fact of what constitutes being, on solid footing; consciousness cannot deceive us. Thinking is, even if mind and matter, self and not self, are illusory. It is, even if we deny both the external and internal causes of consciousness. We know our own consciousness, that alone. All is inference beside. When we consider what inferences are most probable, we are led to build up a constructive philosophy. Consciousness says we have a body, body a brain, and pressure on the brain stops consciousness; hence a close connection between the brain and consciousness. The two go together, and in the brain we must lay the foundation of our philosophy. The mental faculties create the world of individual consciousness, it is the outside world. We know only what is revealed in consciousness. Matter and mind are one. Life and mind are correlates of physical force; they are the forms assumed by physical force when subjected to organic conditions. Yet there is no such thing as mere physical force. Every atom of matter acts intelligently; it has so acted always. The conscious intelligence of the universe has subsided into natural law, and acts automatically. This universal agent of life in all things is God. All consciousness and physical force are but "the varied God." There is in reality no agent but mind conscious. God is nature; nature is mind solidified. Matter is force as revealed by the senses. It is the body, force is the soul. In nature, as in man, body and soul are one and indivisible. Mind builds up organisms. There is a living will, conscious or unconscious in all things. The One and All requires the resignation of the individual and personal, of all that is selfish, to the Infinite whole.'

There is no doubt truth in this philosophy, but its foundation is too circumscribed. Charles Bray omitted to take everything into account. As it is, his philosophy, like an ancient house, projects over the area of its foundations. A philosopher must have a range of vision broad enough to take in all facts, and he must construct his philosophy accordingly. Facts relating to the supra-mundane are ignored. The assertion that man loses his individual consciousness after death and is re-absorbed into the universe is inconsistent with facts well authenticated in this department. It is beside the mark for the philosopher or the scientist to say that such facts do not concern him. He should welcome facts from all quarters. If occurrences take place that do not conform to 'natural laws' as he has hitherto understood them, he must remember that the laws are not of his making, and that possibly he may not yet have discovered them perfectly or in their entirety. Upon attention being drawn to a new order of facts or experiences, he in effect keeps them at arm's length, and demands that they shall be 'well established' before he will condescend to touch them. But while not being credulous, he may yet give respectful attention to any well-authenticated facts. Indeed, he ought to welcome new facts and set about testing and investigating them – track them down for himself to whatever department of the universe they relate. Great as have been the achievements and discoveries of modern science, the possibilities of the future are even greater. The nineteenth century has been eminently materialistic. Its scientific researches have related to matter; in a future age, sooner or later, sooner probably than later, researches on sientific methods will be extended to the realm of spirit which is now unfolding itself and inviting investigation. An era is dawning, nay, has actually dawned, in which facts relating to the spiritual, to man, his nature and ethical concerns, will be investigated. The possibilities of this realm promise to revolutionise both the scientific and religious worlds. Even if no noisy revolution is brought about, they will at least considerably modify the conclusions held in both departments of thought, and will especially tend to convince the sceptical of a future state. Lord Brougham, who had investigated the phenomena of Spiritualism, in his day could say that in the cloudless skies of scepticism he could see a rain cloud, as yet no bigger than a man's hand, and this was modern Spiritualism.

In the presence of men like Charles Bray, it will be readily understood that some difficulty was experienced in getting a footing for the discussion of such a question as individual consciousness after death.

The substance of the paper was as follows:—After some introductory remarks as to the differences of opinion upon this question, and the impossibility of the various notions to alter the real fact, it was maintained that the probabilities were in favour of the opinion that human beings did not lose their individual consciousness after death. There is scarcely a nation on the face of the earth that does not cherish a belief in a future existence in some form or other. Natural phenomena also prove that nothing in the material universe is annihilated, but that things merely change their constituent forms by a re-arrangement of atoms. Embarking from this analogy upon the ocean of probabilities, it was asked – Does it seem consistent that man, with his almost unbounded powers and knowledge, standing supreme in this beautiful creation, should be annihilated? Is it possible that such a superior intellectual being could have been made in vain? Does it not point to the conclusion that the great Author of being made man the type of Himself destined to an immortality suitable to his capacities? Can we in the presence of every day's experience, that man rewards virtue and punishes vice, deny the great Author of our being the power to place after the change called 'death' our principle of life in a state of existence merited by the manner in which as a responsible being it has spent its earth life?

The sceptic might seemingly have the advantage in a discussion of this character, for his arguments rest on what he calls purely natural sequences limited chiefly to outward observances, not knowing that any hidden condition exists beyond the experiences of his senses. As showing by analogy the probability of a future state for man, it may be mentioned that much lower conditions of life are in existence prior to their full development. This is exemplified in the series of changes of the entoza from their lowest forms to their highest development. Similarly with insect life in the many changes that intervene between the pupal state and the perfect form, each change being a perfect life in itself, so perfect indeed that the larval state in some instances has been mistaken for a new species until the life history of the insect has been studied. If the bud of a plant be examined under a microscope, it will be found to contain within itself all the future developments of the leaf and blossom necessary to the propagation of its species; it is as much a leaf and blossom in its embryotic state as in its full development, though this would be doubted by the sceptic because it would not be tangible to his unaided senses. Who can say that this condition was the advent of its creation? Is it more difficult to believe in a future existence after the dissolution of man's organic structure, than that this structure is the most ingenious and elaborate of which the mind can conceive? Who can analyse the human mind or the principle of life? 'The beginning of life is not dependent,' says Andrew Crose, 'upon those laws by which man has hitherto framed his belief, but upon an unknown and unseen power of which man at present knows nothing.' Some hold that man's existence upon earth is in accordance with natural laws totally independent of a Creative Power, and that man's mission is to enjoy life as best he can, irrespective of any care about a future existence. Such a man, with moral and social organs well developed, would be amiable and moral but would lack hope – the feeling that upholds the sufferer on his couch of sickness and that disarms death of its sting in the cheering prospect of happiness hereafter. Hope, the antidote of despair, is the principle that lifts the Christian out of the difficulties and dangers of this ever-changing world, and fits him for another and better state of existence. This hope and expectation is universal. The belief in a future state is not confined to the various sects of Christians; it has existed for all time among mankind, and has been the means of swaying the destinies of nations, changing their character and lifting them out of extreme barbarism to a high state of civilization. The rude and uncultured Red Indian in his death throes rejoices in the prospect of his speedy removal to the happy hunting grounds which his Manitu (God) has provided. The Moslem braves death with pleasure, in the certain hope of enjoying the company of the heavenly houris for ever. What is it that upholds the upright man in his day of desolation but the cheering hope of a happy and glorious life hereafter? The belief enables him to stand aloof from the follies and vanities of the world and not to return evil for injury, this feeling of responsibility deterring him from the committal of offences towards his fellow-men.

Contrast with this beautiful trait of character the conduct and character of the self-important and supercilious athiest who owns no responsibility to man or God, and believes that everything exists by and through a process he calls Nature – a blind fortuitous concourse of atoms. Such a belief satisfies the selfishness which looks only to this world and its pleasures, but it is universally voted low and unworthy of man's highest destinies. Who breaks an organic law breaks the law of God. This axiom the sceptic denies, affirming the non-responsibility of man and giving to 'Nature' the credit of having produced him as a potter produces a vessel of clay; but while the pot is the product of thought and intelligence, the man is said to be the outcome of a blind force – a pot superior to man! Absurd.

Tradition hands down from the remotest antiquity the belief in a future existence for the spirit after its separation from its earthly tenement.

Science proves that nothing is annihilated, reason induces us to believe and expect that the soul – that Divine emanation from the great First Cause – cannot sink into nonentity. It may be asked, How do we know these things to be true? but in return let us ask, Is there sufficient evidence to disprove that which the general opinion of mankind universally accepts as a fact?

The study of Nature compels a belief in the existence of a Primal Cause. To believe in such a Primal Cause is to consider Him (or it) Infinite, and Infinity must be an embodiment of futurity. Who can assert, with the undeniable evidences of design about him, that this world came into existence without a Designer? The perfect uniformity of structure, the peculiar adaptation of parts for a specific purpose, the bewildering ages through which it must have existed, its beautiful appearance, its nicely adjusted machinery-like processes, its marvellous vital functions, its adequate compensation of parts and its harmony as a whole, must convince any one that such an unfathomable Effect could only have been brought into being by a great and Infinite Cause, beyond which it is impossible to penetrate.

You may ask, What have these considerations to do with the question of a future life for man? Everything; for this question of a future life for man must necessarily involve the belief in or denial of a God or Infinity. Does it not strike the mind that Nature is only the outward manifestation of an unseen and omniscient Cause? The mind of man is the outward and visible semblance of the soul – that mysterious agent which gives impulse to our sensations and desires, enables us to unfold to each other our varied acquirements and defects, to confide to each other our varied anxieties and fears, and by the union of sympathetic thought and fellowship, places man at the head of God's beautiful creation. So with Nature. It is the vestment of the Unseen. Does it seem difficult to believe in a future existence for man when things around us prove a future for everything else? Every day's transactions imply a future. The morrow is the future of to-day? What induces a man to strive to overcome the difficulties of the present but the hope of a better condition in the future? The very conditions of man's life are centred in the future, all his earthly hopes and desires are bound up in it. The absence of hope produces the most direful consequences, giving rise to inattention to the duties of this life, causing improvidence and recklessness, and often tending to fearful misery and hopeless despair. You admit this with respect to man's sojourn upon earth, but what has it to do with the immortality of the soul? The evidence is most conclusive that the soul of man is the agent whereby the energies of the human mind are developed, and the mind is the sub-agent through which are exercised the qualities and attributes of sentient beings constituting man the typical representative of the great Power who called him into being. As God is infinite and immortal, so is the soul of man which is the offspring of God. As God is a Cause, planning and making provision for the future, so is man. Man depends upon the future to bring him happiness in this world through the exercise of the mind. The mind being only the outward manifestation of a more subtle agent, the soul, how can we reasonably suppose that God will deny a future for the soul, when He has given man a mind to be the guide and hope of his earthly future?

The belief in a future life dates from the earliest times. Look at the care with which the ancient Egyptians embalmed and preserved their dead! They believed that the spirit would still live on, but that it would be subject to many and various transmigrations, until it had become sufficiently purified to claim again the body it had been separated from, in order to take from it the characteristic form of its earthly existence to be reincarnated as spirit to a state of happiness for ever. Though wrong in detail, the main principle of this, the hope of immortality, is sound. The monotheistic was the prevalent belief in the most ancient times, especially among the Hindoos and Egyptians, and although corrupted in more modern times with crude and uncouth notions, yet nothing can excel the grandeur and sublimity of the Vedas, the Institutes of Menu, and other sacred writings of the ancients, in which the Infinite has always been recognised. Well might Kepler, in deep devotion and with a feeling of dependence upon this great and Infinite Cause, exclaim – 'I give Thee thanks, Lord and Creator, that Thou hast given me joy through Thy creation, for I have been ravished with the work of Thy hands. I have revealed unto mankind the glory of Thy works as far as my limited spirit could conceive their infinitude. Should I have brought forward anything unworthy of Thee, or should I have sought my own fame, be graciously pleased to forgive me.' Though scientific men are usually sceptical respecting God and the existence of a future life for man, there are exceptions. Moving in a humble sphere of life, I have met many reverential scientists, who, studying Nature in the true spirit of humility and earnestness, have looked through its outward vestments into its clear, unfathomable, infinite soul, of whom and of whose works a Psalmist sung – 'In wisdom hast Thou made them all.' In providing for the future of lower orders of creation, we may rest assured that He has not overlooked the necessities of His dearest creature, man, but has provided for him a future exactly suited to his capacities, in which he may still strive and strive after Perfection. 'Be ye therefore perfect, as your Father in Heaven is perfect.' To attain perfection man will need an immortality.

The reading of the paper gave rise to a lively discussion, in which several members, to whom I had not looked for support, upheld the views expressed.

VIII

Spiritualism

Attracted to Spiritualism by American investigators – Michael Faraday's conclusion – Other theories – Phenomena – Sceptical as to the cause – The 'Circle' – Timothy Morris, of Birmingham – Bedworth spiritualists – 'A statue of ice' – A modern version of Gideon's Fleece – A personal message – Set thinking – Sleeping in a haunted room – Caught up – A vision of John Peirpont – Flowers brought by spirits – A glass of ale solidified – The purpose of occult phenomena – The only theory to account for them – The higher aims of Spiritualism.

To be faithful, more than a passing reference must be made to the so-called spiritual forces in Nature, because of their benign influence upon my life. It is not too much to say that Spiritualism set at rest effectually the doubts and questionings which had haunted me through life as to a continued existence beyond the grave. Hearing of it in the first instance through the American newspapers, and finding that it was attracting the attention of some of the greatest scientists of that country, it seemed that the subject was not to be despised as throwing light upon the problem – 'If a man die shall he live again?' It was not to be expected that a Free Thinker should take kindly to the supernatural. At any rate, I and some others of a similar turn of mind commenced investigations. Had these evidences of the supernatural merely come through American newspapers, it is very doubtful whether they would have been of sufficient interest for serious notice, but finding their truth vouched for by a host of men eminent in science, literature, art, and religion, who could be implicity trusted in other matters, these occurrences at any rate commanded respect. On reading the accounts of researches by scientific investigators, and other literature upon the subject, one point that impressed us favourably as to the sincerity of the convictions of these pioneers was their firm and noble bearing, not only under criticism but under persecution. This of course did not satisfy us of the correctness of any of their conclusions; of this we could only be convinced after personal investigation.

It was only when scientific men like Professor Hare, Professor Mapes, Judge Edmonds, N. P. Talmage, Governor of Winsconsin, and many other men of note had publicly acknowledged their belief in the genuineness of the phenomena, that English savants considered it within their dignity to notice them. Before making investigation they ascribed the occurrences to imposture, and the belief in them to hallucination. With this prepossession Michael Faraday set himself to expose the 'gross delusion', and after a series of ingenious experiments with elaborate mechanical appliances, gave his conclusion that the phenomena were not in any way connected with electricity or magnetism or any other known force, but that they were due to 'involuntary and unconscious action of the muscles.' This verdict was very unsatisfactory. If no hitherto *known* force could produce the phenomena, what *unknown* force, it might be asked, has power to control the muscles of a human being against his conviction and will ? The conclusion was too absurd. The verdict of this celebrated master in science would have remained unquestioned, but for the fact that in the presence of other scientists, whose honesty and good faith could not be doubted, supernatural phenomena occurred and were declared to be genuine. Other scientists attributed what took place to 'unconscious cerebration,' stating that the occurrences were not really seen by the physical sight, but that the persons witnessing them only thought they saw such and such things, the whole business being but a freak of the imagination. This theory was more untenable than Faraday's. Could it be an unconscious act, for example, to visit a certain locality in search of a particular species of shell, expecting to find it if conditions were favourable ? The propounder of this theory might as well have said that the act of walking to the spot for that purpose had no connection with one's thinking powers, or that one had no control over one's voluntary muscles. Surely the originator of this theory could not be ignorant of the fact that human beings possess nerves of sensation as well as motor nerves. Or did he think that the great sympathetic nerve had as much influence and power over the voluntary as over the involuntary muscles ? Experiments convinced us that Faraday was right in averring that no force or power known to science could elucidate the mystery, and we were equally convinced that he could not, or would not, give a name to the force or power that, to his mind, produced the phenomena which comprised amongst other things the moving of heavy articles of furniture without any expenditure of physical force. Such feats he held were performed by the involuntary action of the muscles!

Although phenomena occurred in our presence, such as violent rockings and upheavals of a table, and many movements of heavy articles of furniture diametrically opposed to the law of gravity, with raps and concussions that seemed powerful enough to split the furniture into fragments, yet, like Michael Faraday, we were prepared to give in to any force that could be proved to give rise to these disturbances rather than attribute them to any supernatural agency, such as the return of departed spirits, a theory savoring too much of the legends of olden times, when every feudal castle of note possessed its spectral form revisiting periodically the pale glimpses of the moon.

A few particulars of the way in which we proceeded may be interesting. We followed the instructions laid down in books consulted. A 'circle' around a table being recommended as the best method of encouraging spiritual phenomena, we sat in this way, but were so grossly materialistic in our ideas that we rigidly excluded from our circle all who were not similarly inclined, and there need be little wonder that our first experiences yielded but a very meagre harvest of facts ascertained or impressions received favourable to the subject. It was at my house in Tower Street, in the year 1849, that we began sitting. Nothing more than the tilting of the table and tappings underneath occurred for a long time, but these could not be accounted for. The only point on which we were satisfied was that they were not produced voluntarily by any of those present. The table moved with our hands placed above it without actual contact. A scientific friend named Timothy Morris, of Birmingham, at our invitation made a journey to Coventry on purpose to see the table, which not only moved without being touched, but rose from its feet and followed our hands, placed above it, as high as we could reach. Timothy, a thorough materialistic, as most scientific men are, could not solve the mystery.

By the way, Timothy had some strange experiences once at a seance in Birmingham, at which both Timothy and I were present, four mediums were standing at the same time 'entranced' and conversing together. Timothy, regarding it as all 'moonshine,' said to the spirit supposed to be controlling one of the mediums, 'If you can go to my room while I am away and disarrange the things, I shall be more satisfied.' He thereupon produced the key of his room which he had locked, explained that he was about to deliver a lecture and would be away for some time, and asked the spirits to do what they liked in his shop. The next time I saw Timothy I asked him whether they had complied with his request. He said they did more than ten pounds' worth of damage that night. On returning home he went to bed as usual, and in the morning a neighbour said to him, 'Your men were at work very industriously at the lathes and benches last night while you were out, and the shop was lit up.' Timothy knew that the men were not at work, and on going to the shop adjoining, and only to be reached through his house, he found things turned topsy-turvy. There was no evidence of any one having entered either by ordinary or extraordinary means. On another occasion Timothy was called up by a policeman, who informed him that all the gas jets in his workshop were alight. On getting up to see what was the matter, nothing unusual could be discovered. On another occasion he was called into a temperance hotel to set right some bells which had a habit of ringing at unusual times without any apparent cause. He overhauled the bells, and assured the landlord that they would not ring again unless pulled. No sooner had he said the words than they recommenced ringing most violently. He then told the proprietor that it was out of his power to stop them, and advised him to make the case known to some Spiritualists. These people were called in, with the result that it was ascertained that the agitation of the bells was caused by the attempts of the disembodied spirit of a man who had committed suicide in the house some years previously but whose identity was not established at the time, to make himself known. He communicated his name and place of abode in earth life, and on his friends being told of it, his identity was established, and the hotel was not troubled again with mysterious bell ringing. I do not suppose Timothy was ever moved from his dogged materialism. Indeed, physical manifestations do not produce conviction of the reality of a spiritual world. They merely arrest the attention. The reason is led to accept a belief in the spiritual by its own operations, aided by the subtle influence of unseen causes after the mind has been directed into this channel by occurrences which cannot be explained by so-called 'natural laws.'

About twelve months after commencing our sittings, we heard of a party of investigators at Bedworth, and found on paying a visit that one or two of their number had developed into 'mediums.' A medium – it may be explained – is a person through whom, as through a channel, spirits can communicate or manifest themselves by speech, writing, or other means. None of our party showed signs of development in this direction. At one of the first seances attended at Bedworth a spirit writing through the medium, who was in a trance, announced itself as 'Satan.' With the bravado and self-consciousness characteristic of a youth with a smattering of the sciences, I was bent on discovering and exposing imposture, and said, 'You are just the chap I want.' I defied the spirit to do its worst, and was about adding that if it could show itself tangibly I would begin to think there was something in it. I had not finished the sentence before I was apparently transported to the frigid zone; I felt like a statue of ice, every fibre in my body being frozen and rigid – a most horrible sensation. Fearlessly and defiantly exercising my will power, which had been momentarily paralysed by the suddenness of the occurrence, I freed myself from this uncanny condition. Another member of the party felt a similarly chilling influence. Other manifestations occurred at this seance which need not be particularised. Not being able to discover the faintest suspicion of imposture, I recklessly impugned the honour of those present, and succeeded in breaking up the meeting in disorder and creating an uproar. Another experience in connection with Bedworth was this:— Feeling uneasy at the loom one afternoon I went out for a walk, believing that I should be more inclined for work afterwards. While out I met a friend named William Bedder, who said he was going to Bedworth to a Spiritualists' meeting, and asked me to go with him. We walked over, and on reaching the house of Job Riley in the Roadway, where seances were held, we were met at the door by the host, who, entranced, said we were expected. They had been holding a seance, we were informed, and a message was written asking them to wait until the arrival of Mr. Gutteridge and Mr. Bedder, from Coventry, who were on the road. On another occasion at Bedworth, a meeting was held in an open field, and a shower of rain came on. As a 'sign' of the genuineness of the manifestations, it was proposed by the spirits themselves, through the medium, that while all the persons standing round should get wet, the medium in the centre of the circle should be kept dry. This sign was literally fulfilled, for while the people around were wet through, not a spot of rain had fallen upon the medium. It may be as well to add that the Bedworth mediums through whom these written and spoken messages came were perfectly illiterate, being neither able to read nor write.

Seances were held at the house of a shoemaker* living at the corner of the Star Yard, Earl Street, Coventry. Attending one of these meetings in a more than ordinarily sceptical mood, determined to ferret out fraud and humbug, I demanded some proof by which I would personally test the

* Mr Rodhouse.

genuineness of the assumption that the messages given through the medium were from disembodied spirits. The request was acceded to by a written message being given through the medium – an illiterate boy – relating incidents connected with my father and mother which were known only to myself. This was no more remarkable than many other things witnessed, but the personal element in the message appealed to my mind and set me thinking. The tenderness of it dealt the first blow at my scepticism. I had no knowledge of thought reading, but possessed some powers as a mesmerist. This, however, was beyond anything that could be attributed to mesmerism or thought reading as an inducing cause. From this time onward I can trace the gradual acceptance of a belief in a spiritual – as distinct from a material – existence.

Some curious experiences followed, but to relate one half would fill a volume. One or two, however, may be told. Invited by a friend to spend a short time at Northampton, I found Spiritualism quite rife in that town. My friend was manager in the tailoring department of a large firm, and the building in which he lived was an old one that had escaped the ravages of a great fire that had devastated that part of Northampton known as The Newlands. The house had dark passages, mysterious nooks and corners, recesses and secret places in the walls in which persons might hide with ease and safety. Sleeping in a room which had the reputation of being haunted, I was disturbed by weird noises and knockings, but was not in the least alarmed. The disturbances prevented sleep, and on that account were not very pleasant. The next night brought similar experiences. I had to get up and inform the host of what was occurring, but he assured me that it was all right. On going to bed again the noises increased. Crash fell something like a cannon ball upon the floor. It was a light, midsummer's night. Believing that a terrible catastrophe had happened, I sprang out of bed; but after reassuring myself and lying down again, the crash was repeated on the other side of the room. My friend advised the burning of a light, and explained that the figure of a man was frequently seen in the passage, but that it receded before a light into this room, which was very seldom occupied. He and the other occupants of the house, however, had become accustomed to the spectre. On placing a light in the room the noises ceased. The next time I visited Northampton, my wife – the second, of whom more anon – accompanied me, and sleeping in the same room, were violently heaved almost out of bed, as by some person underneath, but could not discover anything to account for the strange disturbances. At last an explanation suggested itself. Remembering that one of the conditions of successful physical phenomena in Spiritualism is a dark cabinet formed usually of thick curtains, it occurred to me that the valances – which were of thick, heavy material, reaching from the bed to the floor – formed an excellent cabinet. On turning up the valances and tucking them underneath the mattress, so as to allow free access for the light to penetrate beneath the bed, we were not disturbed egain. A somewhat similar experience happened at our own house in Yardley Street later. The bed on which we lay was lifted bodily up, so that with a pencil I might have written upon the ceiling, the motion being so gentle that it was scarcely perceptible; we were let down as gently, so that it was impossible to tell by any jarring sensation when the floor was reached. This was attempted a second time, though we were not taken quite so high. My wife says a third attempt was made, but I must have gone to sleep, for I did not notice it. A somewhat similar experience in the way of being 'caught up' befel me on another occasion. Visiting a house at Stoke in connection with Spiritualism, where I believed the conditions were not altogether so harmonious as they might be, my wife and other friends missed me on coming out. I had a feeling of repugnance towards the place, and was desirous of leaving earlier but could not. What actually took place is unknown to me, because I have not the slightest recollection of leaving the house, and must have been in a state of unconsciousness. Upon recovering, however, I was running at some distance from the house towards home. My clothes were disfigured and torn, and streaked with a gummy substance. I was unable to account for this, but a friend suggested as a solution, that I had been spirited away, and in transit had been carried through the branches of the trees which formed an avenue from the house, and which were covered with a substance similar to that which adhered to my clothes.

On another occasion I saw two venerable-looking figures at the foot of the bed, and asked my wife if she saw them, but she did not. The one was the exact counterpart of the other, and I was puzzled, being perfectly wide awake. At the next seance I attended, a spirit controlled and told me that it was he who had appeared; there were not two figures, and the fact of my having seen two was stated to be due to defective vision. The optical delusion was accounted for upon scientific principles. The spirit gave the name of "John Peirpont," the eminent American Unitarian minister, spiritualist, and poet. Upon relating this circumstance, and describing in detail the appearance of the figure, to a gentleman from America who had been an intimate friend of Peirpont's – having attended his ministry for many years – this gentleman said the description I had given corresponded exactly with the personal appearance of Mr. Peirpont.

At another seance, fresh-cut flowers were brought by spirits. It was in the early spring, when the daffodils were beginning to appear. At the commencement of the sitting the weather outside was fine, but while we were indoors a snowstorm came on. None of the sitters came in or went out during the seance. The room was darkened, that being the condition most favourable to the production of physical phenomena. At one point during the sitting I felt distinctly a soft, velvety hand pushed into mine, which was closed. I grasped the hand; it melted away, and left behind two daffodils. My wife was sitting in another part of the room, and I wished mentally that she might have a flower too. At that instant my wife called out, 'Joe, I have got a flower; it has just been dropped into my lap, and here is another on my arm.' Upon turning on the gas, we saw that the flowers were wet with melted snow, and that the stems bore the appearance of having been freshly severed. Flowers and freshly-gathered leaves of plants were also showered upon the table in the centre of the room – fifteen or sixteen different species, covered with melted snow – which, by the direction of the controlling spirit, were distributed amongst the company present. At the same seance, a shawl was taken from the shoulders of a lady and carried across the room to a gentleman, and in transit the pin was put into the hand of another gentleman.

On another occasion fruit was brought into the room by spirits. At a house in Bath Street, a medium named Fellowes, prohibited by spirit friends from drinking during the seances, and persisting in the practice, set a jug of ale and a glass on the table, and during the meeting, while another medium was under control, poured out a glass of the liquid. On raising it to his lips to drink, it was a solid mass, and would not leave the glass. It remained solid till the close of the meeting, when presumably the power used to solidify the liquid was taken away by the dispersal of the sitters. This solidification of the ale was witnessed by myself and a number of others, and was tested by each.

It has been my lot to witness many occurrences which to persons unacquainted with Spiritualism would be considered marvellous, but which, among those who have investigated the phenomena, are ordinary events. These occult phenomena should be regarded, not as the essential part of Spiritualism, but merely as a means of directing attention to the teachings which Spiritualism offers respecting the future state, the reality of which it establishes.

The varied occurrences of Spiritualism can only be rationally accounted for upon the assumption that they are caused by invisible agents possessing intelligence. Certainly the force is not physical, and it is assumed to belong to a realm outside that domain, though not necessarily outside the natural. The messages received have in thousands of cases been tested. Frequently they are of such a character that only the 'departed,' from whom they profess to have originated, could have given them. Any person entering upon the investigation of Spiritualism, with the same patience and desire for truth that he would enter upon any other matter of importance, is not unlikely to meet with such instances, appealing specially to the individual. Everyone investigating Spiritualism may become personally convinced, even though he be so sceptical as to take nothing for granted and to receive no second-hand testimony. Scientists who have investigated the subject without bias have been convinced, more or less, of its reality. Professor Crookes and Professor Alfred Russell Wallace may be cited as English spiritualist scientists, while Professor Huxley is a type of the scientist who scouts and condemns the subject, confessing at the same time that he does not even condescend to look seriously into it.

Physical phenomena are the beginning, not the end, of Spiritualism. They are only at the threshold. Upon being convinced by their means of the existence of a spiritual state, the searcher after truth is impelled to pursue the investigation further, and to assimilate the researches of others. The possibilities of research are inexhaustible, and soon the conviction is borne in upon the mind that the spiritual is the Real and the Abiding, and the physical transient and secondary. Upon the full realization of the spiritual, selfishness and cruelty, which have wrought so much misery in the world, are subdued. There is no place for them, love, and sympathy, and character being the means of advancement in that realm, which, however, can be lived in here. What the Churches try to prove by reference to so-called sacred writings – namely, the existence of a life beyond the grave – Spiritualism proves in the accepted scientific way by reference to present day, well-accredited facts within the reach of all, and it appears to be the only means of converting dogged, hard-headed Materialists to a belief in Immortality, or a continued existence for the spirit of man after the cessation of the physical life.

IX

Distressed Weavers

Smitten by Cupid a second time – An introduction to the young women – Favourable reception – Mutual explanations – Similarity of experience and sympathy – Second marriage – Introduction of the silk trade – Early reminiscences – A kind manufacturer – A new loom – Decline of the ribbon trade – Causes of the stagnation – American tariffs and silk-worm disease – Strike and lock-out – No work – Terrible sufferings – Weavers working on the commons – Sixpence and a loaf per day – Help from a brother – A situation offered – Savings spent – Unprecedented poverty in Coventry – 'The Weaver,' a parody on 'The Pauper' – Economies and aspirations.

IT is now time to relate the circumstances which led up to my second marriage. Nothing was farther from my thoughts at the time than to take another wife. There was, however, an undefinable void in my life owing to the loss of the first which nothing seemed able to fill. I was reminded of her at every turn, and felt that though passed away, she was still mine. But Time, though it cannot altogether destroy, effaces the distinctness of such impressions. The first meeting with the lady who was destined to be my second wife came about in this way. An anatomical museum was open in the Corn Exchange – a most comprehensive and excellent collection, which afforded me an opportunity of supplementing previous knowledge of the human frame gleaned from books and diagrams by reference to carefully prepared specimens and casts of human and animal structure. Day after day found me among the specimens; the hours spent there were among the most pleasant of my life. Some lady friends from Bedworth whom I knew were visiting the museum on a special day set apart for ladies, and going to tea afterwards at the house of a mutual friend, they sent for me to explain the various objects they had seen. All except one were well known to me, and it was in conversation respecting the objects in the museum that my attention was arrested by the face of the stranger, which was suffused with blushes. I immediately changed the subject. The face and expression rivetted itself into my very soul. When the time came for departure I accompanied them to the carrier's cart which was to take them home, but, short as had been our acquaintance, the absence of the young woman who had attracted my attention seemed to leave a blank in my experience. I could think of nothing but her face and form, which so instantaneously, forcibly, and mysteriously impressed me. It was clear I was again smitten with one of Cupid's darts.

In the course of a week or so I wrote to the ladies whom I knew, asking for information respecting the young woman whom I did not know – whether she was disengaged, what were her habits of life, and so on. But several days elapsed without bringing any answer. I therefore resolved to visit my Bedworth friends, in order to gain information by personal interview. I had often called at their home when in that district hunting for fossils amongst the débris brought up from the coal mines in the neighbourhood. They were amused at the interest expressed in my letter respecting the young woman, and had chaffed her about my solicitude for her. I learned from them that she had sprained her ankle on alighting from the carrier's cart in which she returned from Coventry after our first meeting. This interested me considerably, and I made it an excuse for seeking an introduction. My friends accordingly took me at once to see her. They gave her an excellent character. She was a constant attendant at the Wesleyan Chapel, kind, truthful, and industrious, gaining her living by weaving; in fact, she was just such a helpmeet as I needed. Suffice it to say that my suit was favourably received.

These Bedworth friends had known me during the lifetime of my first wife, and were well acquainted with most of the incidents relative to her illness and death. Their favourable report as to my character and disposition smoothed the way for the proposal I afterwards made to the young woman to become my wife. It needed but little explanation to convince her of my sincerity. Her experience in early life had been so similar in its chief characteristics to my own that a mutual feeling of sympathy soon bound us together. Like me, she had been obliged to leave home on account of not being able to live with a stepmother only a little older than herself.

It had been a very remote thought that I should ever settle down again in married life, but I had vowed that should such an event happen, for the sake of the wife who had sacrificed her life to save mine, the happiness of her successor should never be clouded by any fault on my part. At a moment when the thought of such an event was totally absent, this strange meeting utterly changed the current of my ideas. It was not beauty, nor the grace of a cultured mind that enthralled me, for the young woman was diffident in her demeanour almost to shyness, and therefore afforded very scanty superficial materials for forming a judgment as to her qualities of mind and heart. The determining factor was an indescribable sensation that drew me towards her, a sympathetic feeling that word-painting cannot depict. A condition of feeling once previously experienced, in which I had perfect confidence, predicted that the contemplated union would be for the advantage of both. We were married on the 17th of May, 1857, and never have either of us had cause to regret the event.

The events which have now to be related in connection with the ribbon trade of Coventry, may be prefaced by some account of the introduction and growth of this industry.

Silk was originally brought to Europe by some Monks from Constantinople in A.D. 551, from silkworms' eggs which they procured in India and China, and from these eggs raw silk was produced in this capital of the East. The manufacture of it soon spread through Greece, and thence to Sicily, settling in Palermo, where the inhabitants were taught not only the method of rearing the worms, but the spinning of silk and its manufacture by weaving into broad and narrow tissues. The first accredited date of its manufacture in England is about the year 1504. In France it was manufactured in 1521, raw silk not being produced until a long time afterwards. Silkworms were reared, and mulberry trees planted by Henry IV, throughout the whole of Southern France in 1559. Broad silken goods were made from raw silk introduced into England about the year 1620, and a Silk Throwers Company was established in London in 1629.

Lombe's famous silk throwing machine was erected at Derby (1719) with great success, making England independent of the importation of the raw material. It contained 26,586 wheels, one water wheel moving the whole, and in less than two days produced 318,504,960 yards of organzine silken thread fit for the weaver to work up. Before the close of the century the silk throwing industry had firmly established itself in Derby, Macclesfield, Leek, Congleton, Coventry, and other places. One of the oldest of these silk throwing mills was Naul's mill in Abbott's Lane.

Jacquard (born at Lyons 1752), the inventor of the machine that bears his name, was the son of a weaver. He was famous for his improvements in cutlery and typefounding. His machines for weaving were broken up by the Lyonese population, and he was reduced to extreme poverty in consequence, but he lived to see his invention used in Lyons, and in St. Etienne and other places.

On the overthrow of Napoleon and the restoration of the Bourbon dynasty, great numbers of Englishmen visited France. It was about this time that the Jacquard machine was introduced to England, it is said, by a gentleman named Wilson, who had some of them constructed in Manchester, where they gained a footing in the manufacture of figured woollen fabrics.

About the year 1820 or 1821 the Jacquard machine was introduced into Coventry by Mr. Sawbridge, of Gosford Street, but improvements made in it by Mr. Goddard, of Bailey Lane, a very clever mechanic, led to a lawsuit between him and Mr. Sawbridge for innovation of prior right, but the case was decided against the claimant, and the right to use the machine was left open to the trade. At this period my father worked for Mr. Goddard.

About this date a large factory was built in St. Agnes Lane by Mr. John Dresser for Jacquard looms, and at the time of his death, in 1826, three of the large flats were filled by these machines. The satin jack and barrel were invented by Mr. Thompson, whom I knew personally, and this improvement added greatly to the value of the hand loom. About 1831 the first application of steam power to the driving of looms was brought out by Mr. Josiah Beck, who had invented the peg batten, but his machinery and factory were burnt down, as already related, by an infuriated mob, three of whom – Burbery, Sparkes, and Toogood, were condemned to be hanged, a sentence which was commuted to penal servitude for life.

Some facts which were inadvertently omitted from an earlier chapter when speaking of my own connection with weaving may be mentioned here.

On the site of the present residence connected with Messrs. Dalton and Barton's factory in King Street formerly stood a very old thatched cottage, in which my grandfather used to ply his trade as a weaving undertaker, with a single-hand loom, in connection with the old ribbon trade of the city. The house was a large and rambling old wooden-framed building of two stories, the upper lights of which were almost hidden by the thick and overhanging thatch. In this house were born my father and five of his brothers some thirty years or more before the close of the eighteenth century. Attached to the house was a piece of ground called the Cherry Orchard, in which it is said my grandfather cultivated the liquorice root (glycyrrhina glabra), and which was not thoroughly eradicated in my early days. Here also the old folks died, at an advanced age.

The old thatched cottage at the time of my apprenticeship was occupied by a carpenter and loom-maker named Thomas Wilkinson, father of Thomas Wilkinson, the eminent loom builder of the present day. He manufactured looms for Jacquard machines for Madam Dresser and Sons, in whose factory – though bound to my father – I served my seven years' apprenticeship. It was in Thomas Wilkinson's workshop that I first received the impulse to become a worker in wood.

I recollect when a child hearing my father and his brothers talk of an old piece of masonry in the form of a cross that stood on the hill near their house. The memory of this is preserved in the name of Hill Cross, which still attaches to that particular spot – the middle of an open space outside the city wall in a line from Upper Well Street to Abbot's Lane, which joins Barras Lane leading to Spon End. The north bank of the Cherry Orchard in its upper part was supported by thousands of ox horns and skulls packed together so tightly as to keep the high ground of the orchard from falling into the lane. The only place near from which these horns and skulls could have been brought in such large quantities was the old tannery in Upper Well Street, now done away with. At that time Abbot's Lane was a narrow and filthy thoroughfare from Hill Cross to its terminus in Spon End. In wet seasons it was almost impassable, bounded on either side by overhanging hedgerows beautiful in their wildness.

About eighteen months prior to my second marriage I engaged to work for Mr. Richmond Phillips, then recently started in business, under whom I earned good wages. He had by some means obtained a knowledge of my peculiar proclivities, and put the question to me one day as to my knowledge of botany and kindred matters. I was much surprised, for at the warehouse counter, as a rule, little else was talked except business, but here, notwithstanding our different social positions, I found a gentleman who could waive artificial distinctions and converse freely and unrestrainedly upon a subject that he seemed to take a great interest in – botany. On one occasion he presented me with nearly one hundred numbers of the *Edinburgh* and *Westminster* reviews, which contained articles upon scientific, social, political, historical, religious, and moral subjects, which were intensely interesting. There were also contributions upon the land laws and tenant right, and stirring details of the evils resulting from the operation of the law of primogeniture and entail, a law which hangs like a heavy mill-stone about the neck of this country, depriving the population of many of the benefits which the earth could give were the responsibility of its cultivation committed to the many instead of to the few.

Another intended benefit I received from Mr. Philips was the offer to have built for me a Jacquard loom for the making of brocaded ribbons, the cost of which was to be repaid out of my weekly earnings. The mounting or fitting up of the loom I did myself, in order to secure as nearly as possible perfection in its working parts. The batten was of a special construction, patented by an eminent firm, and great things were expected of it, but it was disappointing. I had got the silk into the loom, and was ready to produce a pattern, when it was found that the structural part of the batten – that part of the loom which carries the shuttles – was inadequate for the purpose required, and for twenty weeks I was in this dilemma. The silk was spoilt in the loom, and the order for the goods that were to be made in it was rescinded. In a manner I could not interfere, as the loom was not of my ordering, but when I found that the builders had done all they could without surmounting the difficulty, I bade them leave it and let me try what I could do. In the course of two or three days it was in working order. The peculiarity of the loom consisted in the introduction of a new form of motion for which the builders had received a patent. They wished to see the alterations I had made to make the loom workable, but I refused, unless they compensated me for the trouble of making their patent a marketable commodity, to explain what I had done. Nothing, however, came of this patent.

Before I could realise any substantial advantage from working this loom trade declined, and wages came down rapidly. This the weavers in a body resisted, and the struggle culminated in the terrible strike and lock-out of 1860-1. It is computed that nearly 14,000 people were at that time dependent upon the silk trade in Coventry and district, and the consequence of this dispute was that all looms, whether on hire or purchase, were called in by the manufacturers, who were in a great measure determined not to give in to the demands of their hands, but on the other hand were determined to compel them to work for weekly wages on the factory system.

The factory system of that time was most vile, legislation on the subject being very meagre. Only those who have had experience under the system which embraced the indiscriminate association of adults and young people of both sexes with but little restraint, in a tainted atmosphere, can tell of the moral depravity that like a poisonous miasma enervated, if it did not utterly destroy in too many instances, the respect owed by the workpeople to themselves and to society.

Although the Tories made capital out of this depression in the ribbon trade and averred that the Cobden treaty with France was the ruin of the trade, no greater deception could have been used to further their political ends, for they well knew that other causes than the French treaty were at the root of this terrible stagnation. The most important cause was the revised American tariff, which practically excluded English manufactured goods from American ports by duties varying from 40 to 60 per cent. This also affected both France and Switzerland, who had, like England, largely depended upon the American trade for the sale of their goods. Another important cause of the decline was the silkworm disease in France and Italy. Prior to 1846 the production of silk in France alone had averaged 24,000 tons of cocoons, yielding over 2,000 tons of silk annually, but in 1865 the quantity had gone down to less than one-fifth of that amount. This disease, by enormously enhancing the price of the raw material, practically closed the demand for silken goods as an article of adornment. No wonder then, with the principal market closed by prohibitory duties, together with the failure in the silk crops increasing the price of the raw material almost to a famine price, that silken goods should go out of fashion simply because they were beyond the means of the millions who had previously used them for dress and ornament.

This strike and lock-out, combined with the cessation of the fashion for wearing ribbons, in the course of a few years reduced the number of Coventry manufacturers from eighty to less than twenty, and caused a decrease in the population of the city of over five thousand. Hundreds of looms, the first cost of which was from £40 to £100, were sold to brokers for a mere song to enable weavers to obtain the means to sustain life, and were ultimately broken up for what the wood and metal would realise. The new loom upon which I had bestowed so much trouble was called in and placed in a factory, and I was out of employment for more than a year. No work could be procured. Ribbons, as articles of adornment, were superseded by gimp trimmings, lace, and feathers.

During this period we subsisted upon the little capital saved during more prosperous times. Eventually, as with many others, the last penny was spent, with no prospect of obtaining another meal. At this juncture my younger brother came to inquire how we were getting on, and found my wife in tears, and myself half mad through not being able to work (owing to physical incapacity) with other distressed weavers on the common lands for sixpence and a quarter loaf per day. My brother was the agent under an inscrutable Providence whereby we were prevented from again knowing the want of a morsel of bread. From his own too limited store for many weeks he supplied money to keep us from the suicidal act of parting with our only remaining loom – the future means of subsistence. Although when at work I had subscribed a tenth of my earnings to the Trades' Union fund for the support of the lock-outs, yet when I found myself without the means of getting employment, not one farthing ever came back from this source. Not being quite destitute, like some, through improvidence, it was thought we could forego the money to which we were entitled. I did not apply to the parish, and was taunted with being too proud to ask for help, and therefore deserved the neglect of the Trades' Union officials.

Just at this time two new looms were imported from St. Etienne, one for Mr. Richmond Phillips, and the other for Messrs. Caldicott. These looms were entirely strange to the experience of Coventry weavers, both in the character of the machinery and the manipulation of the tissue. By some means, of which I am still ignorant, I was recommended, as a man well used to the technicalities of Jacquard machinery, to take charge of Messrs. Caldicott's loom. Being an entire stranger to Mr. Caldicott, enquiries were made of Mr. Eli Green, in one of whose houses I lived, as to my character and fitness to undertake this work. Mr. Green stated that I might suit, but that a year's rent was owing, in consequence of there having been no work. He had not asked me for a single payment during the time, believing that I should pay when opportunity served. This difficulty was overcome by Mr. Caldicott proffering to pay the rent and to retain my loom as security until the liability was cleared off. To the honour of Mr. Green, the quarterly notice that would have prevented me from leaving in order to accept this engagement, so fraught with importance in this terrible crisis, was dispensed with.

Prior to the sudden collapse of the ribbon trade, I was looking forward to a brighter future. My wife was well versed in the art of weaving, and being thrifty in household management, we had been able to put by a little money to meet probable losses. Little did I think that before I could again earn a living my losses from the outlay of savings and liabilities incurred would have reached two hundred pounds, a sum which I have never again been able to make good. Terrible as was the ordeal, I found a source of strength in my wife; except for her patient and plodding endurance, I must have given up all hope of ever again being able to regain lost ground.

Such a general state of extreme poverty was never known in Coventry before. Many weavers with large families were compelled to make raids upon the field camps of turnips and potatoes to save their children from utter starvation. The Workhouse was filled to overflowing; the rates went up enormously to supply the out-door poor with a scanty pittance; shopkeepers were on the verge of ruin, and no credit could be obtained for food; the manufacturers one after another were going into bankruptcy, and nearly eight hundred houses were soon without tenants. Hundreds of families emigrated by means of help to America and the Colonies, and at home, besides the relief works on the commons, soup kitchens were opened to appease the famished people who could not get bread. A sheet of verses was circulated through the town, composed by Thomas Rushton, a compositor on the *Coventry Herald*, a parody on Tom Hood's poem 'The Pauper.' This song was sung by bodies of distressed weavers, who marched in procession through the streets, or when they proceeded to and from their work on the commons. The following are the verses:–

THE WEAVER

Who is that man coming up the street,
With wearied manner and shuffling feet,
With a face that tells of care and grief,
And in hope seems to have lost belief?
His wife, I know, has a face as wan;
They've a home, 'tis true, but the furniture's gone,
And when the children the father meet,
They ask him with tears for something to eat.

But take no heed of his sighs and groans,
His careworn face and agony moans,
For wickedness past he now atones;
He's only a weaver whom nobody owns.

He's coming, no doubt, from breaking stones,
With saddened heart and aching bones;
But why should he grumble? he gets good pay,
A loaf and sixpence every day.

This world is a world of change, all know,
And exempt he cannot expect to go,
And the change to him perhaps may be
A blessing he cannot plainly see.

But take no heed, &c.

He thought if he worked both night and day
He ought to receive equivalent pay.
He's evidently an inconsistent man,
Who don't understand the commercial plan
Which in wages rules their rise or fall,
So deserves his miseries one and all.
His presumption, of course, deserved that he
Should experience want and poverty.

But take no heed, &c.

Political economy now must sway,
And say when a man shall work or play.
If he's wanted, his wages may be high;
If he isn't, why then he may starve and die.
Suppose he may have seen better days,
That should not be a meed of praise;
In poverty's toils he now is bound,
So crush him, grind him, into the ground

But take no heed, &c.

You who may give him a bit of work,
Don't let pity within you lurk;
Remember he's down, and can't refuse
To receive in return whatever you choose.
And if you employ him, don't mend the price;
He's starving, you know, and has no choice;
And give him to weave the worst of silk,
For it's only a weaver's time you bilk.

But take no heed, &c.

Give him likewise the weighted shute;
It's only his winding account you loot,
And he may perhaps, when his warps are out,
Be minus a pound to put him about.
Don't spare him, pray, on the score of pity;
Teach him that those he may strike will owe
Him a debt and return him the blow.

But take no heed, &c.

Tho' he put in a new pattern, and has to pay
For compensator, harness, and slay;
Though he lose a fortnight in anxious toil,
And has to pay for the steam the while;
Tho' he often plays for the want of shute,
And has plenty of 'knock downs,' too, to boot;
Tho' threads come down from the roll by the score,
And besides a hundred difficulties more.

But take no heed, &c.

Take no heed of the precept, 'Love one another,'
A weaver's a weaver, don't think him a brother;
And to do unto others as they should do unto us
Is a figure of speech that requires no fuss.
All should be selfish – they need not bestow
A thought on the duties to others they owe;
Need not strive to assist their poor fellow-man,
But endeavour to get for themselves all they can.

But take no heed of his sighs and groans,
His careworn face, his agony moans,
For wickedness past he now atones;
He's only a weaver, whom nobody owns.

It was fortunate that at this crisis I was chosen to manage Mr. Caldicott's new loom. For doing so I was to receive eighteen shillings a week with house and gas light. As a result I was soon able by frugal economy to clear off the debt due to my brother, but not to pay for the redemption of my loom, to which extravagant and to my mind useless alterations were made that rendered it impossible for me to redeem it at the extra value that was put upon it in consequence. It was probably thought I had been well paid for the loom, by the £10 that had been advanced to pay off my arrears of rent; the loom cost nearly £50 only a few years previously. The French looms that had been imported did not fulfil the expectations that were formed of them. The way they were made necessitated the clearing and sizing of the silk, for which process there was no machinery in Coventry, and after making a few choice patterns in five colours for exhibition, and an elaborate portrait of the Rev. Mr. Widdrington and a view of St. Michael's Church, of which he was vicar, it was found that to prepare the silk by hand was unprofitable. I had the privilege to use the loom after this in accordance with trade usage, and to work it for other warehouses, accounting to my employers for the wages earned, they retaining the difference between the amount earned and the amount of my wages as compensation for the use of the machinery. This state of things continued for several years, but it was very unsatisfactory. I was not in a position to extricate myself, not having any loom of my own. The only hope was in saving what little I could with a view to purchasing another loom. If I had had no other hobby to engage my attention beyond working, eating, and sleeping, I must have given up. But in the Summer time, when the labour of the day was done at five o'clock, I was off to the lanes and fields to hunt up some fresh specimen of plant or moss, or land and fresh-water shells, of which I was getting a goodly collection. To this love of natural products, the hunting after which gave me plenty of fresh air, do I in a great measure ascribe the fortitude with which I was able to bear up against the many difficulties and trials that beset us in life.

X

A Visit to France

The Society of Arts and the Paris Exhibition – Chosen as a delegate – Arrival at Paris – Sights of the city – French workmen – Their pleasures – Visit to St Etienne – Lyons – Geneva – Lake dwellings – Meeting Coventry friends – Berne – Basle – Back to Geneva – Disappointment – At Paris again – The British Commissioner – Adieu to France – A rough sea passage – Home again – Reports – French and English weavers – Causes of the Depression – Emigration from England and the Continent.

IN 1867 the Coventry Market Hall was opened, and the event was commemorated by an exhibition. To this I contributed a collection of recent shells and fossils, together with my microscope, which was shown in a carved oak case, imitating Gothic architecture. The exhibition was a great success, and resulted in a surplus of over a thousand pounds. At the same time the Universal exhibition in Paris was being held, and the Society of Arts in London had raised a fund to enable English artisans connected with various trades to visit Paris and report with a view to comparing the conditions of labour and production in the two countries. A grant of £7 was made from the Society of Arts to pay the fare of each working-man delegate sent on their behalf, and £3 more was promised when a report was handed over to the Society. A request was made by the Society of Arts to Coventry to recommend two 'fit and proper' workmen from each of the staple trades – the ribbon and watch – to undertake the duties of this visit. Mr. Lawrence Saunders Booth and myself were chosen to represent the ribbon trade, and Mr. Stringer and Mr. Gregory, employés of Messrs. Rotherham and Sons, represented the watch trade. I had to get the consent of my employers before undertaking the commission, but as trade was at a low ebb, leave of absence for a month was readily granted.

On September 8th, 1867, we started for London, where we had an interview with the secretary of the Society of Arts, Mr. P. L. Foster, and were furnished by him with recommendations to the British Commissioner at Paris to accord us all the help he possibly could. Having transacted our business with Mr. Foster, we set out for Dover, reaching that town about seven o'clock at night. We started by the steam packet for Calais, landing there about nine o'clock on Sunday morning. On reaching Paris, we made our way to the lodgments in the Rue Rapp, temporary buildings put up for British workmen visiting the exhibition. Here we engaged an apartment with sleeping accommodation for which we paid five francs per week. We also exchanged our English money for French. Not having tasted food since we left Dover, we recruited the inner man at a Café close by, where we fortunately found an English waitress. On Monday morning we crossed over to the exhibition from our lodgings facing it, and took a weekly ticket to view a series of departments and out-buildings that covered thirty-five acres of land. After traversing many of these apartments to acquaint ourselves with the bearings of the place, we went to the British Workmen's Hall, the president of which, Mons. Haussoullier, presented us with a copy of the official catalogue and provided us with an 'interpreter' (a book containing French sentences such as visitors would be likely to use with their English equivalents) which enabled us to find our way about through the interminable maze of apartments. For the first week we studied hard to obtain a knowledge of the machinery there used in the weaving trade, the mode of production and cost, and the weavers' prices for making as compared with the prices paid in Coventry, taking copious notes to enable us to make our report. We visited most of the sights of Paris, as well as the exhibition.

When not engaged at the exhibition we threaded the wide avenues that intersect Paris, crossing the Seine in every direction by means of fine bridges of which there are more than twenty within the city. We visited the Hotel des Invalides, with its two fine Churches, the magnificent gilded dome of the more recent edifice, 323 feet high, visible from any part of Paris, serving as a landmark to the stranger. Though designated 'hotel,' this establishment is really a gigantic military hospital, providing accommodation for seven thousand invalids. An asylum for military invalids had existed since 1596, prior to which date disabled French soldiers had no other resources than the charity of monastic establishments. The foundations of the present building were laid in 1670, and the main building and the first Church were finished about 1706. Another object that interested us greatly was the wondrous Cathedral of Notre-Dame, with its chapels and confessionals, the work of nearly a thousand years. The precise date of the original foundation is not known, but it appears certain that a temple existed here in the time of the Romans, the foundations having been discovered in 1711. The present structure was erected between 1010 and 1407, having gradually advanced towards its final state of perfection. The west front especially is superbly grand and magnificent, the towers rising on each side of the great rose window to a height of 204 feet. The length of the interior is 390 feet, and the width at the transepts 144 feet. The general style of the architecture is very early and very pure pointed, those parts that were built in the 14th century being closely copied from what previously existed. The superlatively grand altar at the east end, illuminated by hundreds of candles, is the most exquisite the human mind could conceive. One would scarcely imagine that the Madeleine from its external appearance was a place of worship. It is built in the form of a Grecian temple, reminding the visitor of the Birmingham Town Hall in its external appearance. The internal dimensions, exclusive of the thickness of the walls, are 300 feet long by 130 feet wide and 90 feet high. Its interior is grand and solemn in the extreme, notwithstanding its magnificence owing to the lavish introduction of rich marble in the walls. Chapels and confessionals are ranged along the sides, and the high altar at the east end by Marochetti is surmounted by a figure of the Virgin being carried to heaven by a group of angels. There are also some exquisite paintings on the walls. The first stone of the edifice was laid in 1764. One of the most interesting places visited was the Hotel de Cluny, in which are stored many valuable and rare mementoes of the middle ages and of the Merovingian kings who ruled France after the Roman Empire was broken up. An interest attaches to this place on account of the fact that it is built upon the site of the palace of the ancient Governors of Gaul. The only remains of the ancient palace left are the baths with walls of immense thickness. The frigidarum or cold bath was 65 feet by 45 feet, and the tepidarum or warm bath is still entire. These rooms are filled with ancient monuments and statues illustrating early French history. The museum contains nearly three thousand articles of the utmost value to the antiquary, and of so rare a character that their loss could never be replaced. The present building was erected in 1505, and is regarded as one of the finest remains of the ancient mansions of Paris. After passing through the hands of many tenants, it eventually fell into the possession of a gentleman who has formed the present valuable collection.

The Place de la Concorde is perhaps the largest and grandest square in Europe. In the centre is the famed Luxor obelisk – a granite monolinth, 172 feet in height, standing on a pedestal composed of four blocks of granite, each of which is 12 feet by 5 feet by 2 feet – erected on the spot where in the reign of terror the guillotine shed its torrents of blood. From January 21, 1793, to May 3, 1795, more than 2,800 persons were executed here. The Place connects the gardens of the Tuilleries with the Champs Elysées, which is interspersed with gardens and broad avenues for nearly a mile. In a straight line, looking up the Avenue des Champs Elysées towards Neuilly, stands the Arc de Triomphé, 152 feet high by 137 feet broad, the centre arch being 90 feet by 45 feet, and said to be the largest single arch standing.

To describe the churches, the public and monumental buildings that beautify Paris – most of which are open to the public, with permission to inspect the treasures they contain – would need a volume. Paris seems a city of palaces. In the heart of the city every one is bent on pleasure. The industrial part of the people are hidden away in the lower and more crowded parts. Even among this class the love of pleasure dominates their lives, the café and the restaurant being the places most delighted in during leisure. A good deal of spare time is spent there, especially at meals. There seems to be among the majority of the French workmen, allied with a taste for the artistic and beautiful in their daily avocations, a total absence of that desire for domestic comfort and of the union of the family at meal times which the Englishman prizes so highly. I was told, however, that there was springing up a tendency to emulate Englishmen in this respect. Something may be said in extenuation of the life they lead when the temptations that beset them are considered, and when we remember their laxity of morals. Every inducement is offered by legal enactments to break through the moral law that in England binds together husband and wife.

During our stay in Paris the Fête of St. Cloud was being celebrated in the Park attached to the Palace there, and having a desire to witness the pleasures of the people on one of their greatest holidays, we went by boat to the Palace. The repelling sensations aroused at the sights witnessed will never be forgotten. There were no less than two hundred thousand people congregated. It seemed a perfect Saturnalia, an orgie of uncontrolled passion, where all could exercise their propensities according to their own sweet will.

My colleague had been reared among the Independents, and it was a most terrible shock for him to see a day so sacred desecrated by being used for such vicious purposes. Although perhaps I did not look upon the affair in a religious light, I was equally anxious to get away from such a scene of vice. We left almost immediately, without availing ourselves of the opportunity of making an inspection of the historic old Palace, with its rich stores of treasures and works of art which I had been longing to see. The Palace dates from the earliest period of French history, the name being a corruption of St. Clodoald, grandson of Clovis, who took refuge here in a wood from the vengeance of his uncle Clotaire, who to secure the throne for himself had murdered his brothers. Clodoald, being canonised after his death, the former name of the place 'Novigentum' was altered to its present appellation.

We returned to Paris by the next boat to ruminate over the Sunday scenes left behind – very different to those with which we were familiar in England. In returning we passed the Church of the Madeleine, where, notwithstanding that it was Sunday, workmen were engaged repairing the stone steps leading to the interior. On the side basement, defiling as it were the courts of the temple, were exposed for sale on a long canvas framework an immense number of photographs, many of which would not have been tolerated in Holywell Street in its worst days.

On reaching our lodgments we found a letter awaiting us requesting us to visit St. Etienne in the South of France, a distance of between three and four hundred miles, and then to visit Lyons, Geneva, and Basle. We immediately wrote home to our committee for a remittance to enable us to comply with this unexpected request, as our private resources were inadequate for such a journey. In addition to expenses of travelling, we should have to engage an interpreter. A telegram urged us to start immediately, and promised that a sufficient sum of money should be sent to cover expenses. On the faith of this promise we started for St. Etienne, leaving instructions with the President of the British Commission to forward us any sum that might be sent from Coventry; but no remittance came.

St. Etienne is a very ancient and interesting city, containing nearly sixty thousand inhabitants, with a suburban population of several thousands more. There is a very extensive factory of small arms here under Government inspection, which turns out beautiful specimens of workmanship, and which gives employment to a great number of people. There are also many cutlery establishments, the steel for which is made chiefly from Scottish iron. The coal fields, too, are very productive, yielding iron as well as coal – the only place in France that I know of where both can be worked together at a profit.

The district of St. Etienne, St. Chamond and Besançon in the time of

Julius Cæsar were inhabited by the Gallic tribe of the Sequanii. Many fierce battles were fought in the vicinity between the Roman Emperor and the ancient tribes who inhabited the country in the attempts to conquer this fertile province of Gaul, where the orange, the vine and other fruits flourished in a wild state. Its rude villages formed a veritable paradise, compared with the desolate and ofttimes snow-capped mountains that shut them in on either side. The remains of the old Roman fortifications of this province are still traceable, particularly at St. Chamond, a silk weaving district seven miles north-east of St. Etienne.

It was most interesting to visit a place so memorable in Frankish history. The town dates from before the advent of Christianity. Under the rule of the Sequanii, it was a popular and thriving province, controlled by the sacerdotal and governmental authority centred in the ancient Druidical system which ruled, religiously and politically, the people under its sway.

The modern town of St. Etienne contains many beautiful structures, not the least noteworthy being the warehouses of the manufacturers of silk goods, who at one time employed more than twenty thousand looms in the production of silken and velvet fabrics. At the time of our visit, however, not more than three or four thousand looms were employed owing to the disastrous state of that trade.

At St. Etienne, as at other places throughout France, is an institution called the 'Prudhomme' Society or Council of wise men, which exercises authority over industrial affairs. Its object is to prevent strikes and dissensions in trade matters. All disputes are settled by a joint committee of employers and working men chosen from the general council. The general council itself settles all disputes under a certain sum, and from their decision there is no appeal. For disputes exceeding a certain sum appeal is allowed to a higher tribunal. We met with courteous treatment from the manufacturers, who afforded us every facility for carrying out our investigations into the trade of the district, and gave us an introduction to the Technical School or Trade Museum, an institution for the practical education of skilled hands.

Persons employed in the weaving trade are obliged to hold the certificate of capacity granted by this school before they have the right to be possessed of a loom. The course of instruction comprises amongst other matters the following – The life and habits of the silk-worm and its various modes of culture, the process of spinning silk from the cocoon, the principles which regulate the number of fibres required from various well-known breeds of silk-worms to make threads of certain sizes and thicknesses, varying from No. 1 to No. 24 to suit the various dyes, the coarser threads being used for aniline, and the finer for the dyes which add substance and weight to the thread. Each student is supposed to acquire as much knowledge of design as he is capable of receiving, and the ability of transferring designs to the draft. The paper upon which the designs are 'drafted' is closely ruled with lines forming minute squares, each square corresponding to a separate thread in the woven tissue lifted or refused by the hooks of the Jacquard machine. The number of hooks varies according to the nature of the fabric required, from two to twelve hundred. When a student has passed satisfactorily through a course of instruction at this school, or has gained a certain number of points, he receives a certificate which entitles him to acquire a loom of his own, while unsuccessful students are only allowed to act as helps to others, who, under the law of the Prudhomme Society, claim from them one-third of their earnings for the liberty of using their machinery. Some idea of the extent of certificate holders may be formed when it is stated that out of over twenty thousand looms engaged in the trade, only 2,300 were owned by manufacturers.

The river Rhone runs very near, and after passing Nimes, empties itself into the Mediterranean by two mouths forming a delta. Having completed our business here and visited the workshops of the loom makers, and no remittance from home reaching us, we started for Lyons on our way to Geneva. We wrote home again asking the local committee to send by a certain date a remittance to Geneva, as we should not be able to proceed further without money. We did not make a long stay at Lyons, though we remained a day longer than we ought to have done in the hope of hearing from home, but here again there was no remittance. We were enabled to visit the gardens and grand square that had been erected to the memory of the Girondists, who were massacred here during the Reign of Terror.

Lyons contains over a million of inhabitants, and ranks next to Paris in importance, being the second city of the empire. Its staple trade is the manufacture of rich silken velvets, broad silks for dresses, and velvet ribbons, engaging, in a prosperous time, nearly one hundred thousand looms. The trade at the time of our visit was in a most distressed condition. Nearly two-thirds of the looms were standing idle, and as a result of such a condition of things hundreds were literally starving. It is calculated that in good times of trade the ribbon industry was the means of support for families whose numerical aggregate was between two and three hundred thousand men, women and children. Having gained all the information we could respecting the trade of this place, we took train for Geneva. The route lay in the direction of the valleys as far as practicable, but when we neared the frontiers of Switzerland and entered the mountain range that connects that country with France, the railroad in many places was scooped out of the mountain side, so that we could see the river Rhone over a thousand feet below, meandering through the defile like an azure blue ribbon. We passed one place where only the year before a whole train had been precipitated into the valley in consequence of the road being blocked by a landslide from the mountain side. The loss of life was terrible, amounting to nearly two hundred persons. Soon after passing this place, the road merged into the valley of the Rhone, and brought us in sight of Geneva.

Geneva is situated at the outlet of lake Leman, where the Rhone begins its outlet from the lake, skirting the city in a broad, rapid and shallow stream. The scenery on either side in places is grand beyond description. Mountain masses enclose the lake, which is about fifty-nine miles long, with an average breadth of nine miles. The general depth in mid-stream is about 1,200 feet, but in places it is much more. Its water is azure blue and clear as crystal, and daily trips are made by steam boats to the various places of interest on its banks, as far as the castle of Chillon at the east end of the lake, so forcibly described by Byron in 'The Prisoner of Chillon.' The chief water supply of the lake is derived from the glaciers of Mont Blanc, which at a distance of sixty miles from Geneva can be plainly seen by means of an ordinary telescope. The city of Geneva with its history is most interesting – a kind of borderland which early Roman Catholic supremacy could not easily pass over – a stronghold for those who differed from the Church of Rome. A terrible blot, however, rests upon its otherwise fair fame in the betrayal to the stake by John Calvin of the celebrated Dr. Michael Servetus, who was endeavouring to pass through the city in disguise. The attempt was known only to Calvin, to whom Servetus had entrusted the secret. Calvin however had him apprehended, and given over to the authorities in whose court Calvin himself acted as informer, prosecutor and judge, and contrary to Swiss law Servetus was condemned to be burned alive for his advocacy of the Arian confession of faith. The infamous sentence was brutally carried out October 25th, 1553. I had a most earnest desire to see the building in which Calvin preached his doctrine of Election and Reprobation, and therefore paid it a visit. Never shall I forget the repellent sensation that enthralled me in this ancient, black-pewed edifice.

It seemed as though a darksome and terrible stain still hung over it like a thick pall. Every part of the gloomy interior seemed to echo back the name of Michael Servetus. Hurrying out into the brilliant sunshine, with the glorious lake in full view and the mountain masses, cloud capped, on either side, it seemed in contrast like emerging from the region and shadow of death into the portal of a magnificent natural temple, the worship of which was that of the One only true God.

Some years prior to our visit, the Swiss lakes in consequence of a dry winter had sunk lower than had ever been known before, and the remains of ancient pile or lake dwellings were exposed above the surface of the water. Twenty-four of the remains of such settlements were found on the lake of Geneva alone, while in that of Neuchatel the relics of fifty separate villages have been discovered. The earliest of these piled works no doubt were of the stone age. The stakes appeared to have been sharpened by rude tools aided by fire. Stone axes in great numbers, rudely constructed vessels of clay badly burned, and implements of household use, all of the simplest construction, were found in the mud below. Some of these pile buildings were more modern than others. At Morges on the lake they were very extensive, and judging from their area, they might have accommodated a population of between two and three thousand. This settlement was supposed to be of a later age, as bronze and stone weapons for war, the chase, and domestic use were found associated together. All show the agency of fire in their destruction, which no doubt was accomplished by the Romans when they conquered the original tribes, and annexed this country with Savoy and Piedmont to their province of Gaul. We might at first be puzzled to account for the peculiar preference of our prehistoric forefathers for lake-dwellings, but when we remember that the earth was inhabited by gigantic wild animals, who preyed upon human beings in their savage and uncivilised state, we may easily conclude that man chose to live in caves and on the surface of lakes for security.

Geneva was the last place at which any remittance could reach us, but none came, and we were about to return to Paris by the shortest route, when the two watch trade representatives from Coventry – Mr. Stringer and Mr. Gregory – unexpectedly came to our hotel. On being informed of the difficult position the Coventry committee by their neglect had placed us in they were much annoyed, and generously offered us the means to continue our journey to Basle, and thence back to Paris, where if we found no money awaiting us they offered to deposit in the hands of the British Commissioner a sufficient sum to meet our wants. We gratefully accepted their offer, and after spending a few hours with our townsmen, we took train for Basle. Reaching Berne late at night, we found that our ticket at the fare we had paid was not available until morning. We were therefore obliged to look about for food and shelter for the night. After some little trouble we procured both, but no rest. The concern on which we were supposed to sleep was a hard wedge with a bed-like covering for counterpane, in striking contrast with the comfortable English beds or the spotlessly clean sheets at Geneva. However, we made the best of it, and stripping off the huge hard wedge, we used the covering instead as a substance upon which to lie. This allowed us to recline in a more natural position, and glad indeed we were when morning relieved us from our night's unrest. As an agreeable set off to this, we found our host and hostess kind and hospitable at the breakfast table; we enjoyed the meal very much, and the charges were moderate. We had no time to spare to see much of this important old Swiss town, but the frequency with which the bear – presumably forming part of the civic arms – was everywhere prominently displayed, reminded us of the old armorial escutcheon of the Earls of Warwick – the bear and ragged staff.

While we were waiting at the station for the Basle train, two chamois hunters – in picturesque costumes, with rifle and alpine stock, each bearing a chamois killed in the chase slung over his shoulder – made their appearance, and created quite a sensation among some of the travellers who had never previously seen such a sight. Among the passengers were an English family taking this route for Germany, who, hearing from our conversation that we were English, spoke to us and furnished us with some English newspapers, which gave us most interesting and welcome news from home.

Berne stands in the valley of the Aare, and is nearly surrounded by that river at an elevation of 1,700 feet above the level of the sea. From this town can be seen about twelve snow-capped peaks, some of them reaching the height of 10,000 feet – a sublime and wondrous sight. It is interesting to know that these mountains are geologically of comparatively modern date. Tertiary fossil shells have been found where the strata joins the azoic, and shells and remains of former life exist in the various strata lower down. These immense peaks of granite and syenite have been upheaved when in a molten state, pushing up what were once level plains to heights exceeding 8,000 feet.

The railway from Berne to Basle is particularly noticeable on account of the long tunnels that pierce the mountains at their very base, and which are marvellous specimens of engineering skill. Very glad we were to get clear of them. The constant jolting and the sound of rushing water was anything but pleasant to persons used to the steady travelling on English railways.

Basle is about eighty miles from Berne by rail, and is divided by the Rhine into Great and Little Basle. It is more like an old German town than a Swiss, the German frontier being within three miles of the place, with fortifications in the immediate vicinity, giving to the town the title of the Gate of Switzerland. On the German side the view is bounded by the high hills of the Black Forest and the stupendous mountain masses of the Jura that connect Basle with Berne. Its population is about fifty thousand. Its staple trades are the manufacture of silk tissues and velvets, though the ribbon trade is the principal staple. It appeared to me that the language was a mixture of German and Swiss, but most of the well-to-do inhabitants speak French. Education here is compulsory, and the State pays for it. Basle may well be considered the most intellectual and scientific of the Swiss cantons.

Much more might have been noticed of this historic town if time had allowed. We were obliged to confine our observation to the business that had called us thither, and as soon as that was done we made our way to the station for the return journey to Paris. A cold and drizzling rain was coming on, which we soon felt the ill effects of. We were shivering fearfully when we reached the shelter of the station. I felt an ague fit coming on, and fearful as to the result with the prospect of such a journey, we procured a flask of brandy. The frequent use of this stimulant warded off the attack, and I was much better on reaching Geneva. The storm had followed us and appeared to have culminated here in terrific force. The huge waves on the lake rose and fell like the waves of an angry sea, washing away from the breakwater large stones as though they had been feathers, destroying or damaging the boats and vessels. A great number of people had congregated in the English garden overlooking the lake. We dare not approach too near the edge of the water, for had we done so the gale would certainly have carried us in. Such a sight we may never expect to see again. With some difficulty we found our way back to the hotel, where our two Coventry friends were awaiting us. Together we went to the Post Office to ascertain whether a money order had arrived, but we were disappointed. We were now in a fine fix. The extra fares we had been obliged to pay in our outward journey had exhausted all our available cash, and had we not fortunately met our Coventry friends again we should have been obliged to have had recourse to the British Council to enable us to reach Paris. After a hearty meal together and the exchange of good wishes we parted, we *en route* for Paris, and they for Neuchatel and Pontarlier, to which their business led them.

We reached Paris late in the afternoon, and secured for the night our old place at the lodgments. Next morning being the last day for which our tickets were available, we visited the exhibition and enquired if any remittance had arrived, but were still answered in the negative. We sought an interview with the British Commissioner, to whom we made our case known. He at once offered us the means to carry us to Coventry. I asked him what guarantee we could offer him for the repayment of the money, and laying his hands upon his heart he said, 'The honour of an Englishman.' Besides that he had our credentials from the Society of Arts.

I was not aware until it was too late to take advantage of the knowledge that Mons. Haussoullier, the British Commissioner, was a thoroughly scientific gentleman. He assured me that had he known earlier that I was interested in the geology of the district, he would have given me whatever assistance was in his power. The quarries of Montmartre, from which gypsum or plaster of Paris is obtained, were especially interesting, and from these he had obtained a large collection of rare geological specimens. Had I stayed a little longer I should have had an opportunity of looking over his collection and of seeing the numerous articles of vertu, minerals, fossils, and curiosities of every kind and character that he had brought together. At our departure he very kindly wished us a safe journey home, expressing at the same time a strong opinion of the neglect of the officials of the Coventry exhibition in urging us to undertake such a journey, and neglecting to supply us with the necessary means.

It was with much pleasure that we bade adieu to this city of palaces, with its fair and beautiful exterior and its temptations that beset the unwary on every hand. No city in the world possesses so much grandeur and beauty in its public buildings nor so many facilities for studying the beautiful in art, and but for the lax morality that pervades almost all classes of society, it would be *par excellence* the place where one could enjoy life's pleasures to the full. Among the higher classes there are those pre-eminent in science, art, literature, and music. But the counterpart to this is to be found in the homes of the clever and intelligent workmen of Paris in the old Faubourgs; and in the purlieus of the lowest class, the gamins, beggars, rag-pickers, and malefactors that swarm in the haunts of vice near the walls of the city. These classes were thinned out from the centre of the city by Napoleon the Third, and driven back to the fortifications at the extreme edge of the city, and even beyond. The old Rues and Faubourgs that at the time of the Revolution sent out their thousands of poor people are now known only by their past history, the sites of the dwellings formerly inhabited by this class having been converted into wide and fashionable streets all converging to the Place de la Concorde as a common centre. Paris at this time contained about two million inhabitants. The city was surrounded by fortifications, and these with the detached forts were over thirty-two miles in circumference.

We left Paris with means so limited, that we had no money to spare to even purchase a meal without incurring the risk of being delayed in our homeward journey from London. The journey from Paris to Dieppe through Rouen occupied about eleven hours. The stay at Rouen, an ancient and historical town, with a population of 102,000, which may be described as the Manchester of France, was too short to allow us even to leave the train, but as it was night, a time unfavourable for sight-seeing, we did not much mind. We reached Dieppe just in time to catch the night packet for Newhaven, and had a sea passage of about six hours. The conditions under which we started portended a heavy sea, and when we reached the open the waves were rough and boisterous. My colleague retired below, but I preferred to walk the deck in the fresh sea breeze, which seemed to bring new life. The sight, too, was glorious, for in the rifts of the clouds the moon peeped out lighting up the crests of the waves with a sheen of silver, and for the time I forgot everything but the grandeur and majesty of the sea. At times it seemed as if the waves would overwhelm us, as they broke with tremendous force against the sides of the vessel, occasionally sweeping the deck. But the sight was too grand to think of inconvenience, and when told to go down into the saloon I begged to be allowed to remain on deck, for it was perfect enjoyment, and besides, I wished to see all I could in so short a voyage. I did go down once to see how my companion was faring, but was soon driven back by the sight – and smell which would soon have reduced me to the condition of limp helplessness in which I found those who had gone below. I therefore hurried back with all speed to check the feeling of seasickness which was already coming on. As morn approached the heavy clouds began to disperse and the sea became somewhat calmer, but still there was no land in sight. I watched very anxiously for the first beams of the sun across the waves. At last they came seemingly from under a dense bank of cloud that was slowly rising. These first beams seemed to set the sea on fire. So vivid and gorgeous was the colour that tinged the crests of the waves that I felt forgetful of all the experiences through which we had passed in the ecstasy awakened by the sublimity of the scene. With the sun's rising we came in sight of land, the headlands of the Brighton coast looming very distinctly as we neared Newhaven, reminding me of the view of the Great Orme's Head from Rhyl. The cliffs appeared to have been cut perpendicularly down to the water's edge. It was a very interesting pastime to watch the coast line. The cliffs seemed huge and abrupt about Brighton, but not so high nearer Newhaven, which was reached about eleven o'clock in the morning. Changing our French money – what little we had left – into English, we made our way to the train that was awaiting the arrival of the boat, and reached London Bridge Station at about mid-day. We had then been over sixteen hours without food, and the question was how in our weak state we could stand another tiresome journey of nearly a hundred miles without further sustenance. We had proposed to ride second-class, because third-class carriages were not attached to all trains, but hunger led us to use the difference between a second-class and third-class fare to recruit ourselves by a hearty meal. This seemed to put new life into us. We had then to take our chance of finding a third-class carriage at Euston. We watched all the trains going out until, as night was coming on, a train started to which were attached third-class carriages, and brought us to Coventry in about four hours. Notwithstanding that it had all three grades of compartments, it was, contrary to custom in such cases, a fast train. At the end of the journey we were pleased to find ourselves at home once more.

We had written to our wives stating particulars of our embarrassed financial position, and desired that the letter might be shown to the agent at Coventry (Mr. Ebenezer Price), who had the management of this affair on behalf of the Exhibition Committee. This was some time before we reached home. My wife and Mrs. Booth – naturally in a state of anxiety – sought out the agent, and found him at his Mission Hall, Grey Friar's Lane, in the midst of a sermon. Waiting until the end of the discourse, they sought an interview with him, and showed him our letter. Evidently he did not view the matter so seriously as our wives had viewed it, for after reading the letter, he laughingly said, 'Oh! did you not know that your husbands were in pawn in Geneva? We are going to send some money to get them out and bring them home.' This statement put the women into a state of consternation, and they no doubt expressed themselves very strongly on the matter. The sum of five pounds that was sent to redeem us did not reach Paris until we were well on our way home. The Coventry Committee had some difficulty in getting the money back, and we lingered on for two years before we could get our claims settled.

One proviso in our agreement with the agent of the Coventry Committee was that independently of our report to the Society of Arts, we should compile a fuller report for the Coventry newspapers. After much trouble we compiled detailed accounts from personal observation and statistics of the past and present state of the silk industry in France; its Technical Schools, the working of the Prudhomme Society, and the Chambers of Commerce, which latter were very zealous in the protection of the silk trade, claiming it as exclusively their own. My colleague had allowed his report to appear in full, but not being satisfied with the treatment received at the hands of the Exhibition Committee, I merely sent in a report for the Society of Arts. When my short report appeared side by side in the Coventry papers with the detailed account of my colleague, the public wondered at the contrast. Private complaints were numerous, and I made known among my friends my reasons for witholding the report, and my determination, if our accounts were not speedily settled, to write to the papers explaining our actual position. The detailed report upon the French Silk Trade, its origin and progress; upon France as a silk-growing country, and the value of the manufactured article; an account of the laws enacted by the French Government for the protection of the silk trade, with an account of the Chambers of Commerce and local associations to enforce the due observance of the laws, would have been published had we been fairly dealt with, but it still remains in my possession, and its interest has now passed away.

Much was at one time urged by some of our manufacturers, and is even urged now in a few insignificant quarters, in favour of protection for the English silk industry, their plea being the heavy duty that the English have to pay on exports, while French goods are admitted free. Another point the manufacturers made against the English workmen was that the French artisans worked longer hours for less wages and required less money for their living than English artisans, and that under those circumstances English manufacturers could not profitably compete with their continental neighbours without effecting a serious reduction in the price of labour. My own personal experience was that for the few looms employed wages were equal and in many cases higher in France than in England for the same class of goods. The cause must lie deeper than the mere competition between the two countries. When in France I sought an interview with the President of the Prudhomme Society, to whom I put this question:– 'Is it your opinion, sir, that the treaty of commerce with England has been the immediate cause of the depressed state of your silk trade in St. Etienne and Lyons?' He very decidedly replied, 'No. The immediate cause exists in circumstances over which neither your country nor ours has any control. First, there was the terrible national loss through the failure of our silk crops, which so raised the price of the raw material as to exclude all profitable working of it into manufactured articles, and the result was that the enhanced marketable price was too high for ordinary customers. As a consequence the attention of the public was turned to something that would supersede the too expensive ribbon. The substitute was found in the use of lace, artificial flowers, and feathers. Thus, in a great measure, the use of ribbon ceased for purposes of adornment; the mass of the people will only purchase according to their means. Then again,' he said, 'America was the common market for the surplus production of Europe prior to the passing of the Morrell tariff, which at once, by its prohibitory enactments and high import duties, closed the market against the profitable introduction of all our manufactures. Thus you will perceive that as the use of any article of luxury is dependent upon its marketable value to bring it within the reach of the people, so it must follow that the world of fashion should seek some cheaper means of adornment. Hence the decadence of the silk industry arises from the use of cheaper modes of decoration.'

Then, both in France and England, an attempt was made by the introduction of cotton to cheapen the ribbon, but without success, while the price of labour for making this mixed article became so low that, even with a tolerable amount of work, enough money could not be earned to meet the requirements of the household; indeed, so general was this, that homes were continually being broken up through the inability of weavers to live by their labour. Their machinery was sold for a merely nominal sum, and artisans in numerous instances sought refuge in the Poorhouse. Many hundreds, seeing the inutility of such a desperate struggle for existence sold up their homes and with the proceeds emigrated to the United States or to Canada and Australia, lessening the population of Coventry by many thousands, and so immense was the influx of weavers into Paterson, U.S., that the population of that town soon doubled itself through the thousands pouring into it from England and the continent. It may be interesting to note that Paterson, which is now the seat of the American silk industry, has just been celebrating its centenary. The city was founded as a manufacturing town by the Society for Establishing Useful Manufactures (a corporation conceived by Alexander Hamilton in 1791), and is named after the Governor, William Paterson, who signed the Society's charter. When the first factory was built there were about ten houses within the limits of the present city, so that less than a century has changed the primitive wilderness into a bustling, thriving city of 80,000 inhabitants.

France suffered as much as or more than England, for if this country counted its unemployed by hundreds, those of the continent might be counted by thousands. The conclusion I came to from personal observation of the silk trade, both in France and England, was, even considering the enormous quantity that France could produce when the fashion of the world was in favour of ribbons, that England, with her limited means of supply, cheaper labour, and purer article, could still hold her own against foreign competition. It costs the continental manufacturer very much more to prepare the raw material for the weaver by sorting, sizing, and clearing the silk, whereas the bulk of this trouble is thrown upon the hands of the English artisan, who is obliged to employ subsidiary help to do that which the Swiss or French manufacturer pays for himself. English looms are much larger than French, and will make considerably more in a given time than theirs, thus in times of demand the English manufacturer is enabled to sell his goods cheaper than the French or Swiss makers.

I may here state that on reaching Paris from Geneva we found a letter awaiting us describing a public meeting at Coventry in favour of the adoption of the Free Library and Museum Act, and informing us that we had both been chosen as working-men representatives to act on the Committee. This was a source of gratification to us, and I still remain a member of that Committee. We did not have time to reply to the note, and our wives being under the impression that we were 'in pawn,' did not expect us home. When, therefore, I stepped in home on the Saturday night of our arrival, my sudden appearance rendered my wife for a time almost speechless with astonishment.

Having in due course reported ourselves to the Committee, we wrote and asked for a settlement of our affairs at once, as we were so much out of pocket in consequence of the extra journey the Committee had imposed upon us. We were put off from time to time, until at the last meeting, when the Committee was to dissolve itself and dispose of the surplus, we waited upon them personally. Some of the members no doubt were much surprised at the statements we made and the proofs offered in support of our claim, but all we got was the five pounds, less expenses, which had been returned from Paris, leaving us losers to more than double that amount.

XI

Visits to Northampton

Dissatisfaction with extent of the collection – Fortunate intimacy with an importer of shells – Making cabinets and cases – Wonders of shells – Thoughts suggested – Collection reduced to order – Visit to Northampton – Geological and other impressions of the district – Thoughts on the study of natural science – Pleasures and benefits resulting.

UPON fairly settling down to home life after visiting France, as related in the last chapter, I began to realise more fully than ever the scantiness of my collection of fossils and shells in comparison with what I had been permitted to see in France. Stimulated by the impressions received from the sight of the fossil remains of Montmartre and the splendid display of land and marine shells of the Maldives and the Pacific Ocean at the French Exhibition, I was determined not to be content with my limited collection, and accordingly directed my thoughts towards augmenting it. The idea took such complete possession of my mind that it became a sort of consuming passion, which I was powerless to resist. My limited means, however, seemed entirely to preclude the possibility of gratifying even to a limited extent the desire that had taken such a firm possession of my mind. At this juncture I had the good fortune to become acquainted with a large importer of shells, Mr. John Drayson, of London. This gentleman was simply a dealer, who knew nothing of the scientific names of the shells. The little knowledge I had of conchology interested him much, and he gave me every facility for increasing the size of my collection. At a reasonable cost he procured for me many rare and beautiful specimens of shells and corals, and during the many years I dealt with him I have purchased over two thousand specimens. I am sorry to say that for the last few years I have lost sight of him, but have learned on pretty good authority that his establishment was broken up as a consequence of his reckless and improvident living – he was known as 'Gentleman John' – and that he died in a workhouse. Many a fine specimen has he let me have for a nominal sum, for the pleasure of hearing the life history of his wares, and I should feel much regret to know that this report is true. With this accumulation came the necessity for safe storage, and for a time my spare hours were occupied in making wall cases and cabinets in which to stow the additional specimens.

Now that they are arranged, one never tires of contemplating their beauty. The perfection of form and the harmony of colour are so perfect that one is involuntarily led to wonder how forms of life so humble as the inhabitants of these structures should be able to build up or produce such strange homes, so intricately and delicately marked, to say nothing of the formation and fashioning of the structures themselves from the calcareous molecules contained in the waters in which these animals live and move and have their being. No wonder that the human mind, confronted even with a shell, should be bewildered in considering the questions of Cause and Effect. In what consists the power of production and development? An intelligent power seems to be shut up, contained in, or at all events to exist behind that proto-plasmic mass which, though not cognizant to our unaided senses, appears to be the basis or starting point of future life. Can we find the life-power in this jelly-like mass that apparently has no structural form? The scientist knows the chemical character of the constituent atoms, but what does he know of the atoms themselves – of their causation, or the advent of their existence? At every step taken in the descending scale are found life and form, tending from a lower to a higher development, but we can scarcely tell where life begins. It eludes our grasp, and we cannot at any point say with certainty that we have tracked it down to its beginning.

It took nearly two years of spare time to get my treasures safely housed in their new cases, and although all the wall space was occupied, I still could not find room enough, and so had to crowd them together irrespective of classes, orders, or genera, at the same time classifying them as completely as the limited space would permit. This, I am afraid, was much to the discomfort of my good wife, on whom developed the care of keeping the cases in good order.

About this time I received from an old friend who had left Coventry an invitation to visit Northampton. The principal inducement that led me to accept the invitation was the glowing account given of the fossils to be found in that neighbourhood. My friend lived at the village of Duston, within a short distance of the ironstone quarries, which on arriving I took an early opportunity of visiting. I obtained many specimens of shells. A large number of them, however, were encrusted with ferruginous sand, but others were as sharp in their outline as if they had been taken from a mould. The ferruginous beds in which these shells are found are in places covered by patches of the lower beds of the great oolite, but this occurs only in the Duston beds, which are much higher than the level of Northampton. These higher places comprise Hunsbury Hill and the Danes' Camp, through which a railway tunnel has been cut, affording a good section for observation. The shells in these Duston beds are all marine, and the beds no doubt were extensively worked by the Romans, whose mining instruments, with human remains, together with articles of pottery such as were used in the preparation of food, have been found in the deeper deposits. The skulls that have been found are in a good state of preservation, and can be seen in the museum. The strata is a singular formation, in many places being severed by extensive faults* or rents in the rocks. These 'troughs' have apparently been filled up by an after deposit, which are the sands containing the iron ore. They are supposed to be an equivalent to the Stonefield slate, but there seems to be but little resemblance between them, for here the shells of pecten, gervillia, and trigonia are embedded in a very pure ironstone matrix, and when released are as clean and sharp as if taken from a plaster mould. The fossils found here by R. Etheridge, F.G.S., were Astarte, Cardium, Bucklandi Pecten, Trigonia, Hillites vellotus, remains of Megalosaurus, a large reptile, and other remains.

A few miles from Northampton, leaving Kingsthorpe to the left, is the hamlet of Moulton, where the limestone of the lower oolite forms extensive beds. From these beds I obtained a great quantity of palate teeth, some fine specimens of a crustacean (Limulus), large numbers of a species of mussel akin to Gervillia, with various other shells, also some fine vertebral joints of a large saurian, and some very large cardiums in perfect condition beauti-

* 'The ultimate cause to which faults are generally ascribed is the cooling of the earth. This cooling causes a shrinking of the globe, to which the rigid crust adapts itself less readily than the interior, consequently a crumpling and folding of the crust ensues, causing cracks and rents in various parts. As a rule faults appear to be the result, not of a sudden and violent fracture, but of a slow and long-continued strain, to which the rocks of the earth's crust generally yield. This movement is believed to have been so slow that denudation could in many cases keep pace with it. Trough faults are faults slightly inclined to each other, and enclosing wedge-shaped masses, in which there has been sinking relative to the surrounding strata.' – *The National Cyclopædia*.

fully crenated. Returning on one occasion from Weston Flavel, where James Hervey ministered and wrote his 'Meditations among the Tombs,' which was published in 1746, I paid a visit to Kingsthorpe. A shaft for coal had been sunk through the lower beds of the oolite, passing through the lias (which is very thin here) to the trias. The water rose in this shaft to within 227 feet of the top, the entire depth of the shaft being about 976 feet. At that depth the mine was abandoned. The water was salt. The particulars of this search for coal were exceedingly interesting. As a result of this excursion I returned heavily laden with many new found treasures illustrating the geology of the neighbourhood.

About two years afterwards I visited the place again, the inducement this time being the sinking of two shafts in search of water for the supply of the town. The public supply had hitherto been obtained chiefly from the surface drainage of the higher lands of the neighbourhood, but as the population increased this proved to be inadequate. One of these water shafts was sunk within sight of that at Kingsthorpe, and cut through the same beds. The marlstone here was very hard and compact, dark green in colour, and full of fossil remains, very few of which, however, could be obtained perfect. I was told that a heading had been run from the bottom of the shaft to meet a fault in the hope of finding water, but this was not successful.

The other shaft was at a place called Sunnyside, within the grounds of the waterworks. In this lias fossils were found in abundance, both in the blue clay and thin limestone beds. Those from the clay were not very durable when exposed to the action of air, but from the limestone I obtained a fine and rather rare Ammonite (Turnerii) about nine inches across, with its beak or pointed end nearly perfect, also Ammonites Bifrons and others, with great numbers of Belemnites, one about eight inches long, with the chambered portion called the phragmacone very perfect, the nacreous formation of which is still intact as the receptacle for the ink bag, though that was not present.

The Northampton museum has a fine and unique collection of fossils and minerals of the district, and the archæological remains deposited here are of the most interesting character. The immense and valuable collection recently bequeathed to the town by the late Marquis of Northampton is not excelled by any of the kind I had hitherto seen. Their monetary value is set at over four thousand pounds.

Northampton has many natural beauties to interest the student, and is full of relics of past ages. Its monument to the memory of Eleanor, wife of Edward, on the London road, is one of the three that still remain intact, and is a beautiful specimen of the memorial architecture of the Middle Ages. It stands on elevated ground near the Dano-Saxon village of Hardingstone. From it is obtained a splendid view across the valley of the Nen of the town rising like an amphitheatre from the level of the river as far as the eye can reach. In one part of this lower level, where the Nen is now confined to its banks, the ground rises in regular escarpments, like the receding levels of an ancient sea beach. The view – looking towards Hardingstone, with Delapré Abbey to the right – is a sight not easily forgotten. At the entrance to the Cow Meadows from the town stands the celebrated well of Thomas à Beckett, which legend says was built by him to supply the town with water. The water until lately was supposed to be endowed with most miraculous powers in the cure of diseases. Over this extensive piece of land called the Cow Meadows the inhabitants claim a common right. At the time when the Romans made a settlement in the Midland Counties, it must have been a sheet of water and morass nearly a mile wide. At the lower end of these meadows the railway to Bedford crosses by a series of arches, and from the excavations here have been exhumed an immense quantity of human remains, together with those of horses and cattle and rude weapons of war, showing that a terrible conflict had taken place here in the far distant past. It is quite a common saying that these arches were built on a foundation of dead men's bones.

The environs of Northampton are studded with interesting relics of past ages. On the London Road at its lower end are the remains of Delapré Abbey, leading up the hill to the monument. On the other side of the town in Gold Street are the remains of the old Castle, nearly opposite to which stands the Church of St. Peter, a most quaint and remarkable building in the enriched Norman style, but here and there showing its Saxon origin. About five miles westward, leaving Duston to the left and nearing Althorpe, is seen to the right an extensive plantation of conifers, the largest assortment of species in the kingdom.

Althorpe, the seat of Earl Spencer, has a splendid collection of articles of vertu, an immense library of books, many of them of the rarest value, constituting, perhaps, the largest private collection in the country; a picture gallery of the old masters, with portraits of the family from the earliest date, occupying room after room until the eye seems to tire. The Church of St. Sepulchre on the north side is a round edifice, built by the

Knights Templars. It is one of the four that still remain, although it is supposed that the Templars had an establishment at Temple Balsall, near Coventry. Another interesting relic of the past is Abington Abbey, standing in beautiful, park-like scenery. Many abbeys and priories formerly existed, but have disappeared, and the seats of the country are very numerous. About nine miles from Northampton, through Billing, stands that splendid castle called Castle Ashby, the residence of the Marquis of Northampton, a most magnificent pile, dating from early Norman times, and still in a fine state of preservation.

In British times the district now called Northamptonshire was inhabited by three or four tribes, the principal one being the Coritanii in the south-western part, with the Debuni in close proximity to them, Catyeuclani in the south, and the powerful tribe of the Iceni to the east. The forests of Rockingham, Whittlebury, and Salcey at that time were continuous with each other, separated only by the clearings or settlements required by the tribes for permanent occupation. These have formed the nucleii for the existing towns, many of which date back a long time prior to Roman occupation. In various parts of the country burial grounds have been disturbed, the human remains from which prove indisputably the character of the inhabitants of prehistoric times. The terrible struggles between the ancient Britons and the Romans, and afterwards with the Saxons, and in still later times the conflicts of the Saxons with the Danes, are well marked features in the history of the county.

The next few years found me an annual visitor to Northampton, for I had enlarged my circle of acquaintances among friends with similar tastes to my own, who found pleasure in the study of Nature's handiworks. Some of them were prominent inhabitants of the town, and helped me materially in studying the features of the district, giving me facilities to enter the museum when it was closed to the public.

A working man is by force of circumstances precluded from studying geology in a scientific manner. To study the science properly, a man must have time and means at his command, and education as well as a natural inclination. Otherwise he would feel no interest in the wonderful formations from the Azoic and Laurentian, in which it is supposed that the first intimation of organic life appears, and then upward through the various deposits to the tertiary, the last formation of this wondrous series of rocks that form the crust of our globe, and in which we find the earliest record of the human race. Every change in the earth's history from whatever cause points most forcibly to the conclusion that life first commenced in its most simple form in the first deposits, and that life, whether vegetable or animal, has progressed through these various changes. Whole genera and species of animated creation have become entirely extinct and replaced successively by higher and still higher forms of animal and vegetable life, fitting the earth as it were by natural selection for the advent of the genus homo. At what time in the remote past man obtained his ultimate character as a sentient and thinking being may only be known by inference. The remains of man have been found with those of extinct mammals, and undeniable evidence of man's agency in connection with them proves that the period that has elapsed since his advent must not be reckoned by thousands, but millions of years. All geologists agree as to the immense lapse of time required to bring about the present condition of the earth's crust. When we attempt to form an estimate of the approximate age of the earth, we become bewildered in contemplating the immense eras that must have elapsed. As a first step let us consider the accumulation of desert sand at the statue of Rameses the Second, at Memphis. This has occupied three thousand two hundred years for the deposit of a depth if nine feet, four inches; the total accumulation further in the desert is forty-one feet, showing that this deposit must have been going on for a period of fourteen thousand years. Again, take the cataract of Niagara as an indication of the enormous periods necessary for the bringing about of natural changes. Leaving the base of the falls, the river rushes on with great velocity for seven miles through a ravine that has been excavated by the water in a table-land which terminates suddenly at Hamilton in a steep escarpment or inland cliff facing north towards Lake Ontario. Over the edge of this cliff it is supposed the falls originally commenced in early times, so that they have now receded seven miles. At the present rate of recession more than thirty-seven thousand years must have elapsed since the cataract was where the rapids are now, at the end of the table-land above mentioned. Again, the cutting of the Grand Cañon of the river Colorado, five hundred miles in length and in one place six thousand feet in depth, through the hardest rocks, must have occupied a period of time that would read like a fable. The six thousand years commonly assigned as the advent of the creation seem but as yesterday when compared geologically with the immense period of time required to form a stalactite of but a few feet in length, or the æons necessary to complete an astronomical cycle. Sir Charles Lyell assigns a period of two hundred and forty millions of years for the cambrian formation alone. All geologists agree that man must have existed on this earth countless thousands of years before the period assigned as his creation by the orthodox. Again, although astronomers reckon that the circumference of the earth's orbit round the sun is about five hundred and fifty-two millions of miles, yet they are aware that this mighty elipse may vary by about thirteen and a half millions of miles; we are thought to be at the present time eleven millions of miles short of what the elipse may be contracted to, and for this, Lyell states, 210,065 years would be required for the return to its normal condition. Lyell depended upon the calculation of Mr. Stone at the Greenwich Observatory.

These thoughts and speculations on cosmical phenomena, the antiquity of man, and his progressive stages of existence, are suggested to the thoughtful student. He is also struck with the order that reigns. At whatever point of limitless expanse the telescope be directed, order, design, and grandeur are evident in the myriads of systems, suns, worlds, and satellites unfolded to view. Well may these themes, the study of which is open to all, be esteemed some of the lights that have dispelled the shadows of an ardent and eventful life. Though chequered with many shadows, there has always been a silver lining to the heavy clouds that caused the shadows which threatened to overwhelm one. When the silver lining is seen, then does the heart unfold itself in thankfulness to the Giver of all good, from Whom alone providential aid comes at a time when human help looms in the far distance. Time has never seemed to lie very heavily on hand, for when in work I concentrated my energies on that, and when the working hours were ended recruited myself at the bench or lathe, or as opportunity served went into the lanes and hunted the hedgerows in quest of natural productions. The finding of a choice or rare specimen of shell or plant would enhance the pleasure a hundredfold. Although not able to write a learned dissertation upon the various subjects that have given me such intense pleasure, that pleasure has been increased by opportunities of sharing this acquired knowledge with others who may not have had the opportunities or the means of obtaining information upon subjects so foreign to an ordinary school education. Just at the close of the school period more than at any other is it necessary to lay a firm, moral and intellectual foundation for the future man. If the attention of the young mind at this period can but be engaged in the contemplation and study of the wonders that nature has in store for the willing student in every direction, a field of research is ever open that well compensates for the loss of those venial pleasures in which the young of both sexes in this age of sensational enjoyment too often indulge to the injury of both mind and body. The study of natural phenomena elevates the mind, enlarges the understanding, gives the student an insight into the mystery of 'cause and effect,' and enables him to look up through Nature unto Nature's God.

XII

A Visit to Yorkshire

Exhibition at Great Horton, Bradford – View of the town – Kirkstall Abbey – Comfortable lodgings – Public interest in the loom – Geological peculiarities of the district – An unpleasant incident – Altercation with the inventor of the Needle loom – Sequel – Evidence in a law case – Manufactories of Yorkshire – A grim historic association at Halifax – A large reservoir – A funeral custom – Attacked by robbers – Music at the Exhibition – A pleasant surprise – Reconciliation with the Exhibition officials – Returning home – Historical notes of Yorkshire.

DURING the years succeeding the visit to the continent I had to settle down steadily to work, but another change came. Early in August, 1870, I engaged myself to Mr. Thomas Stevens, celebrated for his artistic and beautiful specimens of brocaded book-markers and portraits woven in silk, to work a loom of six tiers of shuttles at an exhibition at Great Horton, one of the townships of Bradford. It was not for want of work that I took this engagement, but to satisfy a craving to visit the largest and most important county of England – Yorkshire.

This county is unique both in its history and the vigorous independence which characterises its people, and its immense coal and iron deposits render it peculiarly suited for extensive manufacturing industries such as those of wool, flax, and cotton which are carried on. The chief inducement to make this visit to Bradford was the fact that the place was within two miles of the celebrated Low Moor Ironworks, the largest in England, and redundant with fossils of the carboniferous formation.

On reaching Bradford, two miles had to be walked to the Exhibition. This was no easy matter with my heavy load, uphill too, and I felt faint and weary with the task. Having gained the top of the steep hill, the ground became more level, and the view of the valley of the Aire in which Bradford is located was grand. Horton stands several hundred feet above the level of Bradford, with an unobstructed view of the town across the valley, while on the left the ground continues rising to the table-lands of the moors.

Between Bradford and Leeds are the beautiful ruins of Kirkstall Abbey, their quietude and desolation offering a striking contrast to the activity of the industrial sites adjoining. Very near are large and extensive ironworks, and the beauties of the country also contrast strongly with the noise, din, and clang of the busy workers in iron here located. The back-ground is well clothed with trees, and the ground rises steeply from the valley to a considerable height like an immense screen to protect this beautiful abbey from further spoilation.

About mid-day on the day following my arrival I visited the Exhibition buildings – which were some new schools and premises for a Nonconformist body in the town – and had an interview with the President, Mr. Myers, who took me over this great pile of buildings devoted entirely to education. The corridors on the upper storeys opened into convenient class rooms for children and adults, each separate from the other, with every convenience, while underneath these was a great hall, which, when used for festive occasions, would seat four or five hundred people.

With the assistance of the President, lodgings were found at the house of a middle-aged person. She was not of the ordinary vulture type of landlady, but had a kind and sympathetic face, and owing to lameness was unable to labour beyond household duties. I was very glad to find a place so much like a home. My landlady was a member of the Nonconformist church which had built the schools where the Exhibition was being held, and therefore was known to Mr. Myers. She was a kind-hearted and cheery woman, towards whom I felt grateful for many acts of kindness received while under her roof. Her name was Elizabeth Holdsworth, of Well Close, Great Horton. There were three other boarders besides myself, one of whom, Joseph Darling, was a cousin and playmate of the immortal Grace Darling. It may be interesting to note here that Mr. John Kidd, the last of the survivors of the wreck of the 'Forfarshire,' rescued by Grace Darling and her father, died at Carnoustie, April, 1889.

The next day the loom came, and I had a most difficult task, owing to dearth of assistance, to get it together, but after it was started there was no lack of visitors, who wondered at such a strange piece of mechanism that could weave eleven different colours of silk into a bouquet of flowers, and form letters on the fabric that was being woven as though they were printed. Ofttimes the number of people round the loom was so great that I had to stop it working, or the barriers that protected it would have been broken down. Next to the loom was a stall well stocked with the richest and most elaborate of Mr. Steven's manufactures.

Just opposite my lodgings, about a quarter of a mile from the Exhibition, was a very abrupt and steep ridge of elevated land about two hundred feet above the level of Horton – one of those strange formations so frequent in Yorkshire. On the table-land of this ridge there was a seam of coal within a few feet of the surface, from three to four feet in thickness. When exposed to the air it would break up into cubes highly bituminous, making an excellent furnace fuel, but I could not find any indication, either in the roof or its bedding, of the vegetable life that had given it birth. For miles along the edge of this Wibsey slack, as it was called, I sought for its outcrop, but could find none. Grass land covered and hid away the outlying edges. It seemed a most singular freak of nature that this black, pitchy mass should be so located with no indication of its derivation from the plant life that must have been the primal cause of the deposit. No doubt by sinking deep enough some fine seams of coal and ironstone would be found. Leaving this moorland and descending toward Low Moor, abundant evidence in the shape of fossils could be found of the origin of the coalfield. I found here some fine specimens of several species of lepidodendrum, sigillaria, with its singular root stigmaria, calamites, well preserved specimens of pecopteries, neucopteries, annularia, and many others too numerous to mention.

The pleasurable experiences connected with this visit were somewhat marred by an untoward incident that occurred in the Exhibition. One day something happened to the driving power, which prevented me allowing the loom to work, and several times a self-important visitor had used very disparaging expressions respecting both the loom and its action, but as they were not addressed personally to myself I took but little notice. The man at length however accosted me with: 'Now, you fellow, how long will it be before your bit of a loom will be going on again? I want to come inside and examine it.' I turned to him and said, 'You are both rude and insolent, and I would like to know by what name the world calls you that you assume to yourself such self-important arrogance.' By this time the motive power was moving, and I was ready to go on again, when with a coarse laugh he said, 'My name is ————, and I am the inventor of the needle loom, that will eat up your paltry Coventry trade altogether.' So saying he endeavoured to pass inside the barrier, but I prevented him and told him his place was among the rest of the visitors, and that as an inventor he was the last person I should admit into the space reserved for those in charge. He was still more chafed when I explained to the people around that he was not the inventor he claimed to be, but a mere copyist of a principle of motion which I had seen at work long before he could have known anything of machinery at all. I refused to start the loom while he was present, and begged him to retire, as an anxious crowd was waiting to see the machinery in motion. He said he would fetch the President and compel me to allow him to examine the loom. He went, and as soon as he was out of sight I re-started the loom, much to the delight of the visitors, with whom this man did not seem to be much of a favourite; but I stopped it again as soon as he re-appeared with Mr. Myers, the President. Mr. Myers ordered me to re-start the loom, but I refused to do so in the presence of the man who had behaved so insolently. The President authoritatively ordered me to start it again. I told him it was not of the slightest use ordering me; he might as well try to drive a wooden peg into an iron anvil as to make me swerve from the course of action I was resolved upon, and in which I considered myself justified by what had occurred. The place was crowded with visitors at the time of this altercation, and although previously I had been on very good terms with Mr. Myers, I felt that in resisting his authority I had probably put an end to our amicable relations. He informed me he would write to Mr. Stevens requesting him to recall me as an unfit person to manage his affairs at the Exhibition. I told him to do as he pleased, as I was just as independent of Mr. Stevens as I was of him, and that no doubt I should be able to justify myself at the proper time. While this wrangling proceeded I was covering up the loom to show my determination not to set it going while this person was present, but when he and the President had gone I resumed work as though nothing had happened.

A young gentleman who gave the name of Ripley requested a few minutes' conversation with me respecting the city of Coventry and its trades. He asked me if I was a fair sample of the Coventry weaver, and added that he was the son of the Mayor of Bradford, and took the liberty of putting the question as he was an admirer of pluck, in whatever grade it was found. He insisted upon my taking a glass of sherry with him for the determined stand I had made. My fellow-workers in the Exhibition were jubilant at the result, and if I had lost the friendship of Mr. Myers I had gained the respect and esteem of others in the place who were both ready and willing to afford me any help they could in visiting places which without their goodwill I could not have visited. Next morning I had several invitations from mill-owners to visit their establishments, which in due course I accepted, much to my gratification and instruction.

As a result of the President's representations to my employer, a stormy and rude letter reached me from Coventry, to which I responded giving every particular respecting my conduct. I informed Mr. Stevens that my only object was to uphold his honour, and if he was dissatisfied I held myself in readiness to come back at a moment's notice. By return I received an answer, exonerating me from all blame, and thanking me for the stand I had taken. I was also informed that if any interference again took place to tell those who interfered to mind their own business.

It soon became bruited about that I had disputed the claim of this visitor as the inventor of the needle loom, but I neither saw nor heard any more of him till 1874.

Mr. Lister, of the Manningham Mills, it appears, had bought the patent for this particular loom, and finding that it was a failure, sought to compromise his contract. The inventor refused, and entered an action for damages against Mr. Lister for £30,000 for breach of contract. The action was remitted for settlement by arbitration before Mr. James Fitz-James Stephens, Q.C. On the 30th October, 1874, I received a summons to attend the court of arbitration to give evidence as to my knowledge of the loom in question and its adaptability for the pretensions that were claimed for it, particularly as to its power to supersede ordinary shuttle looms. The evidence went to prove the needle loom not altogether a success, and the plaintiff had to be satisfied with considerably less damages than the amount originally claimed. His gains after the payment of his law costs would leave him but a scanty margin, and he would doubtless have been better off had he accepted the compromise offered, which would have given him a competence for life. The following is an outline of the evidence I gave on this occasion:–

'I, Joseph Gutteridge, fifty-eight years of age, of 18, Yardley Street, Coventry, have been a weaver forty-four years, and during that time have made every kind of figure and plain silken goods the trade required. I am also able to make the loom machinery, which business I have followed at times. I have been foreman to three of the largest Coventry manufacturers for a period of eleven years, but am now working my own machinery. I was sent out in 1867 at the instance of the Soceity of Arts to examine and report to them on the nature and character of the silk trade on the continent, paying particular attention to the kind of machinery used for the production of such intricate fabrics. Thus, from long experience in the trade, and knowledge of the mechanism of the loom, I consider myself competent to give an opinion as to the capacity of the needle loom to compete with the shuttle. Whatever loom is used, it will have to meet the requirements of the trade, and in this the needle loom fails, for in the manufacture of silken fabrics it is considered of the greatest importance that the weft should be entirely hidden. This the shuttle loom does, the warp completely covering the weft. In the needle loom the weft, by looping round the needle, must of necessity show at the edge; where the body and edge are of different colours the weft would show through and prove a fatal objection to the sale of the woven fabric. This hiding of the weft is considered of the greatest importance by Coventry manufacturers and others. Independently of this, the complication of parts involves the risk of serious derangements and loss of time in the needle loom, and the necessity of being compelled to use a weft three-fourths finer than that used in the shuttle looms would render the loom liable with such extreme tension to at least one-half more stoppages than the shuttle loom would be liable to. Thus I consider that the complication of parts, the extreme tension required for the weft, the liability to derangement, the incapacity of the loom for making fine goods, and the consequent limitation of the number of pieces that can be made at the same time, will preclude the possibility of this needle loom competing commercially with the shuttle loom. About forty years ago I saw in the factory where I served my apprenticeship needle looms used for the production of figures upon narrow gauze ribbons, but the looms were given up because of their liability to derangement.'

Whatever feeling may have been entertained against this gentleman at the time of our altercation in the Exhibition, it had passed off long before I was subpœnaed to give evidence in this case, and it was with pain I went.

To return to 1870 and the Exhibition. After the recontre just described I had no more trouble. Indeed, in consequence of it I gained admission to many mills at Bradford, and had opportunities of examining every department of silk and other textile manufacture that was carried on. One of the most interesting mills visited was at Batley, where cheap cloth is made from shoddy or waste woollen stuffs. The fibres of the waste material are first separated by a machine called 'the Devil,' then sifted and sorted into long and short fibre, the latter being spun around a cotton thread to be made into the very cheapest cloths. The refuse of these processes is used as a valuable manure, and from the manufacture of these woollen stuffs immense fortunes have been made. The mills of Mr. Lister, of Manningham, are stupendous in their character, costing over £500,000 in their erection, and employing over four thousand hands in the manufacture of every kind of woven article, from a simple tape to the richest velvets. I heard Mr. Lister say at a public meeting that it had cost him over £30,000 to buy up patents and royalties in connection with silk manufacture, and that the profits on this branch of his business alone had exceeded seven per cent., besides recouping him for the original cost.

I visited Halifax twice, but at a time when it was impossible to avail myself of an invitation to visit the mills of Sir Francis Crossley, where costly carpets and other fabrics were manufactured. He was supposed to be the largest employer of labour in the county, the report being that he paid over twelve thousand hands weekly. The worsted mills of Mr. Acroyd, at Bankfield, filled with machinery of the most complicated character, were also visited.

A curious, though at the same time grim historic association connected with Halifax and Hull is the fact that until within comparatively modern times an old gibbet law existed, under which the penalty of death was inflicted upon the convicted thief without any appeal to common law. The relics of this sanguinary enactment are still to be seen at the end of Gibbet lane, in a little court where the platform was raised on which stood the instrument of death. The axe itself is preserved at Wakefield, while another portion of the structure is in the Halifax museum. This custom of beheading a convicted thief dates from the time of Edward the Confessor. The Sheriff of the Liberty was the executioner. But in case the theft was of an animal, the stolen animal itself (if recovered) was made the executioner, by being tied to a rope and driven forward so as to draw the bolt that released the fatal axe.

A most pleasant and enjoyable excursion was to the reservoir of Chely Dean, which supplies Bradford and district with water, and is four miles from Horton. This was a vast undertaking, and in appearance it is more like a natural lake than a reservoir of artificial construction. It is situated in one of those romantic valleys so often met with in the mountain chains of this locality. The lower end is closed in by a strong and massive embankment of stone-work, and the upper end nearest the elevated moorland is excavated to the required depth. The stone taken out was coal measure sandstone known as flagstone. In this stratified deposit are found immense quantities of sigillaria, with their roots stigmaria *in situ* and other well-known forms characteristic of the coal formation. The watershed is very extensive, draining a considerable area, which is wild and sparsely populated. It was certainly the largest sheet of water embanked for the supply of a town I had ever seen, and while observing it I shuddered at the thought of what fearful havoc would be caused in the valley below if the embankment gave way. This visit was merely a hurried one, as I had to start about five o'clock in the morning to be able to get back to the Exhibition by ten, but a better idea of the upland country forming the watershed was obtained by walking from Horton to Halifax one Sunday on a visit to a friend. The road is uphill for about eight miles, when there is an unobstructed view – a grand sight – across the valley in which Halifax is situated, the high ridge on the left terminating in the celebrated Beacon Hill. The fields in the valley, looking like a large patchwork quilt, stretch for hundreds of feet below, between this spot and the huge mills with their chimney stacks, which, however, in such a gigantic setting, appear merely like small homesteads from this elevation. For the last two miles the road gradually declines to the foot of the Beacon. Though tired, we could not resist the temptation of climbing this remarkable headland. From the summit it could easily be seen from what source the vast supply of water came.

We found our friend superintending a funeral, and, conforming to a local custom, we purchased a ticket each at the price of one shilling towards defraying the expenses, entitling us to a cake and cup of tea. This practice was general in the West Riding. Sometimes the profit was sufficient to set up the survivor in a small way of business.

October was to have closed the Exhibition, but the Committee decided to continue it for another month. This arrangement did not suit me, but Mr. Stevens held me to the contract to remain as long as the Exhibition was open. Mr. Myers, the superintendent, now became more friendly, and expressed his great regret at the unpleasantness that had occurred. In testimony of his goodwill he asked me to accept on behalf of my wife a dress piece of his best manufacture. As my wife was coming to Horton before the Exhibition closed, I referred him to her direct.

About a fortnight before my wife arrived, I had a narrow escape of being robbed of the results of my nearly four months' labour. The house I lodged at was one of four that stood somewhat back from the main road, and was approached from the Exhibition by a footpath across a field, the entrance at each end of which was guarded by upright stones, somewhat awkward to get through. Only a few weeks previously a daring robbery and maltreatment of a gentleman had taken place at the exit nearest the houses. Since the robbery I had taken the main road at night, though this was much farther, but one evening, as it was particularly rough and tempestuous, I chose the nearer way, and in spite of a premonition of danger that made me hesitate I started across the field. At the farthest end I was met by three or four men, who penned me in at the upright stones and refused to let me pass. I at once saw their object, and in an instant made a straight thrust with my umbrella at the face of the fellow who barred my progress. He uttered a cry of pain and left the passage free, and I hurried off in safety, thanks to a knowledge of fencing acquired in youth. The thrust went straight home, and no doubt hurt the man severely.

Being again on good terms with the Exhibition officials, I turned my attention to the exhibits, which were of a very superior character, considering that the affair was a local enterprise. There were works of the most eminent masters in painting and sculpture, loans from South Kensington, comprising ancient weapons and armour, gold and silver ornaments, and rare articles of vertu, with local exhibits numbering nearly two thousand. The concerts were of rare excellence, a principal feature being the Bradford Choral Society, which then stood unrivalled. I scarcely knew which most to admire, their marvellous performances of difficult pieces of vocal and instrumental music, or their wondrous ingenuity in mechanical skill. At one of the concerts a scene occurred which I shall never forget. A young lady, a general favourite, was on the programme to sing 'Angels ever bright and fair.' The concert hall was always crowded to hear her, but she did not make her appearance this time when called upon, and other pieces were sung. She entered the room later in deep mourning, fresh from the funeral of a sister who had suddenly passed away. A buzz of admiration went through the hall as she stepped upon the platform. For a minute or two she stood unable from emotion to articulate a word, while the audience were awed into death-like silence. She commenced in a low but pure tone, with the tears streaming from her eyes, 'Angels ever bright and fair,' and her very soul seemed absorbed in the theme. The audience was spell-bound, so intense was the feeling, and when she had finished and the spell was removed, such a burst of applause followed as I never heard before or since.

In the early part of the season there were almost daily trips from Bradford to places on the coast. The districts I most wished to visit were Whitby, with its wealth of fossil remains, Scarborough, and Morecambe Bay, but hesitated to go lest it should give cause of offence to my employer. I had therefore to be satisfied with excursions into the immediate neighbourhood. When amity was again the order of the day, it was too late to go, as winter was fast setting in. I was heartily glad when the last week came.

Some few days before the Exhibition closed my wife came, and the morning following the close we commenced to take down the loom, and in the course of two or three days it was on its way to Coventry. I had nothing further to do, as accounts were settled from week to week. My kind landlady would not hear of taking any remuneration for my wife's entertainment; she said it had been a pleasure to her, and wished we could make it convenient to stay another week as her guests, but I had to follow the loom as quickly as possible.

Before our departure from Horton my fellow-lodgers had prepared a little surprise. Two of them had been to Low Moor, and being acquainted with the foreman of the works, had procured about half a hundred weight of choice fossils from the coal and ironstone formation. It was with regret we parted from these kind friends. On our way to the station we called at the warehouse of Mr. Myers, according to promise and at his request, but he was out, and we were unable to await his return. In a few minutes we were journeying to the city of the three tall spires. Woman-like, my wife was uneasy about the promised new dress, and supposed she would hear nothing more about it. In a few days after our arrival at home, however, an elegant piece of dress material came with Mr. Myers's compliments and the hope that it would meet with my wife's approbation.

We arrived in Coventry on Saturday night, and on the following Monday I waited on Mr. Stevens to settle up. He was rather surprised to see an account of every day's transactions, and laughingly said, 'You don't expect me to get through this in a hurry, do you?' He cut the matter short by asking what was the difference between us. I told him I had to pay him 10s. 6d. 'Oh,' he said, 'it will be worth that to go through this account; put your signature to it and keep the balance.'

This Exhibition was a success, the promoters realising a surplus of nearly two thousand pounds. It was well patronised by the nobility and gentry of the West Riding, and the contributions sent were of the highest merit and rarity.

Yorkshire is a most interesting county historically. It was over a hundred years from the invasion of Julius Cæsar before the Brigantes – the tribe which originally peopled the district – were subdued, in the reign of Vespasian, A.D. 71. The city of York was chosen as the centre of Roman domination, and thence their power extended over the whole of Britain. From this point they could effectually resist the incursions of the Caledonians

(Picts and Scots), who had harrassed this part of the country from time immemorial, but after the departure of the Romans, about A.D. 427, these northern clans broke down the ramparts and ravaged the country. The Britons then called in the assistance of the Gaulish Saxons, by whose help the northern clans were driven out. The Saxons having begun to settle in the land, had no intention of leaving it, but one hundred and eleven years passed between the landing of Hengist and the conquest of Deira and its formation into the Saxon kingdom of Northumbria, the royal city of which was York. The Danes in their turn superseded the Saxons, their first important invasion being about A.D. 787. They were never expelled, and history seems almost blotted out under their domination; little authentic information is known of them except the wholesale massacre of the Anglo-Saxon inhabitants, the spoliation of the towns and places of worship, and the merciless slaughter of all who professed the Christian faith. From the time of Alfred, who reduced the Danes partly to subjection, first one and then another of these opposing nationalities obtained dominant power until the conquest of England by William the Norman, who parcelled out the conquered land among his chosen followers. There was a sanguinary resistance by the conquered people. The struggle was a long one, this northern county, the stronghold of the Danes, being among the last to succumb to the domination of the Norman. It was most interesting to learn whatever facts could be gained respecting this important county, its extensive and barren moorlands, and deeply indented vales, redundant with vegetation, and studded with large towns, whose workmen and mechanics are not to be excelled by those of any other county in England, while the mineral wealth of the hills and moorlands seem inexhaustible.

XIII

Reflections

The Franco-German War and the Silk Trade – Slackness of trade – Cases for fossils and shells – Illness – Prodigal son returned – An accident – Son's death – Remorseful reflections – Books on Science – Honour to Scientists – The physical and the spiritual – The golden rule and social conditions – Footprints of ancient peoples – The antiquity of man – Pleasures of study.

WHILE I was in Yorkshire the Franco-German War broke out, and the Germans in Bradford were ordered home, on pain of confiscation or outlawry, to take their place in the various regiments into which they were drafted. In consequence of this edict, the able-bodied young men who had not served their engagements had to leave at once, or their families and possessions would suffer from their refusal, unless they had become naturalised British subjects.

Trade of every kind in Germany and France was at a standstill during this short but sanguinary war, as nothing but war material was required. The call upon the silk industry, what little there was, was transferred to England. The demand for silk goods from the English however soon diminished, and once more our artisans had to succumb to a scanty demand for these fabrics. One country was quite sufficient at that time to supply all that were needed.

The stagnation in the ribbon trade, which came as a sort of reaction after the Franco-German War, left weavers with plenty of time on their hands. Through lack of work I was able to pursue my favourite hobbies. They were not expensive ones, and were never allowed to trench upon the household income. The cases already referred to for the reception of shells and fossils were soon finished. The collection had increased to such an extent that I was obliged to use every bit of available wall space for their preservation. This carpentry work was very exacting, and kept me within doors a good deal. When it was completed and the pleasurable excitement over, it appeared that I had over-taxed my strength. I was smitten by a dangerous attack of brain congestion, a disorder to which I had been more or less subject for some time past, due no doubt to reserved and studious habits and lack of outdoor exercises. The principal remedy for these attacks was the total abnegation of everything that would affect the nerve centres – a quietude entirely free from mental and physical labour or excitement of any kind.

At this juncture my eldest son, who had been wild and reckless, became married to his second wife, settled down in life as an engine-driver, and was now as careful of his earnings as he had previously been prodigal. With higher and better thoughts concerning both his physical and his spiritual future, he scarcely ever tasted the accursed drink that had been the means of shattering his formerly robust constitution. As often as possible I would visit him, and he now willingly acted upon the advice offered, so to live as in a manner to compensate in some small degree for the wrongs formerly done to himself and others. I knew that in all probability his tenure of life was short, and urged him to make the best use of the time at his disposal by trying to live so that death might be disarmed of its terrors, by true reformation and by trust in the mercy of a loving and forgiving Father.

Having recovered somewhat from my own prostration, I was one day early in June in the shop at the top of the house, trying to work at the loom, when the news came that my son was dying. Although the event was not unexpected, the message caused such a shock to my nerves that I instinctively felt a serious crisis coming on. Without alarming my wife I made my way downstairs, in the hope of finding relief, but was only able to reach the bedroom just below, where I recollect trying to throw myself on the bed. I must at that instant have become unconscious, for on recovery I found myself in bed with my head bandaged to prevent the flow of blood from an ugly wound in the temple, received in falling. The blood thus liberated relieved the temporary congestion and no doubt saved my life. It seems, from my wife's account, that after I left the shop, she heard a heavy thud as of some one falling, and being in the shop herself, rushed downstairs after me, believing that I had fallen headlong, as I had had several narrow escapes previously. Finding nothing amiss on the stairs or at the foot, she went up to the bedroom and found me lying by the side of the bed with blood flowing freely from a wound in the temple. There I lay while my son was passing away, unconscious and unable to be near him. Urging my wife to leave me in the care of a neighbour, I begged her to go and see my dying son. She went, and was just in time to witness his peaceful departure. I lay on a sick bed while he was buried, and my wife attended the funeral. These were hours of mental torture. Only those who have had this sad experience can tell the agony of mind that comes to one who feels that though he did not, he might have taught his children a higher principle than that of mere non-responsibility.

As soon as I knew with certainty, through the investigation of occult phenomena, that the spirit of man survives the dissolution of the body, and realised that man is responsible for the life lived on earth, I urged my son to the same investigation. From this I am pleased to say he obtained such demonstrative proofs of the continuity of life after the change called 'death,' that it completely altered the course of his life, and made his last days on earth his happiest. The remorse felt at not having led him to this change earlier was intense.

Thoughts as to the nature of God and the spiritual state were continually recurring to my mind during this illness, and I felt my faith strengthened in the Unseen Power that had intervened to change my son's current of thought, as it had changed my own, from notions of non-responsibility to a belief in and a sure and certain hope of a life beyond the grave.

For five or six years the difficulties of the Coventry weavers were most trying, sometimes without hope of any better condition for the large numbers dependent upon the silk industry. Yet fortunately for me it so happened that by making specialities and doing odd jobs, I managed to ward off the distress that was pressing very heavily upon many families. I was also fast increasing my stock of books on science, and had but little fear of losing them by lending, for they were not congenial to the ordinary novel reader. They were to me invaluable, imparting knowledge that could not be gained by a working man without such help – knowledge on subjects that were the life studies of the authors, requiring ample means in the research, but which in this manner was brought within the reach of the thoughtful artisan. The researches in science by such master minds as Brewster, Faraday, Tyndall, and Huxley, with many others, though wide and extensive, have merely opened the door of a wide vista of truth for future exploration. Each in his own sphere did not look beyond the physical. A certain point reached would be designated 'ultimate.' Tyndall and Huxley, having extended their investigations somewhat beyond this point were credited with propagating athiestical doctrines – a calumny they could well afford to ignore. Huxley's investigations were specially directed towards the discovery of the laws which govern the lower phases of animal life.

To such men as Charles Darwin, Huxley, the German Haeckel and Balbiani, we are largely indebted for the knowledge of the laws that rule the production of these lower forms of life which previously seemed so mysterious that nothing less than a special creation would account for their existence. All honour to such men for having studied their life's history for the benefit of the thoughtful and enquiring mind, and for having solved many a doubt that had hitherto been a stumbling-block to progress in knowledge. For this and much more we have reason to be thankful that such men have devoted their lives to discover as far as possible the laws governing the lower forms of creation that had hitherto baffled any attempt at elucidation. How much I feel indebted to such men my pen would fail to record. Many a doubt has been removed and many a difficult problem solved through the unwearied labours of these our noblest men of the age. It mattered little what creed they professed or whether they were thoroughly agnostic, the point to my mind was whether their scientific researches would help me to reach or pass over the line of demarkation that separates the purely physical and tangible from that other state of existence – the spirit essence of the present physical life and the germ of the life that is to be, that passes on to a newer phase of existence at death.

Specially commendable are the efforts of some other eminent men who have had the moral courage to differ not only from materialistic philosophers, but from the orthodox teachers of theology. Alfred Russell Wallace, the eminent biologist and naturalist; Professor Crookes, the celebrated chemist; William Howitt, Cromwell Varley, the electrician, Lord Adair, Lord Lindsay, Dr. Elliotson, Professor de Morgan, the mathematician, and very many others eminent in science and literature, too numerous to mention, have bravely dared to step across the line that separates the physical from the spiritual, and by their investigations have proved that the life beyond is only a continuation of the life that now is, and that under certain favourable conditions the essential or spiritual part of the human being which passes out of the body at death can and does communicate with the denizens of earth, as it is recorded it did in the olden times. This knowledge of a future life, as has been recorded in a previous chapter, I have personally proven by investigations extending over a series of years. It has proved a blessing to me both in the home and in every-day life. I have found, too that the future condition will depend entirely on the characteristics of the earth life, and will be happy or miserable according to the measure of our obedience to that principle of right expressed in the golden precept – 'Do ye unto others as ye would that others should do unto you.'

It is a most lamentable fact that under the present fictitious social conditions we cannot absolutely conform to that principle, which, if carried out, would no doubt make those conditions more endurable. The barriers that stand between the capitalist and the wealth producer would be levelled, and no longer, as under the present régime, would the profits of labour be absorbed by the few to the social degradation of the wealth-producing bees of the human hive. Throughout nature we find design and fitness of purpose, and it is most humiliating to find that the only mal-administration of this beneficient law is on the part of men who arrogate to themselves, because of their possession of wealth, the right to dominate over their fellow-men, who by the sweat of their brow in their serf-like labour have been the agents by which those immense fortunes have been made. This state of things exists too in direct contravention of the truism religiously accepted by these lords of men, that everything is derived from one great Creative power, and that all are equal in God's sight. Jeremy Bentham, I believe it is, says:– 'God has abundantly supplied man with all the requisite means of support, and where he cannot find these means we must look not to the arrangements of God, but to those of men and to the mode in which they are proportioned out to all. To charge the poverty of man on God is to blaspheme the Creator instead of bowing with reverence and thankfulness for the profusion of His goodness. He has given enough and for all, and if one feels that he has not enough, we must look to the mode in which the gifts of God have been distributed. There is enough, enough for all, abundantly so, and all that is requisite is the right to labour on the soil and to extract from it that produce that God intended for the support of man.'

From an early period I was an earnest reader of all kinds of books, but precedence was given to those of scientific and elevating character. I was particularly fond also of the history of the old dynasties, their rise and fall, their mythologies, and the influence exerted by them on modern civilization. There seems no reason to doubt that to the people in the far remote past we are indebted for much that we boast of as exclusively belonging to the present day.

The ancient Egyptians and Chaldeans possessed a knowledge of the motions of the heavenly bodies, especially of those planets connected with our solar system, and in even modern times we are to some extent indebted to them for a knowledge of eclipses through their ancient monumental hieroglyphics.

No doubt Upper Egypt was peopled by the Nubian race long before the delta of the Nile was formed or the pyramids built. The regions upward prove a more ancient civilization still, the monumental and other relics found there being of a ruder construction and more difficult of explanation. Yet these ancient people seem modern, compared with those strange races of South America who built the colossal cities and temples in Yucatan, Nicaragua, and Paraguay. Nothing now remains of them or their history save immense ruins covered with floral inscriptions and sculpture of such a peculiar character as to defy all efforts hitherto made to decipher their meaning. The monuments and ruins of Lower Egypt, great as they are, become small in comparison with these wondrous buried cities whose civilization must have been exceedingly advanced. Whole nations seem to have been blotted out, leaving behind no trace of their history except stupendous relics of their existence, the history of which is as surely lost as the supposed Atlantis, until a key is found to unlock the mysteries that now enshroud them. The American museums teem with remains, and antiquaries are endeavouring to find a clue that may throw light upon these strange people, the remains of whose buildings of cyclopean structure in many districts extend for a great number of miles. Some suggestion as to the unravelling of this inextricable mystery may perhaps be obtained by studying the history of those conquering nations who drove out the aboriginal inhabitants of Mexico, Peru, and Chili, before the Conquest of South America by the Spaniards, but the best evidence seems lost in the immense lapse of time. Their origin may have been from the more northern territory, now the United States, from which they may have come conquering the peoples in Florida and along the Mexican Gulf, crossing the mountain ranges and taking possession of all the land from Utah, California, and Yucutan down to Panama. The colossal ruins found in Yucutan, Honduras, Guatemala, and Nicaragua coincide in great measure with those found in Venezuela in the more southern part. The question arises, Whence did this immense migration take its rise? From the north, through the districts mentioned, or from central South America – those extensive regions ruled by the sovereigns of Mexico and Peru until the period of the Spanish Conquest? The ruins here seem to be more ancient than their own history can throw any light upon, but their legends say that in the first occupation of the land by these peoples, the ruins of these immense cities were all that remained of nations that had vanished from the records of time. No doubt they were as much a wonder to these early occupants of the country as they are to us at the present day.

The antiquity of man has always been a most interesting theme. Man seems to have buried his origin in the myths of the remote past – so remote that hundreds of thousands of years must have elapsed since his advent upon this earth. We find that ethnological characteristics of races have not changed within historical times, and that the brain capacity of human skulls found in association with the remains of extinct animals proves the volume of brain of pre-historic man to be equal to, if not greater than, that of many savage tribes at the present day. What evidence can be offered by legend or history of the people who constructed the immense mounds in Ohio and other States, which show a decided plan in their construction for a definite purpose? Not a single clue has been found to point to the nature or character of these ancient builders, and even the legendary lore of the Red Indians, who look upon these remains with wonder and awe, can offer no evidence as to their probable origin. Time merges into the myths of the past, and we are lost in wonder when we try to imagine how or at what period these stupendous structures arose.

All geologists agree that man was contemporary with the later manifestations of mammal life that were dominant in the tertiary period, and that for countless ages these mammals have been extinct. Man alone by his powers of thought and reason has been able to survive the changes to which the earth has been subject in the almost infinite past.

In reading upon these and other matters my time passed with many pleasures and some vicissitudes. In the ups and downs of life I could not dominate my own prospects in a financial sense, but I have been taught a lesson not soon to be forgotten, that man may in all conditions of existence make life much happier by conforming to those principles which will lead him to seek the highest good not only of himself, but of his fellows. What can confer a greater pleasure upon a man than to share his knowledge with those who may not have had the opportunity of acquiring what he has? The pleasure is increased and satisfaction is also felt when as a result the character and aims of the man who shares these benefits are raised to a higher plane.

XIV

Nearing The End

State of the ribbon trade in 1889 – A falling off – Shadows – Destruction of the Coventry Cotton Mill – Relief fund – Surplus to distressed weavers – Publication of extracts from this diary – The notes to be published in full – Thoughtful generosity of friends – An annuity – Thanks – Public museum wanted – Illness in 1892-93 – Joys and regrets – Beauties of shells – Matter and spirit – The starting-point of life – A retrospect – Looking forward.

THE year 1889 was a prosperous one for Coventry weavers. By taking advantage of these improved conditions we were well able to provide for coming want when the trade fell off. It was well for us that we did so, for the succeeding year commenced with much time lost for want of work. The prices went down fully fifty per cent. Scarcely anything was wanted but narrow ribbons, which, woven in looms capable of making broad ones with but comparatively few spaces, rendered it still worse for the weaver. Things went on until September, when, fiinding my resources at an end, I took out a set of warps at a greatly reduced price. They lasted for three weeks, and our united earnings amounted to twenty-seven shillings a week, out of which we had to pay rent, steam hire, and help, with other incidentals, leaving but about eight or nine shillings for food and other necessaries. Then came a thorough stagnation in the ribbon trade, hundreds of weavers were silently but patiently starving, this being the worst time experienced since the great strike and lock-out of 1860

Just prior to 1860, that is, about the time that the American markets were closed against England by the passing of the Morrell Tariff, which practically excluded all goods of European manufacture from that country – until then the principal market for English productions – things came to a climax. Up to this period there were over eighty ribbon manufacturers in Coventry and neighbourhood, employing about 18,000 men, women, and children; now the number of employers could be counted on the fingers. Yet the capacity and skill of English weavers cannot be excelled by any other weavers in Europe. Christmas, 1890, was within two days of coming when I received a note to attend the warehouse, and was jubilant at the thought of a probability of work, but instead of that I had to carry home a fine piece of beef. Although it was not what I could have wished, viz., the means of earning my own bread by labour, still it showed a most thoughtful care on the manufacturer's part for his employees in such a time of distress.

Deep and gloomy shadows affect the mind for the moment to such an extent as to make one overlook the gleam of bright sunshine that will overpower them. In a real sense it is true in relation to a superintending Providence, whose workings are hidden from our finite capacities, that

'The clouds ye so much dread
Are big with mercy, and shall break
In blessings on your head.'

In 1890 occurred the entire destruction of the mill belonging to the Coventry Cotton Spinning and Weaving Company, built upon Freemen's land, throwing out of employment some hundreds of men, women, and children. As the workpeople had to divest themselves of superfluous clothing, they escaped from burning in a semi-nude state. The weather was very severe. A fund of several thousand pounds was raised for the immediate relief of those thrown out of work. This help was extended to all connected with the mill with no niggardly hand – their homes were visited, and in many instances their wages were paid in full. The clothing they had lost was in great measure replaced, and employment was found for many, so that the number of claimants on the fund was soon lessened.

After the distress had been relieved a considerable surplus remained. Upon the question of its future application Mr. Walter Mason, president of one of our philanthropic societies, through the public papers directed the attention of the relief committee to the deplorably distressed condition of ribbon weavers, but for some time the Committee could not see the way clear to use this money for any other purpose than that for which it was subscribed. This letter, however, attracted public attention to the necessity of alleviating the pressing wants of the outdoor workers and factory hands engaged in the ribbon trade. A Committee was formed to establish a fund for this purpose, and an arrangement was made with the trustees of the Cotton Mill Fund to transfer their surplus to the Weavers' Relief Fund, the dispensing of which was entrusted to the officials of the philanthropic societies of Coventry. The representatives of these societies belong to the people who know where and how to alleviate distress. It is no disgrace to say that without making application, or in the slightest way intimating that I was in distress, I became a recipient of some of this fund. A great help it was, for I had not earned a shilling by weaving from September, 1890, to March, 1891, but was happily free from debt. To keep from starving I was compelled to do odd jobs in violin repairing and inlaid or cabinet work, and to sell such articles from the home as could be spared or replaced.

Unexpectedly, as in former times, came a change for the better. It arose in this way; a representative of the *Coventry Herald*, in preparing an article for that paper on the growth of Hill Fields, knowing that I had lived the greater part of my life in the district, applied to me for information as to its condition in days gone by, before it became so thickly populated. I placed my diary at his disposal, and the result was a most interesting narrative. Subsequently he had the manuscript again to make extracts from. These were published weekly under the title of 'Lights and Shadows in the Life of an Artisan.' Letters reached me from all parts asking if it was intended to print the memoirs in book form, but what answer could be made to these requests with my limited means? Several gentlemen interested themselves in the matter, and arrangements were made with Messrs. Curtis and Beamish (Coventry) to print and publish 500 copies, to be issued to subscribers at 3/6 each. It appears that through the publication of the extracts from these notes the attention of several gentlemen was drawn to my particular case. The first intimation of this that reached me was from Mr. Francis Smith, of Coventry, a member of the Society of Friends, a most indefatigable worker for the good of his fellow-men, being earnest and active among the class of misguided working-men who spend their hard-earned wages in intoxicating drink. A good work he has done in this direction by reclaiming many who by intemperance had brought their homes and families to the verge of ruin. Through his instrumentality a number of gentlemen joined together, and in some way that seems to me like an inscrutable Providence have arranged for me to receive a stipulated sum per week. This was done without my knowledge, and came as a surprise. I don't know how it was done; all I know is that it is called 'an annuity,' and that I obtain these payments by cheques from the Savings Bank, Hertford Street. This arrangement commenced in July, 1891, and has continued to the present time. Who to thank individually I do not know, although my thoughts point to many members of the Free Library Committee, with whom I have been connected since its first formation. Whoever they may be, they have my warmest gratitude and most sincere thanks for their kindly consideration.

Just prior to this thoughtful intervention of friends, I began to think of advertising my collection as the only way of providing means to live, but was advised by friends not to do so, as it might possibly be wanted for the use of the city. Public opinion will probably be favourable at some future date to providing a building in which such collections may be deposited as an educational centre, to check in some small degree the growing tendency to venial pleasures among the young and thoughtless of both sexes, and to raise their minds to higher aspirations by contemplating the wonders that Nature has so bountifully set before them. The study of Nature in its varied aspects is a joy for ever. It affects the moral as well as the intellectual life by teaching us the use of those things that confer health and happiness.

The year 1892 was a momentous one, bringing little work, but plenty of sickness. Both wife and I were confined to the house from the middle of November, to the end of January, 1893. Had we been in health there would have been no employment, as in my class of work nothing was wanted. That and the sharp, bitter winter has told terribly upon us, but there is always hope of a happier future. The past, with its joys and sorrows, during this sickness flitted across my mind like an open vision, unfolding the various pleasures experienced in the study of Nature in contrast with the dark shadows that have sometimes enveloped me. Regrets naturally arise at the loss of the collections of plants, birds' eggs, and insects, made in my youth, but this loss has been more than counterbalanced by the acquisition and study of British marine, land and fresh-water shells, with their endless variety of form and colour. Well might Mr. Adams say in his work on beautiful shells, 'They have not only grace and elegance of form, but have also richness and delicacy of tints, with every variety of colouring. In some species the tints are as intensely vivid as the shifting lights of the aurora borealis, or the glowing hues of an autumnal sunset – in others pure and delicate as the first indication of a coming morn. In some the colours are arranged in patterns regularly disposed, in others in masses and blotches of various shapes and degrees of intensity; in some, again, they seem to melt into one another like the hues of a rainbow. Nor is their beauty of an evanescent character, for shells are composed of particles already in natural combination, and almost indestructible, unless exposed to some powerful acid or the action of fire.'

The land shells of the South Sea Islands and those of Madagascar, the

Philippines, Madeira, Moluccas, Ceylon, and lands bordering on the Indian Ocean, with tropical America, vie with their compeers of the ocean in the strangeness of their forms, the beauty and intensity of their colouring, and the immense variety of their species, each united by form and colour to the peculiar locality inhabited. Although the marine and land shells of Britain are more subdued in colour, and smaller than those of tropical regions, still they are quite as interesting, as playing their part in the economy of Nature.

Turning from marine shells, whose formation is ofttimes so dense and compact as almost to resist the action of a file, they may be contrasted with the loose granular structure of the carbonate of lime, of which the majority of coral structures are composed. In general these are very fragile, and easily broken; in fact a common stone skeleton, in the small tubes of which myriads of polypus exist. Then again is the wonder how these minute organisms – little oblong bags of jelly – can secrete for the building of their houses these minute particles of calcium carbonate.

These simple forms of life even at the present time are building up immense reefs, fringes of coral rock, throughout the whole extent of Polynesia; extending for hundreds of miles. Turning to geological periods, we find their remains in the ancient limestones of the carboniferous, and the more recent period of the cretacious formation, showing what an important part they have played in the constitution of the earth's crust.

It is not yet given to man to know the abstract qualities of matter, and we can only reason analogically from the effects visible to the naked eye or revealed by the aid of the microscope. The transformations that take place in lower forms of being towards a higher plane of existence strike the mind with wonder and awe. For every effect there must be a cause; that cause traced to its ultimate source is called God. None the less can we wonder at the power that upholds us in our everyday life and the Providence that is displayed in so many various ways inscrutable to our limited senses. Ofttimes we are perplexed to conceive from what source help has come that has saved us in an extremity, forgetting that it may have been through the instrumentality of the Unseen Giver of all good. The outcome of conduct here, and the consciousness that we are cared for, warrants the conclusion that the faithful discharge of our duties during this physical state o existence will result in a happier condition in the life to come.

In taking a broad retrospective survey of the years covered by a long life, one cannot but be struck with the changes that have occurred in the city itself no less than in the conditions of its inhabitants. In my early days the working classes had to struggle much harder for a livelihood than now, and they did not enjoy so many of the advantages which tend to lighten the burden of honest toil. The necessaries of life were much dearer, and though prior to 1860 the weaving trade was prosperous, the working people did not appear to reap the benefits they ought. The intellectual condition of the poorer classes was low, and the opportunities of advancement were very meagre; the educated few appeared to be jealous lest their inferiors should taste the tree of knowledge and have their eyes opened. The condition of women in this respect was particularly deplorable, the only public institution in Coventry for the education of girls being Katharine Bayley's Blue Coat Charity, and the only scholastic subjects included in its curriculum were reading, writing and summing, but great stress was laid upon a knowledge of household duties, the sole ambition of the school being apparently to train by rule of thumb efficient domestic servants. The schools for boys were the Free (or Grammar) School – which, being at that time practically free to Freemen's sons, merited its title more than it does now – the Bablake School, and the Blue and Green Gifts, which are now amalgamated, and the Black Gift, or Baker, Billing and Crow's Charity. None of the denominational schools were in existence. The National School in Union Street was built during my boyhood, and the whole of the elementary educational machinery of the present day has been introduced since. The result is that intellectuality and morality have risen and criminality has declined. The Coventry of old age is vastly different from the Coventry of youth. The population then did not number more than seventeen or eighteen thousand, but with the development of the ribbon and watch trades it increased rapidly. Old streets were widened and new ones constructed, and whole districts – such as the new town of Hill Fields, Chapel Fields, and Earlsdon – that were rural, have been covered with houses to accommodate the teeming population. Hill Fields is now the centre of the cycle trade, which, since the decadence of the ribbon industry, has done so much to favour the growth of modern Coventry. The city boundaries have been extended, and the title and status of 'County,' which some years ago were lost have been regained, though it is to be regretted that shortly before this rapid municipal development the city lost one of its Parliamentary representatives, and now only returns one Member.

Among the notable improvements that have taken place are the making of the London and Birmingham (now the London and North Western) Railway, and with it the exit of the old stage coaches; the construction of the new Birmingham Road from Spon Street to Allesley, and the making of the Stoney Stanton Road from the Cook Street Gate, opening up a shorter route to Leicester. The new streets within the city, made in consequence of the increasing population, were not immediately taken over by the Sanitary Authority, and remained in a most filthy condition, being practically impassable during winter. The main streets were paved with pebbles or granite sets, but there was no proper system of drainage to carry off the surface water which found its way by gravitation to the Sherbourne, then a most fœtid, pestilential, sluggish stream, loaded with the germs of disease and death. The sanitary condition of the town was most deplorable, and its moral and intellectual state seemed as sluggish as the stream which lingered amid such congenial surroundings. With the passing of the Reform Bill a new public spirit came into existence. Coventry was infused with the new life, and from that time improvements in the sanitary, social, political, and educational conditions of the city may be chiefly traced.

To enumerate all the public improvements that have taken place would be a heavy task, but the Gas, Water, and Sewage Works, the Cemetery, the Market Hall, the building of the Coventry and Warwickshire Hospital, several Churches and Chapels, and many other projects have been carried out. Amongst the more recent may be mentioned the Restoration of St. Michael's, the finest Parish Church in England, the opening of the Technical Institute, made practicable at so early a stage by the large-hearted generosity of the late Mr. David Spencer, and the liberality of other public-spirited gentlemen. Mr. Spencer's noble benefactions will cause his memory to be revered by many generations of grateful citizens. The opening of the Free Library has been previously mentioned. As I write another public educational centre is on the point of completion, namely, the Wheatley Street Board Schools, undoubtedly one of the finest and most completely equipped establishments of the kind in the country. New Public Baths and new Water Works are nearly completed, a large Sewage Farm for the city is proposed on land between Ryton-on-Dunsmore and Stoneleigh, and amongst schemes in prospect are a new set of Municipal Buildings, for the purposes of which extensive properties have been acquired in Earl Street. The city is in a prosperous condition generally, though the ribbon and watch trades are depressed, and it is to be hoped that the efforts of those gentlemen who have spent their energies in promoting technical education may be rewarded by a revival of these old staple trades, and that the citizens may be wise in time in this respect with regard to the new industry to which Coventry owes so much. After a long period of what may be characterised as short-sightedness, if not of gross stupidity, on the part of the past generation, the citizens of modern Coventry appear to have realised their position, and to have braced themselves to meet the requirements of the new times, and are looking hopefully forward to the future.

In taking a retrospect of life I am struck at its various phases. Sometimes its complexion has been bright and beautiful, as in my younger days while roaming the fields and lanes in search of plants and wild flowers. The aspect of Nature transformed the world into a veritable paradise, made happier by the loving care and protection of earthly parents. After this period came shadows – privations and troubles – but viewed from the standpoint of old age these were as nothing in their effects upon manhood compared with the blighting influence of the dark shadows of Materialism which enveloped the mind for about eighteen years of the best part of life. This materialistic philosophy of non-responsibility almost brought me to a state of unreason, so dark and gloomy was the prospect, but from this Slough of Despond – this quagmire of doubt and perplexity – I eventually began to emerge towards the sunlight of reason through the study of the various physical sciences and the investigation of spiritual phenomena, guided by works that were within the means of a working man. The pleasure experienced in these pursuits led to the resolve not to live for self alone, but to place at the service of those who were struggling for 'more light' whatever knowledge I had gained. This power to help others confers a pleasure beyond all expression.

At the age of seventy-seven, looking forward to the future, it would appear that I am fast nearing the end of a long life. Yet there seems much effort still to be made and work to be done that in the past has been left undone. Time was when all was gloom and uncertainty as to a future life. I have found that the reasoning powers entrusted to our keeping, when properly exercised, can discriminate between right and wrong. These faculties aided by comprehension and analogy may bring us still nearer to an understanding of that Prime Cause of all things which to the non-observant seems so utterly incomprehensible. The dark shadows, however, have flitted away before the rays of light brought by the study of Nature in its varied aspects, and the conviction is more strongly than ever borne in upon the consciousness that all things are wisely ordained – in the eventide there is light. This belief enables one to look forward without fear to that change which will usher in a new life perfectly suited to the needs and capacities of the individual, a condition that will be not so much a reward for as the outcome of this probationary experience on earth. The coming change I sincerely believe will bring me into closer communication with dear friends who have gone before, and who no doubt are watching and waiting for a joyous re-union in the Better Land. This is a consummation devoutly to be wished, and one that is expected by all who believe in a Life to come.

A Note on Gutteridge's Autobiography

Although Gutteridge generally recorded events honestly and accurately, there are two points at least in which he is not a reliable guide to the industrial unrest of his time:

He states (on page 101) that Josiah Beck had employed cheap female labour to run his new looms. This is incorrect, though a rumour to that effect may have circulated among the rioters. Another manufacturer, John Day, did, in fact, make a practice of employing women and girls as weavers.

Gutteridge may also possibly have been less than frank in recalling his own role in the strike of 1860. The minute book of the Executive Committee of the strikers records the name of Joseph Gutteridge as one of those who on July 26th were deputed to bring out a 'Figure and Double Batten List' and to submit it to a public meeting for approval or rejection as to the prices suggested. It is possible, but not likely, that another member of the family is referred to or that Gutteridge refused to co-operate with the Committee. Otherwise we must assume that he forgot about the incident or deliberately chose not to write about his part in it. The complete failure of the strike and the shabby treatment he received when he applied for financial aid to the Trade Union officials (page 179) may have influenced him in this.